P9-CLZ-840

Writing for the Internet

Writing for the Internet

A Guide to Real Communication in Virtual Space

Craig Baehr and Bob Schaller

GREENWOOD PRESS

An Imprint of ABC-CLIO, LLC

A B C ⬥ C L I O

Santa Barbara, California • Denver, Colorado • Oxford, England

Copyright 2010 by Craig Baehr and Bob Schaller

Library of Congress Cataloging-in-Publication Data

Baehr, Craig M.
   Writing for the Internet : a guide to real communication in virtual space /
   Craig Baehr and Bob Schaller.
      p. cm.
   Includes bibliographical references and index.
      ISBN 978–0–313–37694–8 (hard copy : acid-free paper) — ISBN 978–0–313–37695–5 (ebook)
1. Online authorship. I. Schaller, Bob. II. Title.
PN171.O55B34   2010
808'.002854678—dc22   2009020844

14 13 12 11 10   1 2 3 4 5

This book is also available on the World Wide Web as an eBook.
Visit www.abc-clio.com for details.

ISBN: 978–0–313–37694–8
EISBN: 978–0–313–37695–5

Greenwood Press
An Imprint of ABC-CLIO, LLC

ABC-CLIO, LLC
130 Cremona Drive, P.O. Box 1911
Santa Barbara, California 93116-1911

This book is printed on acid-free paper ∞

Manufactured in the United States of America

Contents

Preface

Online publishing is now a billion-dollar per year industry that shows no signs of slowing. The opportunities to be a working Internet writer, whether as a hobby, as a supplement to income, as a career path chosen in college, or as full-time employment, are more numerous than ever. Work-at-home publishing jobs are at an all-time high. Online communicators are being employed by public relations firms nationwide to craft online, real-time responses to issues and events, and news outlets are scrambling to train their journalists to be proficient writers of online and new media content. *Writing for the Internet* was designed to connect related theories and methods of Internet writing to working-world application and practice, so aspiring or actual working communicators understand what to do and why they are doing it this way. In a converged, multimedia, Web-2.0 world, journalists not only have more tools at their disposal, the workplace often demands that they think in multiple platforms. While the demands on the journalist are more intense, the future belongs to those who truly understand first their story and then the best way to tell that story in the environments and delivery media available to them. This book is not just for newspaper or magazine writers, but for video and audio broadcast writers and other forms of multiplatform writing and publishing. A secondary purpose of this book is to educate and help train Internet communicators, from writers to designers and literally anyone who writes any form of digital communication, including email, uses social networking sites such as MySpace and Facebook, and uses technologies such as text messaging, content management systems, wikis, Web pages, blogs, and microblogs.

Books on new media have been outdated upon publication. Why is now different? Because newspapers have gone online to either supplement or even partially replace their hard-copy editions. Because the blogosphere is a force not just during elections, but all the time in not only politics but also marketing, framing, and other public relations issues. Because catalogs are online. The real-time news cycle is here to stay, and editors at Web-only publications, newspapers, and magazines are breaking news online in addition to putting their staples online (advertisements, press releases, public announcements, schedules, etc.). This book explores the interdisciplinary nature of Internet writing, from the roles of content provider, subject matter expert, information designer, and single-sourcing content developers for a variety of media. Internet writers, editors, social-networking users and designers, bloggers, marketing and public relations professionals, and Web page designers for all mediums, as well as any businesses that have online communications will find something useful and highly relevant in this book.

While the title focuses on writing, visual rhetoric is a significant part of the book—designing navigable and interactive Web content and understanding why online Web pages are designed with significantly different practices and formulas compared to traditional magazines, newspapers, and catalogs. Catalog writing and design for online display, for example, involves visual rhetoric design and "chunking" ability in terms of writing skills. Hypertext and linking, done correctly and appropriately, is a necessary skill for anyone who communicates using digital texts. Drawing from contemporary research in visual design, new media, and technology theories, the book provides a discussion of critical practical skills as well as related approaches such as technology convergence and multimodality in writing and adapting content for the Internet.

The book is divided into five major sections, including "Online Publishing," "New Media News Writing," "Internet Writing and Technologies," "Visual and Interactive Rhetoric," and "Social Media." It also includes an appendix, "Tips for Writing, Interviewing, and Blogging." The first section, "Online Publishing," traces the evolution of Internet writing carried over from print-based writing and publication conventions as well as important foundational theories, such as transformation theory, which help describe our transition from print to digital writing. Section One also examines specific ways in which technology has impacted everything from writing process to delivery medium. Two important trends influencing changes in Internet writing have been new media and convergence, both of which are addressed separately in this first section.

The first chapter, "From Print to Electronic," discusses the characteristics of Internet writing, including the impacts on technology, authors, writers, publishing media, and related theories. It begins with a discussion of how the Internet and other digital technologies have contributed to the methods used to write content for the Internet. It covers the transformative theory of technology, including ways in which print-based content has remediated itself into electronic form, and what the implications are for Internet writing. It discusses the concepts of technology convergence, remediation, and reusable content. The notion of single-sourcing content, writing once and reusing multiple times, is an important skill in successful online publishing. Chapter 1 also addresses related mass communication theories and how digital technologies have recontextualized and renewed their application in online publishing.

Chapter 2, "New Media Theory," addresses historical, foundational, and contemporary theories and how they inform our understanding information across a wide range of media. Although there is a rich foundation of work, new media theory is still evolving. As the pace of technology outran the intellectual legs of academia, researchers had a difficult task pinning down just what new media is and is not, and how it was similar to or different from existing media and mass communication theory. As the dust begins to settle and in the era of the iPhone and other leaps forward in mobile technologies, it appears that at least momentarily the innovation curve is starting to flatten out. Thus, new media theory is only starting to be fully explicated. As with the new media technology itself, our notions of new media can be built around many of the existing theories, with extensions of many of each adding to a new understanding in this digital era, and into the future.

One of the buzz words in new media is "convergence," which means a place where boundaries between mediums disappear, and it is explored through a variety of different perspectives in Chapter 3, "Convergence." Think of convergence as an online environment where the same story, on even the same Web page, exists as text, audio, and video. Convergence is where all media meet, which gives the user control like never before. It considers a wide range of aspects including the convergence of individual technologies, cultures, communities, and media, as well as various hybrid forms. Convergence has also placed new demands on content providers who must decide how to allocate resources and present stories in multimedia formats, often, however, with no additional resources or revenue. Additionally, presenting in a converged platform demands multimedia storytelling skills, which must be taught, developed, and honed for the working media professional.

Section Two, "New Media News Writing," addresses the important topics of news media writing, media and digital literacy, and narrative theory for online writing. New media news writing involves storytelling across multiple platforms, whether online, in print, or over the air. Along with the new responsibilities of online writing, Internet writers must keep abreast of the latest tools, methods, technologies, and uses of working with media and online content—and maintain a digital literacy consistent with the demands that readers expect. Writers must also learn to use narrative storytelling techniques in real-time media platforms for successful Internet writing.

Chapter 4, "New Media News Writing," addresses a variety of issues news media writers face. What could be more exciting than picking your own hours and writing for a variety of New Media outlets on topics that interest you? Maybe doing it well and developing into one of the better new media writers out there. Writing online demands a new approach to the real-time, 24-hour news cycle, so it requires an attention to detail like never before. However, while news and events unfold before our eyes, only the well-trained and best critical thinkers will be effective new media writers who can provide context, research, and other background perspective to the craft. The tenets of good writing remain largely the same, but new media writing brings with it an urgency that requires practitioners to navigate the busy seas of information with a clear perspective on where their stories are headed, and enough of an open mind to realize stories must constantly be followed up upon as they take on a life, and new directions, all their own.

The idea of a global village assumes and erroneously takes into account that everyone has access and understands how to use the Internet. Chapter 5, "Media and Digital Literacy," discusses the notion that writing online demands a level of media literacy that requires knowledge structures to accommodate the multimedia experience. While the generations of today are growing up in the digital age, those older generations are new to new media and have to be able to learn later in life how to understand and use various forms of digital media. Additionally, though most schools have access to computers and the Internet, not all have the support to teach students how to use it, let alone how to maintain and upgrade the equipment. So before writing online becomes a worldwide vocation, or welcomes a worldwide audience, media and digital literacy are crucial skills for proficient media professionals.

Chapter 6, "Narrative Theory," discusses the concept of narrative, or story-based structure, and its effect upon human comprehension and processing of online messages. Narrative appears to be a fundamental building block of human communication, and when no narrative is provided, readers, listeners, and viewers appear to invent one. News stories often are written in a way that violates traditional chronological narrative. This style, often called the inverted pyramid, is attention-getting and efficient, as it front-loads the most relevant details of the story. However, violating chronological order appears to make stories more difficult to process and more difficult to remember. Finally, readers actively assess the perceived reality of narratives—even narratives unlike anything they have ever experienced. Commonplace narratives appear to blend with similar memories, whereas highly atypical events stand out distinctly in memory.

Section Three, "Internet Writing and Technologies," addresses three important aspects of Internet writing, including an overview of Web 2.0 technologies, important writing techniques of chunking and hyperlinking, and a discussion of ownership and copyright issues related to digital content. Specific features of Web 2.0 technologies, including collaborative writing, content management, structured authoring, content single-sourcing, and syndicated content, have all influenced the methods of successful Internet writing. However, writers must learn more than the tools of the trade; they must also learn how to chunk information into units, types, and structures, and link it in ways that make it usable and useful to readers. Writers, and readers who contribute to online forums, blogs, wikis, and Web sites, must also understand the implications and limitations of their rights to ownership and intellectual property when publishing online. This section addresses all of these important issues.

Chapter 7, "Web 2.0 Technologies," discusses a wide range of technologies used in Internet and new media writing, beginning with a description of specific characteristics of these technologies. Specific applications and trends in Web 2.0 are covered, including content management theory and content management systems, as well as the integral part that markup and scripting languages, electronic stylesheets, syndicated content, and new media technologies play in Internet writing. The chapter concludes with a discussion of important implications for integrating and keeping abreast of development in new Web-based technologies.

Chapter 8, "Chunking and Hyperlinking," provides an overview of the unique characteristics of Internet writing and reading, including the concepts of content chunking and hyperlinking. It includes a discussion of single-sourcing methods, structured authoring approaches, and techniques of remediating content into other online equivalents. Other important concepts covered include content types, cross-referencing, linking techniques, creating context-sensitive content, and implications for Internet writers.

Chapter 9, "Ownership and Copyright of Digital Content," addresses important issues related to ownership and copyright of digital text. It discusses important intellectual property, digital rights, and ownership concerns of online content from the perspectives of author, consumer, and publisher. It also discusses the impact of the Digital Millennium Copyright Act, digital rights management technologies, and some important implications for new media writers and publishers.

Internet writers must be successful designers as well as competent writers. Section Four, "Visual and Interactive Rhetoric," addresses techniques and theories of designing informative, usable, and interactive visual content for online publication. Important design theories that inform the structure and design of visual information include an understanding of perception theory, color theory, user-centered design, as well as important research trends related to online design. Readers have also come to expect content that meets not only their information needs but also the level of interactivity they have come to expect with regard to Internet content, when searching and browsing online.

Chapter 10, "Visual Structure and Information Design," discusses the design of visual information, including the role visual perception plays, how information is visually structured on the page for users, and how visual design is different for online and new media writing from traditional newspapers and print. It discusses specific principles and methods of design theory for Internet writing, including visual structure, color theory, and user-centered design. It also incorporates important eye-tracking and usability research findings, including a discussion of where users focus when they look at a screen as well as the importance of consistent standards and principles in electronic information design.

Chapter 11, "Interactive Content," covers the kinds of tools and interactive content users expect in terms of reading online content, including an overview of navigation tools they expect when reading content in online environments. It discusses characteristics of interactive content, related theories of interaction design, a discussion of user experience and expectation with regard to interactive content, and guidelines for developing interactive navigation tools for users. Principles of interface and interaction design are addressed, which can be applied to developing digital content. It also provides examples of technologies, tools, resources, and specific methods, such as task analysis and user testing, commonly used in developing interactive Internet-based content.

Section Five on "Social Media" discusses the various media platforms, online reading, and cognitive aspects of online writing. Blogging has become more than a platform for online journaling, but also an important platform for news media reporting, commentary, community building, and corporate knowledge sharing. Social networking rhetoric and dialogue have invented a coding all their own, and effective Weblog writing is an essential online writing skill. Understanding the differences in online reading, including reader habits, various media channels, and structural features of online content are aspects for Internet writers to consider.

Chapter 12 on "Blogging" discusses the Weblog (and forms of micro-blogging) as a form of writing, how to prepare and plan before launching a Weblog, and tips for effective Weblog writing. It addresses properly focusing on a topic general enough to be idea generating yet specific enough to draw an audience. It also outlines blog-specific writing skills likely to keep a reader's attention and lead to repeat visitors.

Chapter 13, "Reading Online," discusses the evolution of reading on a computer screen, which has quickly become the norm for reading, rather than the exception. When the computer first became a part of a small percentage of households, no one could have imagined reading on them for extended periods of times. However, technology has made it so that e-books and other online texts are read first, and sometimes primarily, online. In this chapter, we study the intersection of print and text, and where it might be headed to in the future.

And finally, Chapter 14, "Cognitive and Psychological Aspects of Online Writing," discusses the importance of understanding cognitive and social psychological processing of online messages for writers. It discusses attention to messages, including structural features of audio, visual, and animated messages that automatically allocate attention resources and often translate into superior memory for the message. This chapter discusses the cognitive overload that can occur when the audio and visual channels of a message begin to diverge, including the tendency for viewers to focus on the visual channel at the expense of processing the audio channel. Finally, it discusses the media equation, or the tendency for people to treat new media messages and the computers that present them as real people, including team identification, politeness, and personality matching.

ACKNOWLEDGMENTS

The authors would like to thank Samuel D. Bradley for contributing the chapters "Narrative Theory," "Blogging," and "Cognitive and Psychological Aspects of Online Writing."

Section One

Online Publishing

Chapter 1

From Print to Electronic

INTRODUCTION: THE CHANGING NATURE OF INTERNET WRITING

Today, the Internet serves as a major publishing venue for virtually every sector of the working world, from news media organizations to corporations to the academy. Writers now are involved in more than basic prose writing; their work involves a wide range of publishing roles requiring vastly different skills in both publishing and writing. Writers must master content relationships, cross-referenced linking, single-sourcing methods, multimedia development, visual information design, electronic style-sheets, interaction, usability, markup and scripting languages, as well as structuring content. Writing online involves more than mastering the latest software programs; it requires a problem-solving mind-set, adaptability, and a strong literacy in the latest digital technologies. Technology and the Internet have automated the publishing industry and put once-specialized skills and tools within reach of writers. Internet writing has changed tremendously in just the past decade largely due to shifts in technology, expectations of the online reader, content, and methods of online distribution.

New technologies continue to revolutionize the field of online publishing, increasing the range of tools writers can use and the accessibility of online content for users. Content management systems and databases help writers store, chunk, organize, and deliver content using a variety of scripting technologies and templates that make publishing online easier. Graphics software and digital imaging devices, such as cameras and scanners, help writers develop sophisticated visual and multimedia content that can be displayed and embedded in Web sites. Markup, scripting, and programming languages have become increasingly sophisticated, accommodating more interactive and reusable content, which can be used to create complex templates for Web sites. Advances in display technologies, haptic interfaces, Web 2.0 technologies, and improved bandwidth have provided users with high-resolution displays, streaming audio and video content, touch-based interface screens, and downloadable content at much higher speeds, increasing the immediacy of content to user. Convergences of technologies have given computers and offshoot mobile computing devices the ability to capture visual images, write texts, and communicate asynchronously or synchronously, which in turn, allows users to access and share content over the Internet from virtually any location, using a variety of methods and media.

Readers have also become content users and producers, assuming a more active role that requires them to problem solve, search, browse, and interact with online content. Most individuals rarely read full texts online, but rather resort to filtering, keyword searching, and navigating to digest texts for pertinent information. Readers have a remarkable adaptability to navigating complex structures and interactive content found online. This ability makes them avid users and monitors of online content, but also has them seeking more dynamic content, customized and personalized to their information needs. Eye tracking studies have also revealed differences in how readers conceptualize, navigate, and problem solve when interacting with online content pages. Research has also revealed complex patterns by which users locate and discern navigation tools, content objects, and reference links. With serialized content, such as blogs, RSS feeds, and podcasts, readers can subscribe and monitor content on a frequent basis. They can also participate in the evolution of online knowledge bases and Web sites, by attaching their own content, feedback, and multimedia content. These types of skills, which readers possess and writers must accommodate, comprise a digital literacy required to be literate in digital environments such as the Internet. For Internet writers, this further compounds the complexity and level of skill and expertise required of good Internet writing.

Internet content continues to change and evolve, becoming more interactive, customized, and reusable. Content is not just created for one use but, often, for multiple uses and formats for users. It comes in a variety of forms including text, graphics, multimedia, and live feeds. Writers can use a variety of software tools and text editors to add styles, develop media, create layouts, and single-source content from databases and other online sources. Markup and scripting languages are used to specify the structure, layout, and interactive nature of content. The content a user sees on a screen is often composed of multiple layers of information, including text chunks, images, media, templates, and interactive scripts, often from a variety of sources. Single-sourcing is widely used to compile and reuse content from databases and other data sources, based on user needs and input, which is delivered in a variety of formats and media. Social media and syndicated content, such as blogging, wikis, podcasts, and microblogging have created new forms of collaborative, real-time content that is quickly becoming an important Internet writing trend. The relationship between content sources has become increasingly important in terms of cross-referencing and linking to other relevant sources of interest to readers. Internet writing includes the ability to produce these types of content and deliver them in usable, accessible, and interactive forms for users.

While the Internet remains the largest venue for online publishing, the methods of distribution have expanded considerably since the inception of the World Wide Web in the early 1990s. Content sources can be shared, cross-referenced, and highly structured using databases, content management systems, and scripting tools such as Extensible Markup Language (XML). Using personalizing techniques, such as templates and forms, content can be reused and transformed to be highly customized to suit individual users. Serialized content allows users to subscribe, monitor, and even embed content in their own Web pages, allowing for frequent distribution from a single source. Multimedia content can be stored, downloaded, or streamed live over the Internet. Delivery forms include Web sites, asynchronous discussion boards, blogs, wikis, or synchronous forms such as chat rooms, or even online, three-dimensional simulated environments, such as Second Life. These media have broadened the range of distribution methods and collaborative authoring venues available online. Content can also be delivered in multiple formats and uploaded to a wide range of devices for viewing, including desktop computers, laptops, cellular telephones, and other mobile devices. Perhaps the largest distribution issue deals with push and pull media—users can subscribe and download content, effectively pulling it to themselves, or, through subscription, have related content and advertising delivered, which is pushed to them from a variety of sources. Many online publications today serve a variety of push and pull media relevant to individual user needs and information interests.

For Internet writing, change is inevitable, and to be successful at online writing, a writer must keep abreast of the latest developments in technology, reader habits, content development techniques, and methods of distribution. Writing ability is not just basic writing and editing texts but rather requires a breadth of knowledge and skills. Design, structure, software, single-sourcing, scripting, media, and a deep understanding of the interaction between reader and text must all be parts of the writer's cadre. Digital literacy encompasses more than the ability to read and write successfully in digital environments—it has become essential in producing cutting-edge, successful online publications that demonstrate proficiency in the latest methods and tools, which appeals to the modern, sophisticated reader. Online publications with a dated look and presentation reflect negatively on the credibility and reputation of its writers and institutions. This is why it is even more important for online writers to keep abreast of the latest development methods and techniques so their work will remain consistently abreast of the changes in technology, content, users, and delivery methods. A publication's quality and writer's ability are equally reflected in the end product; if either are deficient, it may cost readership, subscriptions, loss of reputation, and more importantly, credibility with its readers.

Collectively, these are some ways in which Internet writing has changed in terms of skills and practical matters. The following sections deal with a number of related theories to provide a brief theoretical background on the development of Internet writing. These include transformative technology theory, technology convergence, remediated and reusable content, and mass media theories. Discussing these related topics helps provide Internet writers with a foundation of theories and methods that have contributed to contemporary practices and methods of Internet writing. Some of the subjects addressed are digital writing characteristics, hybrid technologies, convergence, remediation, single-sourcing, and communication theories. The first section deals with the ways in which print-based writing and technology has influenced and led to electronic or digital-based writing. The second section addresses ways in which technology and content have remediated from earlier forms and adapted to a digital environment. The last section discusses how mass communication theory applies to Internet writing, particularly for publication on the World Wide Web.

TRANSFORMATION THEORY AND TECHNOLOGY CONVERGENCE

Print vs. Electronic Content

Much of the foundation of electronic publication comes from print-based writing, including books and other paper-based publications. Print-based publications have familiar standardized components such as titles, tables of contents, chapters, paragraphs, indices, sequential page numbering, and so forth. Print publications are portable, static or fixed, linear, and not infrequently updated. Conventions for writing, organizing, and producing print-based publications are fairly standardized; however, for online writing fewer conventions and standards exist. A variety of different terms are used to describe Internet writing, including digital, electronic, and online writing, but although there might be subtle differences in terms of where content is published (such as online or the Internet), basically, all refer to content that is written, produced, and accessed in an electronic or digital environment, such as a computer using software. Electronic-based content has familiar structural features, such as site maps or indices, which outline content in the same way a traditional index might. It has navigation menus, which often resemble the organization of content as a table of contents might. Electronic publications offer readers the ability to interact with content, through buttons, applets, and forms, and then customize the output based on user input. They also have the ability to cross-reference or link to other relevant content sources using hyperlinks, which resembles a more robust version of footnotes. They are downloadable and printable, which makes them portable, often with some limitations. But more than print-based versions, electronic publications can contain multimedia, such as audio or video clips, to further enrich the reading experience. A few other major differences include: provides more frequent updates, includes a wide variety of formats, is accessible from a variety of computing devices, and accommodates searching, browsing, and exploring content in nonlinear ways. So, while electronic publications share certain structural and usability characteristics with print-based publications, they also have many new characteristics and features.

Transformation Theory and Literacy

Walter Ong and Michael Heim, two prominent literacy and publications scholars, wrote extensively on the intersection of print culture and electronic culture in the mid-1980s and 1990s. Ong argued that characteristics of primarily oral cultures were emerging in the budding electronic culture, creating what he called a secondary orality. He argued that both cultures focused on group mentality and spontaneity in expression and the notion that the reader (or audience member, user, etc.) would adapt to the medium of expression (1982, 135–37). Ong suggested that print culture was marked by a focus on closure and fixed space, contrasting it with electronic, or post-typographic, culture, which was becoming more open-ended and collaborative (1982, 134). Today, electronic culture is marked by multiauthor collaboration, wikis, blogs, and

other participatory online publications, which serve as socially constructed texts that focus on the collective knowledge of the group in telling stories and creating knowledge. Interaction is often spontaneous,
where the medium itself encourages feedback instantly or at the reader's
leisure. Online publications often vary in the ways in which collaboration,
navigation, and organization are handled; readers often must adjust to
slight variations in how content is presented and in rules for contribution.
These adaptations are oral culture traits in that early oral culture speakers
would often adapt their storytelling to fit the audience reaction. These
secondary orality characteristics are also important aspects of digital
literacy—users learn etiquette for contributing, knowledge sharing, and
interacting from their expertise with digital texts and interactions online.
In fact, when users experience one set of familiar tools or set of conditions
in one digital environment, they can use this knowledge to adapt to new
environments with similar conditions.

Heim was also interested in connections between writing technologies
and the way the human mind works in a given culture (1999, 48). Media
theorist Marshall McLuhan echoed this sentiment, suggesting that dominant forms of media and technology help define the "entire psychic life of
the community" (2003, 209). These notions extend into a theory of transformative technologies, which suggests that each major shift in the dominant medium creates a shift in the ways in which humans think, read,
and write, including the technologies they use to do so (Heim 1999, 59).
Examining notions of author, text, reader, and the tools we use to communicate at points along communicative history can help illustrate how
we are influenced by technology and forms of media prevalent in our culture. The history of human communication has been marked by four
major shifts in the dominant medium: oral, written, print, and, more
recently, electronic. Oral culture was marked by great speakers and audiences and the dominant text was the speech and oral storytelling, which
was often adapted to fit the audience's needs and reactions. Written culture (c. 300 B.C.) had scribes that captured oral stories and wrote new
texts on scrolls and codices, which created a privileged literate culture
that could read and write. Print culture (c. fifteenth century) mass produced texts into books using set type and printing presses, which democ-
ratized reading and writing, creating a larger literate culture. Electronic
(or digital) culture (c. late twentieth century) continues to transform
notions of author, reader, text, and literacy even further. Texts are composed using computers and collaborative authoring, and are distributed
online, resulting in more active readers and requiring greater technical
skill to write. Notions of primary text have changed from their early
beginnings as speeches and scrolls and evolved into printed books and

now Web-based texts accessible online. Conversely, notions of authorship that began as highly collaborative (oral storytelling), became increasingly individualized (scroll and printed book), and reemerged as more collaborative (Web sites, wikis, blogs), also a characteristic of secondary orality.

Literacy has always been skill-based and the baseline level of skills has changed at each shift. Eloquence and public speaking skills and mastery of written language have continued to be important skills in electronic culture, yet added to those are now other skills, such as technical skill with software, human computer interaction, and mixed media, that are becoming increasingly essential. Multimodality, or the ability to work with multiple forms of media, is an increasingly desired digital literacy skill for both readers and writers of electronic content. Literate readers and writers must be able to switch between media forms in composing and learning, including audio, video, interactive, static, visual, spatial, and textual content. These changes in literacy highlight an important aspect of transformation theory—that from each shift in the dominant medium, some aspects from the previous culture are preserved, some are supplanted, and others are remediated and integrated into the new dominant culture.

While early Internet writing was marked with the promise of collaborative authorship, early writing was still focused on individual authorship and ownership of online texts. More recently, technologies have evolved to facilitate collaborative authorship and improved reader interaction with online texts. Wikis, blogs, knowledge bases, and other content management systems are designed and structured around collaborative authoring. While a specific text might begin with an individual author, it expands in breadth and depth with the postings, replies, and contributions of its readers. As such, one trend in online content authoring is the move toward creating knowledge through collaboration between a single text's initial author and its readership. This, in turn, has created issues in textual ownership and digital copyright in terms of who legally has rights over texts.

Transformation theory and secondary orality are important to Internet writing because they illustrate the ways in which communication media and writing technologies have changed the ways we think, write, read, and interact with digital content. Previous notions of authorship, text, reader, and literacy continue to influence the techniques, desired skills, and content we publish and produce today. Many of the conventions and standards in place are derived from previous media forms, as well. For example, many of the structural aspects of printed texts have been carried over into electronic texts, such as indices, tables of contents, footnotes, yet in subtly different ways. The notion of collaborative authorship has early roots in oral culture. Concepts of authorship and textual ownership have come from both written and print cultures. The foundation of electronic culture is based on sustaining and remediated concepts from previous media forms. Indications of where electronic culture is heading are dependent on change in technology and ways in which we adapt to use them in our daily communications.

Convergence of Media and Technologies

Convergence has emerged as a key area of scholarly exploration, especially with regard to Internet writing. We encounter the convergence of devices, media, technologies, and hybridization of forms of digital content in electronic culture almost daily. More importantly to aspiring professional communicators, convergence has become a key for how to reach audiences, whether it is for media, for public relations, for advertising, or through anything related to technical communication (Baran & Davis 2009). The convergence of media types for news reporting and storytelling brings with it options never before available, collectively, until the Internet. One example, hypermediated text, runs the risk of leading the reader away from the story, rather than finishing it, as more information is presented than the reader can handle. Also, the idea of digital storytelling within multiplatforms has made the modern-day professional communicator someone who must understand not just the language, use of audio, visual rhetoric, and broadcast pictures, but also have a working knowledge of how to use the equipment to post stories, load MP3 files, design Web pages, and post video. The convergence of media has allowed those who still like the idea of reading the newspaper but wanting instant access to have the option of logging on and finding the story—often the way they want it told. However, links are not always accessible after the fact, and while the fraying corners of yellowing newspaper are not appealing to this generation, archival and the impermanence of text has a relevance to both new media practitioners and academics trying to understand and then teach the mentality of both the news consumer and the producer.

Peter Morville, an information architecture and technology scholar, underscores the importance of technology convergence and human interaction, citing how many mobile computing devices such as handheld computers and digital imaging devices allow users to capture, download, store, and create portable sources of personal data to carry with them wherever they go (2005, 93). The business sector has fully integrated portable computing devices, which are used by shipping and rental car companies, airlines, hospitals, and retail outlets worldwide. We have not yet reached a saturation point with regard to how technology has been integrated into our daily lives. However, the convergence trend seems to be progressing toward an increasingly unified interface—one where portable content is an individual accessory that can be accessed from any terminal display virtually anywhere. Universal content formats may also become a passing trend in favor of the computer that can interpret and convert content into the appropriate format for display. Another trend in writing content is the move toward remediated and reusable content, which can be created once and used in a variety of contexts and situations. Hybridization has also been an influential technology trend in electronic culture. As we make the transition from a print-based culture to an electronic-based one, a number of hybrid forms have emerged (and converged), such as the electronic printer, printable versions of electronic documents (such as Adobe's Portable Document Format), indices, styluses, and many others. On one hand, these hybrids may be symptomatic of our culture's transition from one dominant form to another. On another, they may be prototypes that reflect emerging characteristics of electronic culture, and related technologies to come. However, with regard to convergent technologies, one important factor to consider is sustainability. The reality is that many technologies and trends may or may not sustain themselves over time. As both remediation and transformation theories suggest, some technologies are integrated or refit into the new paradigm, while others are left behind. While difficult to determine the exact point of saturation or the longevity of any technology, it is important to be aware that every tool or skill may outlive its usefulness eventually. One essential skill of a successful Internet writer is to continually "tool up" and keep abreast of new technologies, tools, and skills, so they can successfully circumnavigate the many trends and fads it left in the wake.

REMEDIATED AND REUSABLE CONTENT

One important skill of good Internet writing is the ability to deliver the similar or related content in a variety of different formats. For example, an online news story might use text and graphic content, but also include links to related stories and resources, or even include video or other interactive content. As such, the same content may need to be delivered in a variety of different forms or media. News reporting on the Internet, such as on various Web sites, is a remediated form of more traditional printed newspapers. With the new format comes the ability to report news in different ways, including interactive applets, video content, related features, and reader blogs. Remediation is the transformation of one form of media into another, often to accommodate a new or different medium. Media theorists Jay David Bolter and Richard Grusin suggest "the very act of remediation, however, ensures that the older medium cannot be entirely effaced; the new medium remains dependent on the older one in acknowledged or unacknowledged ways" (1999, 47). Most forms of remediated content retain some aspects of the original form, and in the case of printed newspapers, the ability to provide static text and graphic content is still widely used. On the downside, Internet news may have some problems with remediation such as accessibility, portability, and archiving. For Internet writers, the ability to remediate, compile, and deliver content in a variety of different forms, while maximizing access, usability, and so forth, is often an essential balancing act in successful online writing.

Another important Internet writing skill is the ability to single-source content. Single-sourcing describes the set of skills related to the conversion, updating, remediating, and reuse of content across multiple platforms, products, and media. Technology has had a significant impact on single-sourcing, more recently focusing on features that support context sensitivity, personalization, content management, and both structured and collaborative authoring. While single-sourcing has many benefits for Internet writing, information development scholar JoAnn Hackos highlights potential challenges with multiauthoring teams, suggesting it "requires that team members collaborate so they share content development and avoid duplication of content and effort" (2007, 225). Reusable content should also adhere to a consistent set of standards and be adapted to fit the purpose and medium for which it is suited. Ann Rockley, publications development expert, suggests that content is not always ideally reusable and must consider context, quality, usability, type of reuse, and appropriateness for the product (2003, 41). Creating reusable content is an important skill in Internet writing for a variety of reasons. It saves the writing team time, effort, and resources by writing content once and reusing it multiple times. It enables greater consistency among products that are based on the same content sources. It also creates flexible content that can be adapted and published in a variety of formats and media, such as Web pages, videos, podcasts, advertisements, and printed literature.

One increasing challenge readers have with online content is learning to successfully search and navigate large volumes of content to find just what they are looking for. As the Internet and electronic culture continue to produce content in many forms, in different media, and from a variety of reusable sources, it is increasingly important for Internet writers to make that content easy to find, access, and use. Put simply, reusable and remediated content must also be findable. Morville defines "findability" as the degree to which something can be located, or more specifically the ability to "find anything from anywhere at anytime" (2005, 6). Ultimately, findability is closely linked to usability. Successful findability is linked to many important aspects of Internet writing, including structure, navigation, layout, style, content chunking, and interactivity. The typical user has a wide range of experience interacting with a variety of different Web sites and content forms. As such, they become familiar with conventions, typical layouts, organizational schemes, and navigation tools. Usability testing can help writers understand the mental models readers/ users create to organize and structure content, and their expectations for searching and browsing tools for navigation. Drawing on this knowledge can help Internet writers learn a lot about making online content more findable and usable.

RECONTEXTUALIZING MASS COMMUNICATION THEORY INTO DIGITAL FORM

Communication theory as taught decades, and even a century, ago might not be the irrelevant, recycled "dinosaur chronicles" that some new media and technology advocates tried to convince professionals and academics it was. Grand theory, postpositivist theory, hermeneutic theory, critical theory, social hermeneutics, causal relationship, and, particularly, the third-person effect need to be pulled from the shelves, dusted off, and applied to the current communicative conundrum. What America has gone through in the past decade is a normative media theory study waiting to happen. Enduring questions have become important again, whether for mediated and remediated communication or for digital literacy and who has the access, means, and working knowledge to make the most of the technology.

The media theory that was developed to guide research in the 1940s was used for what was considered "revolutionary" research in the 1960s (Baran & Davis 2009). As the dust settles on the technology and some sense can be made of it, the theories of the past do, indeed, need to be updated, and in some cases they will not be applicable to particular aspects of the technology. However, the same complaints about the penny press and the telegraph (Czitrom 1982) that were being made a century ago are now being made about the real-time news cycle and instant posting of stories online: that so much information is being put out to the masses so soon that no one has time to wait for all the facts, let alone develop a context. According to a 2007 report from the Pew Research Center, often conflicting information will follow, which does not reach all the users who hear, read, or see initial reports, so the truths to which they arrive are not based on the most recent—and correct—facts.

A great hope and belief pushed upon the world was that the Internet was going to give a voice to everyone, to bring about democratization like never before, and to aid globalization. Yet the lead-up to the Iraq War, during which journalists were later criticized for basically being no more than a mouthpiece for the Bush administration and its bogus intelligence, showed that the old standards of communication still apply even with this new medium (Braiker 2007), that the ruling elite still often decide what information is distributed, and that the voice of dissent, even in the ether of cyberspace, is not always heard by all, or even any. In fact, therein might lay the problem—that the idea of giving everyone a voice is indeed a property of the Internet. The fallacy might be that anyone wanted to listen, especially the notion that everyone would log on to hear everyone else's opinion (Gitlin 2007). It appears that, rather than unite or globalize the world, the Internet as a mass communication instrument has further fractured it, as the rhetorical selectivism of hearing like opinions has pushed out the voice of reason, the voice of fact, in favor of being told what we want to believe, and further reinforce our own beliefs rather than open our minds, emails, and message boards to a different theory or evidence (Baran & Davis 2009).

Chapter 2

New Media Theory

INTRODUCTION

Writing for media has always had direct ties to mass communications theory, whether it was for audience and writers, or for the medium itself being used as the delivery method.

While new media theory is still being developed by scholars within the academic community, there are logical ties that can be made to previous mass communication theory. This is, of course, consistent with the logic of academia, which notes that almost all theory is built on, and an extension of, previous or "existing" theory.

As new media developed as an interactive platform, users were able to, as never before, access the media at their own leisure, or even with their own urgency. The "demassification" of the media has made it so that the mass media is much more a micromedia experience, with each user deciding what kind, what time, and what format he/she wants the news. The interaction is also asynchronous now; this means it can be whenever the user wants. Information is placed online, or received in email, and can be accessed or ignored at the user's discretion.

Mass media theory from the past is still applicable today, just differently from the fragmentation of audience, the wide variety of media outlets, and the fact that the time the public uses media is in the users' hands, not the media.

Critical theory is a theory that seeks change in the dominant social order (Littlejohn & Foss 2008), and notes how communication is controlled by the in-power group and used to exert control over the audience. The belief in critical theory is that knowledge is good only when it promotes democracies and levels out the social classes, taking power away from the dominant classes and giving it to the masses. Certainly, that can be seen as applicable to new media since users have all the information they could possibly want largely at their fingertips if they are logged on and know how to find information online.

Normative media theory is based on how the media should work to attain ideal social values (Baran & Davis 2009). This theory focuses on its being "situational," or applying specifically only to the social system it serves and might not be relevant in differing systems.

The gathering of media, and media theory, into new media is also shaped by convergence, so in a way, the new media theory would also be a theory of convergence. A convergence theory would be based around the idea that there are no longer distinctions, lines, or boundaries from one medium to another, or even among all media.

Mass society theory is something that came to dominate the academic and media landscape in the late nineteenth century (Lowery & DeFleur 1995). This theory takes a particularly negative view of the media but does note the media have an influence on the masses. This is a theory filled with contradiction, largely in part because it was developed at a time when the agrarian business model dominated and the urban format had yet to unfurl with cities filled with workers and factories.

Another significant theory is the limited effects theory that views media as only reinforcing and strengthening trends and power structures and not providing any opportunity to challenge the status quo or offer direction for progress (Lazarsfeld, Berelson, & Gaudet 1944). This theory was researched empirically through election coverage and found that the media were not nearly as influential as proposed in other theories.

Another theory that has application today is framing theory (Baran & Davis 2009), which is founded upon the idea that people use "expectations of the social world to make sense of that social world" (35). Framing theory applies to new media because it believes in the power of the active audience and that users can access media and process it to have meaningful experiences.

The "third-person effect" theory is based on people thinking other people are much more influenced by the media then they themselves are (Tewksbury, Moy, & Weis 2004). People think other people are more susceptible to the pull and direction of the media than they are.

In the past, there was a smaller form of this. Print, such as magazines and newspapers, could certainly be picked up and read or set down and ignored as the reader chose. However, the online format presents not a daily or weekly edition, but a constantly updated series of periodicals with new and different information every hour, even every minute, counting all the publications around the world and constant posts from readers.

This has completely loosened the reins of power for those who have information and readers who crave its immediate distribution and want to personalize it for use. Certainly, cable television has for decades provided 24/7, constantly updated news, though much of that is the same recycled news throughout the day, with often the same stories being run again and again, until news events are covered or reported to take their place. Also, cable television does not allow the viewers what to choose in terms of coverage or which stories to watch. Online, users can choose the text or video of any story at any time, provided they can find it. Again, quality becomes an issue: While there are stories every week or every month from users who send in video for them, those are the exception. The same thing is noticed for public citizens posting blogs with "exclusive" information: The quality and research on these sites is dubious, though occasionally a legitimate news nugget makes the national news and it is rightfully credited to the person who uncovered and reported it, which usually involves direct posting online, thus taking away further the gatekeeping role the media had enjoyed for, some would say, too long.

This attempted explication of theory, the connecting of dots from past theory to where new media is taking it today—and it is more of a drift and ebb and flow than the linear line it was in the past—is not an indictment of academia for struggling to track and develop new media theory. Indeed, in the past, that linear development was easy to track; significant dates and technological breakthroughs were sporadic and not difficult to denote. Today, however, the breakthroughs are constant, the evolution constant, and just when the dust starts to settle on a technology and its use, it changes, from going mobile with laptops and wireless access to the mobile technology of one's cell phone where everything can literally be in the palm of one's hand every waking (and driving) moment of every single day. So in the past, theory unfolded as a series of steps. Print was a step up from orality, though it was an extension of storytelling, "recording," and passing on information (some would argue that the rants in bloggings are not writing at all, and are in fact just stream-of-consciousness jottings that play better orally than in print). Cable news was just an extension of network news, where lesser known stories get more attention, bigger stories get more constant play, and events such as the stock market or sports scores can be reported in real time whether in the evening and then before bedtime only, as the traditional network newscasts did for several generations.

Just as we touch on in Chapter 5, scholars have had to get used to what new media is—and is not—and formulate theories. But to formulate a theory, the knowledge structures have to be in place so these theories make sense, are well grounded, and are connected to whatever is applicable from the past: This, however, is where the new media theory train jumps the tracks. Rather than the past, where theory was a series of somewhat obviously connected principles built on each other, stacking from, say, left to right and building to the latest theory, new media theory does not travel and thus cannot be built in such lockstep fashion. Rather, new media, instead of moving linear, moves up and down, like an elevator, and diagonally, like a "Z," zigging and zagging back and forth, and forth and back, as users decide what they want in technology, business chases those ideas with the new gadgets, then another use unfolds, and the demand for different applications is set by users, and again met by industry. This is moving horizontally and diagonally, at angles that drive demographic trackers—who do not have tenure and need return-on-investment figures today—crazy, and often out of work.

Since many, perhaps even most, of the academic community was no longer working in the media, or was not a part of the technology industry, as these changes were unfurling at a technological speed never seen before in the world, it is certainly understandable that scholars did not or could not unfurl a theory, even one cobbled together with a compound of seemingly relevant past work. In his book *Convergence Culture*, Henry Jenkins of MIT marvels at the viewer involvement in such shows as *American Idol* and *Survivor*, and about how readers of Harry Potter books created on their own such well-thought out communities on the Web. In the past, such book clubs and TV focus groups were all organized and administered by big business at their discretion, not the viewers'. The lines of constant communication brought by the Internet and now mobile technology, particularly the iPhone and BlackBerry, have left print and broadcast media at the mercy of the users. Rather than chart the course, media empires are now slaves to the users—and since the companies still want to profit, they try to anticipate needs and wants. The reality, however, is that technological appropriation is still consumer-driven. Microsoft made a nearly half-billion dollar mistake thinking users would gladly give up their computers to make their televisions a computer with a black-box apparatus above it that could give them everything they want. Other companies thought people would flock in masses to their cell phones to watch movies on a screen a couple of inches high and wide, if that. That has not happened. Media theorists are thus left in the "when-the-dust-settles" stage hoping to get some intellectual traction on these things. In the past, Marshall McLuhan was given little credibility because his theory was not always based on past theory and his data were largely speculative rather than empirical. Year by year, and perhaps even month by month, as the technological development curves bend and straighten, chapters of new media are unfolding before our very eyes. Jenkins has picked up that ball and run with it, and even admits that he is only fathoming guesses on what he is observing—his book cover blurb touts him as the new McLuhan—and yet, because so little is still understood about new media theory, Jenkins is one of the few leaders in the field.

The development of theory is traced back to oral cultures. Without exploring that too in-depth, the theory professor at your university will likely dive farther into the research of Harold Innis, Walter Ong, Neil Postman, and Marshall McLuhan—the four faces on the Mount Rushmore of some mass communication scholars—than we ever will here; the development of communication between and among people is the start of theory. McLuhan, and to a more pessimistic degree Postman, saw media as having a great influence on shaping and developing culture. McLuhan believed that all the technologies were an extension of man, and that the technologies as they evolved contained properties of the ones previous to it. We can see that today with laptops, iPhones, BlackBerries, and all of their derivations. Postman worried that we would be so consumed with electronic media that we would forget about both reading and noticing the world around us. Certainly, both scholars proved to be prophetic to varying degrees, though to which level could depend upon interpretation.

While oral cultures existed literally by word of mouth, placing great emphasis on proximity and memory, the creation of an alphabet and later the printing press changed the proverbial communication paradigm and largely relegated orality to a back seat as word spread by the printed page, and now, by online text that travels farther and faster than the printed page, and reaches around the world in a matter of seconds, rather than the cumbersome delivery method required by ink-on-page print.

From orality to print, the change was substantial. After print, television took center stage, especially as programming pushed long-standing concepts of morality for what could be shown. The theories that developed focused on how people changed their behavior because of what they saw on television, especially sex and violence, and even the promotion of habits such as smoking and drinking. This was a growing concern, and millions of dollars and thousands of research hours were poured into making sense of it. From there, video games dotted the next area of extreme research interest. The violence in video games was occasionally—as in not even once per year—the reason a person took someone else's, or their own, life. These spectacular, though largely isolated, events, consumed the communication academic community.

While sex on TV and violence in video games—certainly two areas ripe for research and valid concerns for intellectual exploration—were being hashed and rehashed, this little thing called the World Wide Web, later and now known as the Internet, was shaping up as something that was going to not just topple all of these concerns, but extend them into spheres that no one—not researchers, users, or businesses—ever understood would come to be a constant presence in people's lives. Though the Internet brings with it a heretofore unseen access and interactivity, it also incorporates much of previous mass communications theory. It also provides a fertile field for research into video games, which are now played via modem or WiFi with users connected around the world, and sex and violence on television, which is largely available online through various Web sites, particularly news outlets, Internet service providers, and the rapidly growing YouTube, which is a user's paradise for posting and retrieving video.

TECHNOLOGICAL DETERMINISM

You never know who might be reading what you have written online. It could be that woman in the library on the computer, but it could just as easily be the traveler staring at the mobile phone in the Beijing airport. Writing online has brought a wider audience than ever before to both professional and amateur writers alike, so be prepared when you put cyberpen to hypertext, because you never know who will be reading the words you write.

The idea that technology would shape culture was common sense (Silverstone 2006). Machines through the last century in particular have become faster and smaller, yet perform more tasks, and in effect become more sensitive to users and their needs, more user-friendly, in a sense.

In the scientific community, machines were used for such concerns as health and wealth (Silverstone 2006). Humans had to first find a way to live with machines, and in time as this technological appropriation and accommodation took place, humans have found it nearly impossible and highly stressful to live without certain technologies, even for very brief periods of time. It is also a goal to understand how this blisteringly rapid pace of innovation was accommodated by citizens, politicians, and business leaders who had neither the practical experience with such devises or technology nor the knowledge structures to understand the rapidity through which this technology evolved (Postman 1992). The compass and gunpowder were as significant to exploration and conflict as writing and the printing press were to communication. However, the understanding and fine-tuning of information is far more theoretically based, and thus depends more on theory to garner a better understanding and predictive powers of where technology will take culture (Silverstone 2006).

Communications scholars took a backseat to history and sociology scholars in the development of technological-accommodation theory (Silverstone, 2006). Science developed weapons with technology that can be, was, and is used as renewable energy sources, yet the theoretical understanding of this technological determinism never took root or grew branches (Latour 1987). Furthermore, the boundaries between machines and humans were rarely identified or understood (Winston 1998). The often intimidating instruction manuals that come with new technology still provide little explanation or understanding of how these will influence the person's life on a day-to-day basis, or in which groups they will thusly better identify.

One of the great marketing tools of Microsoft, for example, is that its software can make its users' days better, can help get information faster, or can calculate information more rapidly, as Excel did when Microsoft introduced the program. While these programs were interactions between a user and a machine, they had a sociological impact that has had limited study (Meyrowitz 1985). These technological strides have sociological consequences. People spend more time in front of computers. For example, in the case of Excel, rather than ask several employees to do the totals for different columns, the entire data set can be entered and then calculated by one person. These technologies are wholly interactive, and allow or even demand the complete attention of the user, which affects the communication the user has with others (Silverstone 2006). There is also the element to consider that the social consequences become technological; a person's relationship with humans also affects the person's relationship with technology. To focus only on the relationship of people among people at the expense of technology never explicates how the technology is appropriated. This lack of focus on the technological accommodation also skips understanding how the spaces for technology are negotiated. Thus, technology had to be domesticated (Berker, Hartmann, Punie, & Ward 2006). Think of the idea of horses for transportation, or oxen to pull farm equipment. These were wild animals, just as we have in essence wild technologies (Silverstone 2006). Without any boundaries, these technologies are both dangerous and, to some, useless. For those technological innovators, these technologies are sources of great wealth and considerable power. As this trickles down, the early adopters have information that has value and power, be it financial or that held within the hierarchical structures of an organization. The machines need a physical space, but it is up to humans to find a space for them in their lives and thus their culture. This is why the rhetoric of innovators is so important; they are telling people to both use and buy their products, and that by doing so the quality of their life is going to be greater, and the horizons that they chase can be wider.

Once the technology is acquired and applied, nothing is ever the same. The person who is on the iPhone nonstop at home misses conversations, might stop reading or watching television as much, though stays better connected with friends outside the home (Silverstone 2006). The person who cannot or will not disconnect from the technology while crossing a busy street or driving in a car will miss not just the noises of day-to-day life and the vagaries that define a culture but also warning signs and noises that could injure someone. How each person negotiates these technological spaces is highly personal and has consequences that affect everyone around him/her, including those who are time zones and continents away who are part of the user's network. The great closer of spaces—the end of geography, as some have said—means someone living in rural Texas could be better plugged in with someone in another country than to a next-door neighbor, and likely knows more about the person farther away if that is a better connection, so to speak.

These are still extensions of past technologies, make no mistake (McLuhan, 1964). The young man who was considered rude in the 1980s or 1990s because he did not take off his baseball cap when entering a building or meeting an adult has been replaced by the person who enters a room or sits down to dinner with a group without removing the earphones to an MP3 player. Each individual has an infinite number of choices to make in terms of how he/she chooses to make sense of the world. In fact, a concern of society from decades preceding the Internet and cell phones was that people were reading news at an alarmingly decreasing rate. Now, online newspapers are seeing readership soar, and people can read the paper wherever they have their laptops or even cell phones. This is a choice the user makes, no longer dependent upon picking up a newspaper at a news stand or from a front porch at a designated time. Yet the newspaper business itself has not negotiated its space within this technology and is suffering financially for it.

Technological determinism theory states that the technology determines a society's cultural values and social structure (Postman 1992). Certainly, media literacy, more specifically, digital literacy, is much more related to uses and gratifications than the advent of cable TV or the penny press, especially since people often believe they only want the skills they need to use the media for whatever they want it for. And for many, that has very little to do with continuing education, or joining public debate about society and the world's more serious issues (Lanham 2007). In fact, with selective retention and exposure, issues like global warming or the need to downsize the SUVs that Detroit continues to produce in the face of environmental and economic realities points to a scary truth: Some very educated people are compiling a lot of the same facts and coming to polar-opposite truths. Is this partially attributable to media-digital literacy, or the technology?

While media literacy has been an area of considerable research since the beginning of information travel, the Internet, with its multiplatform dissemination properties, has brought to life the academic term of digital literacy. This new discipline can be connected to technological determinism, as the technology itself has allowed far more people access to information made possible by the Internet. The question as to whether technology is neutral is still being debated (Christians 1989). Indeed, thinking that technology is "merely a tool which can be used rightly or wrongly" (123) answers no questions and provides no direction.

Christians cites philosopher George Grant who, long before the Internet was even in people's imaginations, believed that the computer is neutral and does not impose on anyone ways in which it must be used. Of course, that was before the phone line, ether, and airwaves were exchange platforms for information and photos, to be used rightly or wrongly or somewhere in between (Landow & Delaney 1991).

Communicating through technology has created an open space that, while creating its own cliques and groups, has also broken down walls to the world (Meyrowitz 1985). Yet, the entire belief or lightly grounded previous theory that technology is neutral is based on the idea that technology was far more linear, even as a mode of information exchange, than it turned into with the Internet (Christians 1989). Christians's two faces of the technological process, the first phase (design) and the second phase (fabrication) are stages in which rapid technological advancement has been in development and evolution for decades, are driven by the need to make what the public decides it needs (also called technological appropriation). The making of these programs, software applications, and hardware products allows us repeatable maneuvers for finding, disseminating, and storing information, which was the same goal of the printing press. In fact, type has been since its conception a repeatable commodity that puts a visual stress on the reader and requires the writer to assemble a narrative or coherent body of information that the user can process and contextualize (McLuhan 1962).

The extreme speed at which technology evolves is forcing users to develop a host of cognitive, social, and technological skills that require a sort of digital IQ that requires training and actual formal education (Eshet-Alkalai 2004). Therein lies the crux of what the Internet is supposed to do in terms of globalization and democratization: The Internet can and should largely be whatever users want to make it to be and use it for. Yet the technological geniuses behind the development of such software and programs tell us that anything is possible without telling us what the opportunities, and drawbacks, might actually be (Postman 1992). Those who develop the technology and create successful businesses form a "new knowledge monopoly" (10), applaud technology, and champion its proliferation. However, such technology creates, by its own definition, an end to various careers, and those "winners will encourage the losers to be enthusiastic about computer technology" (11).

Postman cites McLuhan's often-repeated phrase that "the medium is the message" and extends it to "the medium is the monopoly" on the technology, finances, and even knowledge. It can be a never-ending intellectual tax of sorts, from buying the hardware and all the software, and then hiring by phone or in person "tech support" for even more money to make this costly engine you have purchased start running correctly. These financial concerns are another less talked about barrier to digital literacy, especially for those living at or below poverty level. "Private learning and individual problem solving" (17) are beneficial for those who can afford, and make sense of, the Internet opportunities. Perhaps the ceiling for digital IQ is unlimited, for those who have the means. Pushing these largely public educational achievement places into personal and private environments takes away the group-learning aspects that orality and pencil-and-paper scholarship brought forth, and the social responsibility that came with such a setting and group-oriented approach.

In another work on the subject, Postman (1985) notes how the media itself is a metaphor in the communication process:

The printing press, the computer, and television are not therefore simply machines which convey information. They are metaphors through which we conceptualize reality in one way or another. They will classify the world for us, sequence it, frame it, enlarge it, reduce it, argue a case for what it is like. Through these media metaphors, we do not see the world as it is. We see it as our coding systems are. Such is the power of the form of information. (39)

Technology shapes culture in ways society is aware of, as well as ways that it either does not imagine or is incapable of imagining (McLuhan 1964). It can be as simple as the media platform we access or as complex as how the information is contextualized (Postman 1992). Sholle (2002) moves one more step along the technological determination path, referring to technology as tools we use in our everyday lives. He claims we are still asking questions about old technologies as well as the new ones, and whether technology is an "agent of freedom or instrument of control" (p. 2). Technology has brought change to our lives whether we know it or not, and has, Sholle claims, become a part of a progression that will alter not just our society and economy, but our consciousness as well.

Measuring media or digital literacy is hard to do; no such scales exist. Access can hardly be the meterstick (going global means going metric, even in clichés) by which all are measured. Meaning making must involve context (Postman 1985). In his work predating *Technopoly*, Postman saw where the Victorian Internet itself, the telegraph, "made relevance irrelevant. The abundant flow of information had very little or nothing to do with those to whom it was addressed: that is, with any social or intellectual context in which their lives were embedded" (67). Writing almost a decade before deafening dial-up modems occasionally silenced oral exchanges, Postman saw a "sea of information with very little of it to use" (67), noting that while the telegraph created the first real-time global village, no one knew anything except "the most superficial facts about each other" (p. 67). Such insights offered by McLuhan and Postman add further credence to why it is so important for new media writers to provide context and additional perspective, even in the 24-hour, real-time news cycle.

PROPAGANDA

Ironically, the idealistic concept that the Internet would be the end of lies and the spread of great truths and democracy was hardly the case. Propaganda theory was developed and became a major theory after the Nazis used it under Adolf Hitler to spread misinformation and promote agendas (Baran & Davis 2009).

In fact, the Internet has added a high gear and overdrive speed to the spin cycle. Companies no longer have to wait for the media and hope to get their turn in print or on video when they are faced with negative news: They can produce their own, post it, and, if they feel like it, send it to the media. The government was supposed to be quieted, if not silenced, by the anarchy and democracy that was supposed to dot the cyberlandscape once most had access to the Internet. But a funny thing happened on the way to the democracy party: Not everyone wanted anarchy, not everyone wanted to spend all their time online getting "educated" or better informed, and some just wanted to be entertained or interact with real or virtual friends.

The government, with its big booming voice and vast resources from people to machines, still gets its message out very well, and often on its own, nonmediated terms. And though that message is likely no more or less truthful than before, it is still widely viewed by the public with the same eye, whether it is taken as gospel or discarded, or somewhere in between. The dissenters also have a better platform, but it is hard to imagine taking the word of someone you have never heard of over a well-crafted and presented message from governments and big business. Again, there are exceptions. But the flow of information still largely drifts from government and big business to the masses. In this two-step flow theory that was largely left for the scrap heap as democracy was set to flourish worldwide and totalitarian governments thought to crumble, opinion leaders are still those who are elected or run big companies.

While many have claimed the media no longer have the kind of influence they have, the actual numbers of hits on news Web sites, especially since Google and other search engines have created news platforms and rely primarily on traditional outlets with links, newspapers, television networks (including cable), magazines, and their Web sites, show they are getting more readership and viewership than ever before. Blame the news media for not finding a financial model to make it profitable, but the number of readers and viewers for the *New York Times, Washington Post,* and *USA Today* has never been higher.

SELECTIVE EXPOSURE

Cable news channels and other news Web sites have moved to the Web to create more content than ever before. While a lot of blogs and YouTube videos are user created, much of the content generated by professionals still comes from corporations. Yet, tracking the corporate tentacles led to some very familiar big business sources. From that came a plethora of stations, many of which—sorry, anarchists—are tied to the major media conglomerations. MSNBC is, of course, tied to giant NBC (and business giant Microsoft) and financial channel CNBC is also under the NBC umbrella. Fox News is owned by the same company that owns the Fox network and *Wall Street Journal,* and on it goes. Even the occasional independent successes—such as YouTube—are quickly swallowed up in purchases by the heavy hitters (Google bought YouTube). So while the audience has, by the sheer enormous number of options available, fragmented, the consolidation of the media has actually continued rather than slowed or been further divided up into pies that all the world can get a piece of.

While the network newscasts have lost viewership since the onset of cable television and its own news programs, something else is at work: selective exposure. In the "old" days that your professor might not be old enough to remember (the days were that long ago), the network news was what it was, and if you did not like the news, were tired of bad news, or thought your political party was getting biased coverage, you had to reconcile that on your own through deep thought, reflection, and assembling as many facts as you could to support the truths in which you believed.

The theory of selective exposure is gaining prominence as more media become available, yet people seek out fewer sources and focus instead on media that reinforce their own beliefs and points of view (Baran & Davis 2009). Selective exposure is the "idea that people tend to expose themselves to messages that are consistent with their pre-existing attitudes and beliefs" (146).

We have talked in other chapters about hypertext and linking to stories, which readers can see as highlighted, underlined, bold, or different-colored text: These links provide great citations and references. But there are issues with this "interactive" content. First of all, and most practically, is that the links have to come from reputable Web sites, and the links have to be working—even the most user-friendly mediums and portals often archive information weekly or monthly. Also, remember that when a hyperlink is placed within a story, it gives the reader an "exit" away from your story. Certainly, for credibility purposes, links can and should be included, but where that is—highlighted with the text for easier access, or in the age-old method of footnotes at the end so that the reader will not ditch that story in favor of another—is an issue. And for those practicing selective exposure, that link might be something that fits in better with their point of view. The idea that something conflicts with what we have known in the past or believe to be true is called "cognitive dissonance," a mental and intellectual discomfort when we are presented with information that clashes or dismisses what we think we know or understand. With so many media options, we can literally be told what we want to hear or read on any issue; we just have to point and click or type a few words into a search engine. Is that the great education that World Wide Web proponents were hoping for as the Web unfurled and caught all the bugs in it, or is it a trap of like-minded thinking?

For all the limitations of the media in its previous form—and a lot of effort had to be made to use it in some cases, just as books had to be tracked down and lugged off the shelves in libraries before the Internet brought such info to our fingertips—users were exposed to a variety of sides of the story. They had to sift through a bevy of facts and come to their own truths. Now, the truth is what the user wants it to be, and the user can assimilate "facts" that fit in nicely with his/her upbringing and political views. And if you do feel like watching a debate or government press conference on television, you do not even need to take time to reflect on what was said or let it percolate in your mind before coming to your own conclusion and making sense of things. Rather, the networks and cable outlets provide you with Republican and Democratic pundits to tell you what was actually said, what was really meant, and how it affects you: That these two points of view never intersect does not seem to bother anyone.

Certainly this type of media consumption has not led to the kind of democracy anarchists wanted or that big business feared. In reality, the idea that the Internet would be this great exchange of brilliant and open minds has largely been a myth. The global village forecasted by so many is more like a collection of like-minded clans that are better organized than ever, further fragmenting societies into haves and have nots.

So as a new media writer, you have more access to more people on more issues than ever before. Your voice is potentially more important than ever. But you have to develop the rhetorical and writing skills to articulate your point with the three C's—clarity, conciseness, and credibility. The idea that "everyone is a writer" and that one can post one's own beliefs and rants faster than ever before is also a levee of credibility that you can break easily and irrevocably by breaking the tenets of good research, reporting, and writing. So while it is easier than ever to "become a writer," the demands to do it well and resonate with a wider audience actually require you to be better than ever before, because your competition is everyone rather than a few well-trained scribes who have a platform.

USES AND GRATIFICATIONS

While "uses and grats" is more an application than a theory, it is as good as any to explain and unfold the Internet. It is also something Paul Lazarsfeld was part of defining along with researchers such as Herta Herzog and Frank Stanton (Baran & Davis 2009). Uses and gratifications is an "approach to media study focusing on the uses to which people put media and the gratifications they seek from those uses" (232).

This is a half-century-plus years old theory that revolved around how people used the media and what they wanted—the gratifications they sought—from it. That, in a nutshell, applies to the Internet and the evolution of the cell phone into multimedia platforms, which not only can locate anything online in one's hand but can create context, be it text or photos, and so on.

In uses and gratifications, theories studied how much readers could expect from their media excursion compared to how much effort it required (Baran & Davis 2009). In the past, that might have meant being in front of the television for the nightly news; getting a subscription to the local newspaper, retrieving it from the doorstop, and making time to read it; or even taping programs on television as the first videocassette recorders hit the market in the 1970s.

That, of course, has all changed. Information is available all the time now. The users decide what they want and when they will get it. The effort to get it is almost so easy as to be laughable: Log-on (if you are not already), and point and click. Once again, we are able to pony another theory—and perhaps two or three—onto this one. Though lectures from Ivy League schools to community colleges are available, in many cases for free, online, the number of hits these lectures receive are pitiful. On the other hand, TMZ.com's Web site counts millions of viewers a week and became such a bonanza it went multimedia with its own weekday television show stalking celebrities and posting unflattering pictures of stars, whether from early in the morning, from late at night when drunk, or from a half-century ago compared with today. That is what viewers wanted, and that is what they received—that is a "use" for current Web surfers and TV watches, and the gratification they get based on TV ratings and times the TMZ.com pages are viewed makes news media Web trackers jealous. Is this is the Great Intellectual Enlightenment Web idealists were hoping for, or a dumbing down of the world? Certainly, there is and should be a place for entertainment. Watching too much war, too much suffering, and even in 2009 too much economic-woes reporting can take a toll on even the most even-keeled user.

Ironically, information on Web use is relatively easy to track. Any Web site can utilize analytics that the originators create themselves or get through Google and other companies. This provides quantitative data on how many pages users looked at, how long they looked at it, what they clicked on while there, and which pages within the site they went to from there (if the user stayed within that site). The location of the user, through the ISP provider, can also be tracked, if not specifically, at least regionally. While these numbers are important for tracking and demographics, such as for use in marketing and even resource allocation and management, there must be a qualitative element added and deducted from as well: Why do readers go to particular Web sites? What are the users looking for on a newspaper Web site—do they really want video, and what kind do they expect from journalists? TV cameras are now often in journalism newsrooms, yet these broadcasts seldom produce a fraction of the hits that the news stories produce. Why is that? Is it because of the quality of the broadcast from the print-trained journalist, or is it something else in the reader's mind? Television news Web pages have both the video they showed on television and the print version of the story. Which is more clicked on, and why? Having numbers is great—even essential—both to gauge a return on investment of employees' time and money and to allow for future planning. But researchers, and businesses, will have to ask readers and viewers why they favor one medium over another on particular Web sites before they put in countless hours preparing photo galleries that people might not view—or conversely, not posting photo galleries for a highly visual event such as the New York City marathon or other such events that are best covered visually. It just takes a little more thought than new media practitioners, and researchers, have put into it so far. As we have said before in this book, using bells and whistles just for the sake of it produces only noise, and if users are not following this reckless pied-piper planning all over the place, the focus will have to be narrowed into malleable chunks the users want.

CONCLUSION

In something that either leaves a sour taste or is a delicious coincidence, several of the theories on notable periods from the past have resurfaced in different forms in new media.

Yellow journalism, thought to be largely dead with the accountability of a professional media educated and trained on ethics and foundationally solid practices of reporting and writing, has experienced a rebirth. Since anyone can post something—and anyone or any dozens and hundreds and thousands—can repeat it or link to it, the transmission of half-truths, innuendos, and even lies now occurs at the speed of light. And once something is "put out there," it can never be brought back. With the 24-hour news cycle and the ability of asynchronous exchange, people can learn about news when they choose, when they watch the real-time news cycle on cable, or when they get news online. These rumors and half-truths, ironically, are straightened out for the most part only when a reputable source is finally interviewed, usually by a mainstream member of the media. However, because many people are dipping and bobbing in and out of media for their own uses and grats, they will not hear the rest of the story, which is often the corrected version.

The Libertarian and social responsibility theories of the media are still in place. The Libertarian theory is that the media in free countries still operate rather of their own accord and have a self-righting mechanism for errors, though that certainly does not extend to all aspects of the sensational elements of the media and bloggers—though there are a number of reputable blogging organizations, including several tied to mainstream media outlets. In terms of social responsibility, the media still at times admirably fulfill their role of watching government, and still crusade, sometimes in too participatory of a nature for many media ethics scholars and media critics, to highlight social causes and to combat illnesses, disease, racism, and bigotry. However, every side has a voice, and while the old theory might have been that the loudest voice is heard, that only the squeakiest wheel gets oiled, the reality is that to keep someone's attention and keep bringing users to whatever you have written and posted online, it is going to have to be succinctly and thoughtfully stated. Good writing still wins larger audiences in the end, regardless of the format.

Tracing the flow of information is another area of research ripe for interest. People in different places find information in different ways and at different times, and depending on the source, the information can be framed in entirely different ways. Do yourself a favor and some night, rather than watching the cable news station that best aligns with your political beliefs and voting preferences, watch the BBC newscast from London. You will see more in-depth stories on even issues about the United States, as well as a dose of socially aware issues in foreign countries you will never hear or see on cable. Or, if you read your news on Google, go to the bottom of the main news page and take a stroll through the news pages for Canada, Great Britain, or Australia—or another foreign country if you speak its language. You will be shocked at the differences in how the same stories are reported and what other countries consider more newsworthy than the latest blond American girl to disappear tragically as the manhunt begins for her killer or abductor. Again, the preoccupancy associated with these "news" stories and how people use the media is something no one has a real handle on. Only by following the readers, and asking them about it, will anyone develop a workable new media theory. Until then, it is coffee-shop research that usually starts, "I think that probably . . . ," has very little empirical value, and offers nothing for exploratory direction. We are so far into the Internet age, yet theory is still standing at the starting line. Old theory has new value, but it must be picked through, deciphered, and applied to a new paradigm that no one is confident enough to put out there. Yet to sit on our hands is more than useless; it is irresponsible. Whether the global democracy predicted to come with the World Wide Web ever evolves is to be seen, but with every digitally literate person using the Internet throughout the days and nights, it is high time a new media theory starts to be explicated by the brightest minds in media and communication research.

Chapter 3

Convergence

INTRODUCTION

Though the concept of convergence is often referred to as a place where media forms "collide," it would be more accurate to describe it as a place where they interact, overlap, and gather. The days of single-media interactions are numbered if not gone: the same print publication you now read online has links to other print stories, includes clips of video and audio, and might include a gallery of still photos as well. It is all packaged in a digital format, so it is up to the user to choose the format to experience the media; indeed, the same story might be available in each format or a hybrid of formats.

Convergence has placed a new set of demands upon media producers: it is no longer enough to have a story told in one format and one format only. Readers want to access the stories they want, in the forms they want, and they want it available now—right now.

There was a time-tested saying in newsrooms around the world for more than a century: Get it right, but get it first. That saying is hardly uttered any longer. Once news breaks, it is fair game to anyone who can report anything. It might start with a comment on Twitter from someone's cell phone. But once it is out there, there is no reeling it back in. Data on this information superhighway move at the speed of cable, or wireless, and it does not pause to breathe, much less wait for editing, fact-checking, and gathering of ancillary perspectives for context and complete storytelling.

DEFINING CONVERGENCE

Convergence involves considering many aspects including technologies, cultures, communities, and media. Technology convergence involves the merging of older and different forms of technology into new devices. Some of these fledgling technologies emerge as hybrids, straddling the old and the new, and are particularly obvious during times of transition between one dominant form of communication, such as print, and another, such as digital (Ong 1982; Heim 1999). Some examples of print-to-digital hybrids include cellular telephones, laser printers, Adobe's Portable Document Format, and alphanumeric keyboards, to name just a few. Some are simply "delivery technologies," which have their own time, give life to other technologies, and then fade (Jenkins 2006). Communication culture itself is marked by these specific technologies, in addition to modes, media forms, and how users interact and participate with them. Jenkins underscores the important differences between interaction, which involves the system's response to user input, and participation, which is shaped by both the culture and its consumers (2006). Interactive forms that require user input process data through scripted algorithms and produce a customized response. Many basic keyword searches operate on the same principle, permitting users some control over the flow of digital media.

Through practiced searching and browsing, users adapt to new forms and become adept participants in a convergence culture. These are not inherent abilities users have, but rather, must learn through active learning, concept formation, association, and active thought. Both interaction and participation work together (or converge) to create the experience of user immersion. With regard to media types, users can accept media that is pushed to them, either through elective subscription or by media producers themselves. Increasingly, customization and personalization have become important aspects of digital media, offering users the ability to pull and compile digital media from a variety of sources. The user-mediated push and pull of digital content creates a "synthetic reality" to suit the users' needs (Lanham 1993; 2007).

The Internet has a prominent role in facilitating convergence and participatory content, by serving as both primary publication medium and facilitator between corporate entities and consumer communities. Convergence also encourages users to repurpose and remix digital content through consumer participation. Media remixability, or the ability to modify and repurpose media into different forms and formats, is one aspect of convergence that has encouraged users to participate, perhaps beyond the bounds or expectations of corporate entities. Jenkins argues, however, that "within a convergence culture, everyone's a participant, although participants may have different degrees of status and influence" (2006, 132). Participation encourages immersion within a specific story, medium, or phenomenon and may come in the form of meta-commentary, community building, collaborative storytelling, and even works of fan fiction. Other examples of participatory media include meta-commentary on discussion boards and wikis. Blogs and video blogs permit users to generate their own media and append to other sources they encounter online. Other more customized user-generated media contribute to the culture of a particular phenomenon, building on the core story, archetypes, ideals, etc., to create media libraries, community discussion forums, Web sites, blogs, wikis, and other forms of collaborative digital content.

A wide range of digital media, including online games, movies, popular fiction, television shows, and others have inspired various forms of consumer participation. From a corporate perspective, this serves a variety of useful functions including sustainability of a product and, not to mention, free advertising. The corporate entity provides official fan sites, blogs, forums, content libraries, and downloads for fans. The consumer community, in turn, generates various forms of unofficial fan-based content, user communities, interface modifications, art, fiction, and much more. Convergence of corporate and consumer cultures has led to tension over ownership and control over digital content. On one side, corporate-controlled media, such as official Web sites and forums, permit a more limited venue for users to participate, whereas the other side, consumer-controlled media, such as fan-based content, may be the result of a community growing beyond corporate-imposed limits. One important aspect of convergence is collaboration, where various communities will continue to negotiate the terms of participation and content creation. So, convergence itself can be defined as the intersection point at which existing technologies, cultures, communities, and media merge to create new forms of communication and stimulate new ways of thinking and interacting with these forms.

MEDIA CONVERGENCE

Certainly, once upon a time, the media had a great deal of say—they were the gatekeepers—about when and how news was presented to the public. Now, that gate is wide open. The so-called citizen journalist with a camera phone often sends in the first footage of crashes and fires, and even the more mundane—though more often spectacular—happenstances of daily life are being documented and shared on multimedia platforms of the event's occurrence.

In the "old" days, geography was a great barrier to news dissemination. The telegraph started to close that gap, and even then citizens and governments wondered if such information travelling at such a rapid rate would lose in its haste any semblance of context.

Now, news travels not just from the local gas station to the people in that community but to everyone in that state, in that country, and indeed, around the world. A major reason for that is that the public is no longer simply the consumer of news, but a news producer as well. In the past, story tips were passed from readers to editors and reporters, and the tip was weighed for its news value before being pursued or discarded. Now, the news speaks for itself: Someone can write a blog about it, post it to a message board, or even record it as a video and post it on YouTube for the world to see.

Time was the other great gate through which information passed— even at just the rate of a trickle in the early years of print, nonair travel, and no telegraph. Now, however, time is no longer a factor; stories of a 2008 plane crash in Denver, Colorado, for example, were on Twitter within one minute of the accident. Reports from regular citizens on iPhones have become staples of cable television, in particular, and its coverage of hurricanes and tornadoes. Digital technology has erased borders, erased deadlines, and allowed for a constant, 24/7 news cycle that places a demand like none in history for media and citizen journalists to spread news.

However, convergence has also brought several other issues—problems, most notably—to light, including, but not limited to, the following:

Context: Okay, so we have a plane crash in Denver. In 140 characters, maybe 20 to 25 words, the news has gotten out. But how many are hurt? How are traffic patterns affected? Is there any risk to the public nearby? Context is something the news media, despite its shortcomings, were always good at providing. Newspaper stories would have accompanying sidebars with reactions, similar events in history, and even stories about what to do facing certain circumstances. In the real-time unfolding of news events online, context is often lost and never recouped as other events break and the early news is stowed at the expense of current events that draw the readers' and viewers' interest. In the past, people would find out about a tsunami on the evening news or the next day. In real time, the news unfolds literally as it happens. The analysis and contextual pieces in the newspaper arrived on the doorstep the following morning. Now, users are left to find their own context. However, readers can also chime in with their opinions and own expert—or amateur—analysis, facts, and perspective about what has transpired. This has made the flow of information much more back and forth, but it has also somewhat stifled the elements of the news-gathering process that simply took time and hours on the street or phone to gather all the facts, all the sides, and to present a coherent report of events that offers context.

Editing: In the past, a reporter would come back from a fire or accident, or even a meeting, start writing a story, look up some background, and send the story to the copy desk. The copy desk, which would also be laying out pages, would usually get to the story then or over the course of an evening, perhaps ask the reporter a few questions about adding something, taking something out, clarifying something, or fact checking such items as names, dates, and times. These stories were then outputted on news pages, which were proofread rather than edited for any mistakes. Not anymore. The news process is not a 500-lap NASCAR race like the one you see on Sunday. The news cycle is a one-lap, winner takes all race to get things out the fastest. Stories given even a cursory read are sitting in the equivalent of the pits while others cruise at high speeds on the information superhighway. Ironically, the consequences are still the same, and even higher, for the media: those who get information wrong lose readers who drift to news sites that are shown to get the stories right. Misinformation from shoddy reporting and hurried editing are just as libelous as those that appear a day later in print. All of this places an immense amount of added pressure on reporters, and even copy editors and Web editors, to edit on the fly as news travels at the pace of the ether through which it is presented and delivered. The Web does provide the ability for newspapers and magazines to correct errors in stories as soon as they are discovered and the correct information is verified. In the past, corrections did not run until at least a day later in the next edition of the newspapers, or in the case of magazines, in a week or even a month. Now, the errors are not only caught but responded to as soon as the story has been posted and been read by users. This raises an ethical issue when correcting the story. Some news operations will go in and physically make the change, and move on. Some will append the corrected information— and this is usually the case in online archives of print publications—at the top or bottom of the story. However, if readers are commenting on the story and that is where the error is posted, then fixing it in the story thus overrides the correction notes in the post at the bottom—which makes that person look as though they are not very bright readers (since the correction was made after the comment). This can turn into a back-and-forth guessing game: After fixing it, does the paper hyperlink to the correction, thank the reader at the end of the story, simply delete the comment once the error has been fixed, or "comment" on the comment noting who caught the error, telling future readers it has since been corrected?

Quality control: There are countless examples of citizen journalists capturing important images on video cameras or picture phones—and that is a fraction of 1 percent of those that are done on a daily basis. There is a reason the evening news is not blurry, that images are framed properly, that sound is clear, and that graphics are sharp—because the people doing it are professionals, and are both trained and paid to do it. Likewise, there is a reason the editorials in the newspaper—whether you like them or loathe them—are so well written and researched, why the rhetoric is so salient and even moving. That is the same reason news stories are written so sharply and crisply in inverted pyramid, with only a few quotes used to make a poignant, unique, or interesting point—and the reason for all this is that the writers are professionals, who are trained in the craft and get paid for it. For the person at home whose spouse has a good income, being a citizen journalist or blogger can be an interesting and rewarding hobby. But it is hard—some might say, it is a job—to do it every day, do it ethically, do the research, and write at a professional, engaging level that is going to draw in the thousands upon thousands of regular readers to make it financially salable for a career. Those nice $10 to $40 checks from Google Ads for blog views are nice. But for the professional in another field who has at least 40 hours of responsibilities at the office or even home office, crafting a well-done story or essay takes the kind of time and skills that not everyone has. So the idea of "everyone being a journalist" is quite different from everyone actually being a paid, working journalist. This does not mean every squirrel will not find an acorn. However, it does mean that to do it well enough, and with enough credibility and ethics to be respected and believed, it cannot simply be something to dabble in—not for a career.

Misinformation: This should probably be in 72-point type with blinking lights and sirens going off around it. Citizen journalists not trained in gathering research and practicing ethical behavior certainly might pick these skills up on their own or through their education in another discipline. However, for as many truth seekers as there are out there, there are at least as many, and probably exponentially more, people with their own agendas trying to put their spin on things. Some companies pay bloggers to help mitigate bad news or downplay potential crises. Only the discerning eye can sift through such "facts" and come to any sort of meaningful truths. Everyone has an opinion, and while that is lesson 101 in journalism school, it is actually the reason most people take to the blogosphere to let loose a rant about a person, place, product, or issue. When someone drops a spectacular number in a story, without the proper context or even citing a reliable source, it often does not keep that from spreading like wildfire around the planet, especially if it is something people want to believe. For example, with the unemployment crisis in 2009, the unemployment rate early in the year was just over 8 percent in late March. The alarm was sounded that a "formal education"—that is, going back to college—obviously would not help. However, digging deeper into the same statistic, unemployment for those with a college degree was still around just 3 percent, and those with a graduate degree was at about 1 percent. So a quick look at the data—something most people do who blog or write as citizen journalists only recreationally—might sound certain alarms, but if the data were looked at completely and in the proper context, the information might help others feel more secure. And it also might help people make well-informed, smart decisions about their future. As a side note, unemployment rates of those who had dropped out of high school were in the high teens and, as the data were broken down further, as high as 26-percent unemployment rates existed in March 2009. The irony of this is, of course, that the big push for the Internet was as the global village that would spread knowledge and prosperity. Yet people can go onto the U.S. Department of Labor Web site at any time and check unemployment for any demographic they want, even breaking it down by sex, gender, ethnicity, wage level, and education. But they would rather see something they want to believe—for whatever matches their personal belief and personal reason—and spread that instead, even though it is at best inaccurate and misleading, and at worst simply wrong. Cognitive dissonance and selective exposure are two concerns that proponents of "information for everyone" certainly did not envision becoming major obstacles to enlightenment, education, and open-mindedness as the gates of the gatekeepers came tumbling down.

Fragmentation: If gatekeeping is somewhat a thing of the past, it would be hard to make the case that the public is better educated, better at self-education through user-created content than media-produced content, or that democracy is flourishing because the walls of information no longer keep anyone from learning whatever they want to know, whenever they want to know it. Many of the best Ivy league schools post videos of their classes online, complete with syllabi, and those get a fraction of hits compared to a celebrity photo Web site. Those claiming intellectual anarchy when the Internet knocked out the windows and maybe the doors of the media establishment did not count on one thing: that not everyone wanted anarchy. A good percentage of the population likes to be well informed and certainly uses the Internet to find information they seek regularly. But the idea that everyone is a journalist simply has not taken root. Even the viral-marketing dream of publishing on demand or becoming self-published was darkened by the 2007 figures that of the record 300,000 titles self-published or publish on demand titles sold fewer, on average, than 100 copies each, which meant the writers who paid to publish were spending more than they made back. Since books like this are not carried in bookstores—though they can be ordered in bookstores—they are not marketed, distributed, or even produced like they are by the trade or even smaller bona-fide publishers, business that have for decades and centuries made a life publishing books. Has the new platform brought a change to the book publishing industry? Absolutely, and both e-books, though it has been slow, and Kindle, which appears more promising, are exciting and potentially profitable options. But the idea of your neighbor's random musings on bathroom smells hitting the *New York Times* remains a solitary dream, for the most part. Whether you subscribe to the masses ruling the publishing universe and everyone being a working writer or not, the harsh reality is that newspapers and magazines not only drifted slowly toward the online format, but have yet to find a way to make it profitable. With all online newspapers viewable worldwide, it is hard to tell advertisers who is reading their text and looking at their pictures, as well as for how long and why. Research from academics in this area has been woeful: Programs at universities will talk ad nauseam about how the paradigm does not yet exist for a financially salable online model, yet the student newspaper at state university X still produces its print paper, along with an online version, because it is not subjected to most of the financial exigencies (including the free print version college newspapers almost always produce) that regular newspapers are.

However, convergence has also brought with it significant benefits—including some the news business salivated over the idea of—for a long time, including:

Dialogue with readers: Actually, it is a dialogue and working relationship in some cases with users who also produce their own content. This is one of the many doubled-edged sword relationships media must deal with. Since anyone can read the media and put their own thoughts and versions of events out there, journalists must have an eye that is as wary as it is curious. Get bogged down or build a relationship with someone who has his/her own agenda and little integrity, and a journalist might bring discredit to the entire Web publication. But this is much more of an exciting turn of events to have users who can also supplement content or simply provide names, numbers, and emails for sources who know the inside on a particular story. Again, verification is very important for footage, information, and even e-files produced to show fraud, or to demonstrate a lack of fraud, for an investigative piece. Dan Rather's long, respectable career at CBS ended on a whimper rather than with a bang because of a shoddily produced forgery related to President

George W. Bush's service career. In a day and era of electronic databases, this information—though it happened long before the microchip—should have been verified and could have very easily been checked. Multiple sides were weighing in, each trying to sway coverage of the story toward one political party's advantage over the other. The result was bad information, bad journalism, and a bad ending to what would otherwise have been a legendary career.

Production costs decrease: Loading content to news Web sites is a lot easier than printing (and delivering) thousands of newspapers or magazines, or going through all the applications for a radio or network affiliate broadcast TV license.

No space issues: On 30-minute, or even 1-hour, broadcast news programs, time is of the essence. Online, a piece could go on as long as the reporters and producers want. However, this is actually a quality-control issue, because even though some pieces are cut to seemingly too short lengths, editing is a skill and telling a story in less time, or fewer words, is a talent news professionals hone over the course of their careers. Likewise, rather than have to shorten or cut stories, sidebars, and charts or tables, print publications can run stories of infinite lengths. Again, do readers want to commit to reading 6,000 words on a city council vote on trash pickup fees, or will that same 300 words and 10 column inches suffice online? One of the tenets of good reporting and writing is word economy, and stories that go long inevitably have more words thrown at ill-thought-out ideas or run-on sentences, when the solution is to cut words or find the right ones, rather than add on aimlessly.

On a pragmatic level, the Internet gives media the chance to present stories in every format—print, audio, and video—something that could not be done because of ownership issues in the past where regulations kept media companies from "controlling the media" by owning television stations, radio stations, and the newspaper in the same cities. With the Internet, each Web site is potentially all three and, as a converged model, a hyper-print-broadcast platform.

Storage: This is another area of convergence with both extraordinary positives and negatives. On the one hand, digital material can be stored—and probably is—forever with the click of one or two buttons. On the other hand, not everyone will have access to it, there are often multiple versions of everything, copyright issues for print, photo, audio, and broadcast content have been kicked to the curb like yesterday's trash, and there is the issue of whether all content should really be saved. Do we save 10 years of John Doe's blogs about bathroom tissue when only one contained a useful nugget? And who decides these things? Where are they stored? Is misinformation countered—is there a responsibility for archives to be fair and balanced?

PERSONALIZED CONVERGENCE

Convergence, as both a concept and emerging new media theory, has its own breathtaking characteristics as something on a personal computer that users can access from an office or home. On the go, a laptop computer makes this concept even more lively, especially with wireless capabilities. But with the advent of the mobile phone, convergence has opened a whole new set of possibilities, and the paradigm around which the dust was just beginning to settle is now alive—and on the move.

Having the Internet on cell phones has unleashed access to information that could hardly have been imagined even in the great heyday of library building and expansion, or even archival storage ability on the microchip. Want to watch a clip or even a full favorite program? You can find it, and probably even buy it, and then watch it from the cell phone. Tired of hearing stories from your parents digging around used record stores to find an obscure song they listened to while dating decades ago? It is online now, probably for less than a buck, and you can probably get it within one minute of reading this text. Did you like that episode from an old sitcom on one of those high-numbered cable channels? If you want, you can get every episode on DVD, or you could just as easily—probably even easier, in fact—download that particular show. Or, you could TiVo it, and watch it again and again at your convenience, if you do not mind the "hassle" of sitting in front of a television *and* using the remote.

Your vote really does count, whether it makes a big difference or not, on *Big Brother* and *American Idol*. You can vote nightly on best plays and most valuable players on several sports Web sites. So audience involvement—and the opportunity for it—is at an all-time high and is ever-expanding.

Yet for the remarkable evolution of technology, these are all still branches from the media tree; they are just incredible, multidimensional extensions that overlap, intersect, and run parallel in ways that make life easier, and make artistic and scientific parts of life more accessible.

On an interpersonal level, or even an individual's experience with the media, there are sociological and psychological factors that are only now starting to get some salient research attention. Indeed, though the cell phone keeps you plugged into everyone around you, at what expense does it come? Are we aware of the strangers on the street who may be potential friends or attackers? The noises of day-to-day life are often drowned out by cell phone conversations, the beeping of instant messages, and even the tireless ringing of the cell phone. Convergence has brought not just the baseball card–thin mobile media player but now music on that cell phone, so students, joggers, and people walking across traffic are oblivious to the innocent and dangerous noises with their earphones in and volume pushed too high so they can listen to favorite tunes rather than the noises around which their lives exist. Again, this is an extension of the Sony Walkman, a bulky cassette player that with any luck clipped to a healthy belt or waistband, which in turn was an extension of the "boombox," itself a direct descendant of the home stereo—the boombox just made it mobile. Certainly, there is irony in that the boombox took the experience of a personal music player and at times annoyed those in the vicinity trying to gather their thoughts, while the personal music players of today let people slip by the days of their lives without having to either make or hear a sound outside of their earphones. The psychological and sociological values and even dangers of being so plugged into what we want and failing to make friends or notice the world around us surely has some sort of consequence, though it is also reassuring and a security blanket of its own to have friends and family at the push of a button no matter where we roam and to have our personal entertainment system on our mobile phones.

Section Two

New Media News Writing

Chapter 4

New Media News Writing

INTRODUCTION

Textbooks today drop the word "Convergence" and are off and running with the idea that a story needs to be told only in "its best medium"—visual, audio, or print—and that the journalists of tomorrow must take with them to every story a reporter's notebook, digital audio recorder, and two cameras—one to shoot still photos, and one to record video and sound.

That might be the recipe for a news reporter on "Fantasy Island," but there are enough untrained writers on the Web blogging, commenting on message boards, and writing pithy comments between conferences or sales appointments at their full-time jobs, but it does little to present the day's news to a public that still, according to page views on news Web sites, has an insatiable appetite for news.

Certainly, academia has its hands full making sense of what the real-time, 24/7 multimedia should spend their time doing. But readers still go to their local newspaper or national newspaper of choice to read the news in online text—and to look at photos, and while readers might click on a video or the now-overdone photo gallery, the dominant majority of clicks still are on text-written stories. They look at CNN and the network and other cable Web sites for video and online text stories, and many of the television Web sites include Associated Press and other text-based news outlets. Even Google News, though it has plenty of links to still photos and the occasional link to video, has predominantly—as in more than 85 percent on a typical weekday—a news front dominated by print news, from newspapers around the world, and wire services. Google does highlight the occasional credible blog—though many of those are from news Web sites—and the occasional spectacular or fun user video, the Internet "news webscape" is still dominated by reporting by those trained to do it.

If you are out covering a story that is highly visual, get pictures and video. If there is an interview and you can set up for a video broadcast interview to record, do it. But by all means, treat it as a journalist would and do what you have to do to get the story for your readers, regardless of format. It is impossible to come back and file the same story in four completely different formats—especially in the real-time news cycle—and do all of them well. In this area of "do everything" all the time, do one thing very well, and learn how to use the equipment to tell the story in other formats when possible. This could be simply an extension of the reporter writing a story from an interview, and posting an audio file for users to listen to, if they so choose: But how many people are going to choose the entire 60-minute interview over the well-written, tightly focused 400-word story that gives them all the information they want right there? Probably a few, but a precious few. You are a journalist first. All the bells and whistles out there now are just noisemakers if they are used only for the sake of using them.

That is not to suggest that reporters should not know how to put together a podcast, shoot video, edit tape, write stories, take photos, crop those pictures, and so on. But there are only so many hours in the day, and if the push is for reporters to get more—perhaps shorter—news stories, then having them present the information in every multimedia format available is probably not the best way to go about covering the news—or to keep reporters motivated. Reporters still go to press conferences, school board and city council meetings, and athletic contests and come back to write stories. The great shot that wins a game, the salacious quote from a council meeting, and outlandish claims in a courtroom still make great video or audio. But to provide a "good read" requires the same basic writing and reporting tenets it has for more than a century. Putting together a minute of videotape can take up to an hour; it is hard to imagine anyone putting together an hour-long video broadcast from a city council meeting or game, or anyone watching it—or any network dedicating that much time to one event when so much else is going on. Text can still run without limitation; indeed, that was a big concern of reporters in the "old" days of print, that editors were too punitive in cutting stories and publishers were too stingy in allocating news holes for stories. The Internet brings a bottomless news hole, and reporters can write—provided they are doing it well—to their heart's content, giving the readers longer, better reads than ever before.

NEW MEDIA PRINT WRITING

Newspapers in the 1900s were a thriving business. As the century moved into its later half, certainly television, and then especially cable television, took a chunk of advertising revenue away from newspapers. Cities that had two newspapers—morning and evening—were in most cases down to one, and one either folded or operated jointly with the other.

However, in the 1990s, all that started to change as the Internet became the delivery platform of choice. It was easier and faster, and people liked it better than the paper—or hard-copy—version. With advertising all over the Internet, as well as all over sports stadiums, school buses, and other media, newspapers found a shrinking advertising base, and at the turn of the century, the slide was quite pronounced, with circulation numbers dwindling and newspapers laying off people in every part of the operation. This is, of course, among the greater ironies of the twentieth and early twenty-first centuries, that newspapers would be in this position, because while the headlines and stories are about how newspapers are going broke, the reality is that readership is up hundreds of percent, and in many cases thousands of percent, though with free distribution via the Internet, circulation revenue has plunged.

The New York Times, for example, went from a circulation of several million to as many as 40 million readers per day—so readership is anything but down. Newspapers, a source of producing and disseminating information, misjudged the speed and power of the Internet from the very beginning of the World Wide Web. They never embraced the idea of doing business any differently than they had for more than two centuries, and they underestimated the influence the Internet would have on the business model that newspapers had survived by—and depended upon. Newspapers sold space on pages, be it a one column by four inch ad, a two- or three-column by however many inches ad, or a full-page advertisement. Classified advertising for selling and buying items, or finding work, was another source of income. Revenue also came from selling subscriptions; however, the idea that newspapers made much money—if any, in most cases—from selling the paper is largely a myth; most newspapers barely covered back shop, print, and delivery costs with circulation revenue.

So the Internet, in theory, wiped out the biggest expenses for newspapers. No longer would newspapers have to pay people to paste up (which faded out in the 1990s) or paginate pages, and with an online edition newspapers would not have to spend a dime on gas, worry about insurance for drivers or carriers—or keep claiming they were "independent" contractors.

The cost of newsprint, which skyrocketed in the 1990s, was no longer an issue for an Internet edition.

If the picture was so good, what went wrong?

The problem was that as whiz kids and graduate students embraced the new technology and created the likes of Yahoo and Google, newspapers sat on their collective hands. They did not want to change the way they did business, did not want find a new business model, and did not want to acknowledge that the shattered pieces on the floor of their newsroom was the paradigm under which they had successfully existed for so long.

It is unthinkable that an industry in charge of news gathering and distributing would sit on its hands as the Internet and search engines became financial cash cows. Newspapers for a long time had a great financial resource in their customers' addresses, phone numbers, and even shopping habits from coupons and advertisements. The search engines found great value—and accrued Wall Street value—in part from a limited number of advertisements, but another primary source was where people were visiting online, for how long, what they were clicking on, what they did not like, and where they did their shopping. Newspapers missed that boat.

Newspapers' first reaction, when they finally collectively reacted (though to this day there are newspapers with no or nearly no online presence), was to sell subscriptions to an online edition, even though people could go to Yahoo, and then later to Google, to get news from around the world updated constantly. What newspapers found out was that their online readers had little interest in sending in credit card numbers for information that they could get, for the most part for free on the Web— local news remains an exception. Other newspapers, rather than sell subscriptions, required online registrations, so that each user had a username and password. That information allowed newspapers a potentially small revenue stream for a while, but with *USA Today* and other newspapers going entirely online, impatient readers did not want to have to even register for subscriptions.

"For generations, newspapers didn't change much. They didn't have to," *Colorado Springs Gazette* editor Jeff Thomas wrote in a March 2008 column. "Those days are gone, and change is the new constant."

It is constant, but it is still an evolving model. The advertising dilemma is still one newspapers have no financial traction on; when newspapers grudgingly went online, the first plan to generate revenue was the same as it always was, to sell space, such as a one-column by two- or three-inch-deep advertisement. Many newspapers had "full-page" advertisements that readers would have to sit and wait for to disappear. Readers did not like this, and would leave the Web site. Some news Web sites still have such advertisements but offer a "click here" button to get rid of the ad and proceed directly to the story, but how do they guarantee to advertisers then that the advertisement is working for the business?

NEW MEDIA WRITING

Working in new media is everything you have heard it is—and more.

It is not, and for the sake of credible research, reporting, and writing, the free-for-all approach that many bloggers seem to think it is.

A lot of the excitement around "everyone being an author" and "everyone writing a blog" brings into question a lot of dilemmas: Is there a market for "everyone being a writer" and does the "citizen journalist" have the writing skill, reporting expertise, and ethics many readers expect from their media professionals?

If you are writing for a public relations firm, or working in advertising, you now have a platform to get the word out about your product, to deal with crises, and to promote your co-workers and the good work your company does in its particular communities. However, think about it: How many times a day do you seek out the Web site address for Procter and Gamble or Wal-Mart to read what their public relations staffs have written about the good they are doing in their communities? Probably not very often. The reality is people look to credible news sources online for news, commentary, and features. Most of these credible news Web sites and even bloggers are tied to media organizations, including news papers and television stations. Your neighbor might blog several times a week, but where is the information coming from to back up their claims? Are they doing any research? Is it just a rant about politics? Does he or she have access to local news makers to confirm or deny facts or events? And maybe more importantly, does your neighbor have the time and expertise to write at least several times per week? Blogging is nice, and it is a craft, but with so many millions of bloggers, few blog sites will even be financially sustainable. It is true that there is no salable news model at this time for making actual news Web sites profitable or simply breaking even. However, it is hard to imagine America, or any country, remaining out front as a world leader without news organizations to play watchdog, to uncover the bad news, to report about the truly good news, and to help set the agenda for readers and viewers.

Blogs are a great source for news tips, and the reporters who do not pay attention to the particularly credible bloggers do so at their own peril.

However, less than 1 percent of bloggers are trained journalists or even published writers, so they have neither the writing nor the reporting skills to provide a bona fide service that readers can count on daily. And those who do form their opinions based only on blogs—speaking at their own peril—are choosing a questionable, at best, form of facts to arrive at the hard truths through which we live, work, and even exist in a democratic society.

Using social media for news gathering is fine, as long as you know what you are getting. For interviewing celebrities and athletes, which I do a lot of, I have to make sure the blog or pages from Facebook and MySpace are maintained and updated by the athletes themselves, not a public relations firm or fan club. What you will want to do is establish contact through a personal interview, whether that is in person or via phone—or better yet in the case of the latter, by videophone—to ask the source personally if he/she writes his/her own blogs, how often the blog is updated, and so on.

Because people speak differently than they write, in most cases, you should always cite how the information is attained. The stream-of-consciousness tone that comes with hearing someone speak in a question-and-answer interview is far different from quoting from a blog post, or even from an email (more on email interviews in a bit).

NEW MEDIA ETHICS, A CASE STUDY: THE REAL-TIME NEWS CYCLE

> *What he doesn't get is that journalism is not Hollywood. It's not about closing the deal. It's not about face time. It's about, simply put, telling the truth.*

That paragraph was written by Mitch Albom in the *Detroit Free Press* in 2003, referring to Jayson Blair, the disgraced *New York Times* reporter who admitted fabricating stories.

Yet when Albom himself wrote about an event that had yet to happen—but presented it as if it had—the media scrambled to make sense of it.

The questions raised were all about ethics: Did he mislead? Did he fabricate? Does the media operating in real time justify making assumptions in "advance" stories? However, the discussion that followed the investigation into Albom's wrongdoing, his hollow mea culpa, and his celebrated return to the *Detroit Free Press* sports pages seemed to show a different set of standards for the widely read multimedia maverick Albom.

Albom, the award-winning columnist who has evolved into a celebrity, wrote a 2005 column after interviewing two former Michigan State basketball players who were by then in the NBA. The players' alma mater, Michigan State, was playing in a Saturday NCAA Final Four game, and

Albom was writing for Sunday's "bulldog" edition, which would run before the game was played Saturday. Rather than write a feature, Albom plopped both former players—Mateen Cleaves and Jason Richardson—in the stands at the game. He even wrote about the beer-drinking students around them and what the duo was wearing.

The only problem was that the game had not been played. And when the game was played, neither Cleaves nor Richardson had followed through on plans—which they had relayed to Albom—that they would be sitting together in the stands.

To understand where Albom is coming from, one must know where Albom is—and when it comes to the media, Albom is everywhere—books, TV, radio, magazines, radio stations as a talk-show host and songwriter, and newspapers. He is one of the most hailed sports columnists, winning national writing awards, appearing on ESPN, hosting a highly rated daily radio show, and writing three best-selling books. Though he might have climbed the journalistic ladder by writing a newspaper column, he is by no means a one-trick pony. His best-selling books include the nonfiction *Tuesdays with Morrie* and the fictionalized *The Five People You Meet in Heaven*, both of which spent years on the *New York Times* best-seller list, where his new books always enjoy long stays.

His first two books were made into movies. Albom has also written songs that have been recorded. In addition, he penned a play that played in Jeff Daniels's (whose most famous film credit ironically might be *Dumb and Dumber*) playhouse in Michigan.

Albom apologized in a follow-up column, saying that he had been wrong. "You can't write that something happened that didn't" (Albom 2005). Albom's apology did not address the idea that his writing something that did not happen was ethically wrong. Indeed, Albom seemed to think if the players had gone to the game, the point would have been moot.

Albom wrote in his column explaining why he did what he did by claiming he had "weird" deadlines, blaming the players for not going ahead as planned for the games. But this is where Albom loses this author and former sportswriter. No such "weird" writing of any kind was needed. The arc of the story was the nostalgia and the players' heartfelt comments about professional versus collegiate athletics. All he had to do was say the players would watch the game Saturday and be on a sort of intellectual memory lane. He could go one step further and close the story and say that at the final buzzer, Cleaves and Richardson would be back in the NBA, where they found their riches but had not yet found happiness. That would be consistent with Albom's optimistic narrative style.

If the editors were complicit—and Albom blamed them in part in his apology, his editor also put a big share of the blame on the editors after her in-house team "investigated" the incident and went through past Albom columns—then the paper does not have high standards.

The newspaper suspended Albom. Executive editor Carole Lee Hutton wrote a note to readers claiming the issue was about credibility, and that the column was written Friday for a Sunday edition. However, the overriding problem and issue is that Albom wrote something that had not happened. Had he simply said, "both players plan to be at the game," then he could have done his trademark detail-oriented scene setting as he wished, as long as readers knew it was a forecast of expected events, not a review of actual events that had already occurred.

While the incident was still unfolding, some thought Albom's reign at the *Free Press* should end. "I don't see how they will have any choice at the end of their investigation but to fire Mitch and the editor or editors who read the column before it was published," said Randy Harvey, the *Baltimore Sun*'s assistant managing editor for sports (Joyner 2005).

Karen Brown Dunlap, president of Poynter, said she was surprised Albom committed such an obvious infraction: "I think it's very sad, very serious and very disappointing. And this was done by a very fine writer with a great reputation and a lengthy career. This was not a new reporter in journalism" (Hirsley 2005).

Bill Gallagher, a TV journalist for Fox2 News in Detroit who won, among other awards, a Peabody, wrote a story about Albom for the *Niagara Falls Reporter* (Michigan): "Saying you are somewhere you are not, describing scenes and events that have not occurred and manufacturing conversations certainly are rare deceptions for reporters and columnists—but even one is too many . . . Albom has long been a privileged and pampered figure at the *Free Press*" (Gallagher 2005). In an article in the *Chicago Tribune* detailing the fiasco, Michael Hirsley interviewed Loren Ghiglione, dean of the Medill School of Journalism at Northwestern University, who did not understand how Albom could possibly be allowed to wiggle out of the ethical blunder—though Ghiglione did not want to see Albom's career destroyed, or even see him lose his job. "[The issue] doesn't sound ethical to me," Ghiglione said. "When professors at Medill read a student's story and find something that is untrue, it gets an 'F' " (Hirsley 2005).

Yet Albom was given a pass.

Many in the media took time to question whether the news reporter as a news maker—a media celebrity, as Albom is—fits into journalism ethics. Roy Peter Clark, senior scholar at the Poytner, wonders if newspapers know what to make of, and how to manage, their multimedia stars:

I think this case will present an opportunity to examine the world of the elite newspaper columnist. I'm talking about the columnist who becomes the franchise player for the newspaper. Such columnists get to write in their own voices. They attract a crowd. They become identified with their newspapers. They earn big bucks. They keep the cash registers ringing for the business side. Many of them, such as Albom, are in sports. But others, Mike Barnicle [formerly of the *Boston Globe*] comes to mind—work the news side. Something happens to these newspaper writers over time. Because of their profile, they become celebrities. Because of their celebrity, they become cottage industries. The siren song of fame and fortune is seductive enough. Not only is Mitch Albom one of the most celebrated sports columnists in the world, he is also the author of two astonishingly successful best-sellers. (I'm sure I'm not the first writer to express envy.) He offers his opinions on ESPN and on his own radio talk show. (Clark 2005)

Bob Steele, a journalism ethics professor at the Poynter Institute in St. Petersburg, Florida, blamed Albom for being "dishonest" and also did not think Albom's apology went far enough, or even addressed the issue: "I would say this is a significant journalistic and ethical failure. To write that something happened before that event actually takes place is not only presumptuous but deceptive" (2005). Lost in the debate about Albom's ethical lapse (or lack of ethics) is that in the article in question he was preaching a widely embraced belief that young college players should not forego their college years to enter the NBA (Albom 2005) to embrace its riches before their senior year is completed. Indeed, Albom's angle is that college sports are purer, more meaningful, and even more important than the dollars and glory of the NBA.

Just as troubling to many journalists was that Albom's column was edited and laid out by a team of editors—though it should be pointed out it is a handpicked group of editors (Steele 2005) who always work on Albom's work, not the normal-shift sports copy desk—who put it on the page knowing the event had not happened, thus making the column a fake. "Did editors know Albom was writing a column based on assumptions?" asked Steele. "If so, why did they allow this to happen?"

Yes, they did know (Voas 2005), and why they let it pass their hands onto the page will never be known. Common sense tells any journalist—or any reader—that this problem was easily avoided. Albom could have written it as a feature story, saying both players were proud to be from Michigan State and planned to attend the game. To try and write it in the real time that the game happened was Albom's mistake. Still, any editor could have changed it. Showing how deep this culture ran, the Freep (*Detroit Free Press*) followed its usual process and sent it out on the wire via Knight-Ridder's syndicate to member newspapers who subscribe.

Only one newspaper—the *Duluth News Tribune* (Minnesota), where then-recent University of Kansas journalism-school graduate Nikki Overfelt was working the sports copy desk—took preemptive measures to correct Albom's column. Overfelt changed the wording to indicate that the game had not been played yet. She rewrote the parts about the players being at the game, noting they only said they "will be" at the game and "will sit" in the stands. While the column certainly loses some flair from not unfolding in the excitement of college athletics, the impact of the message of staying in school comes through perfectly clearly. "I thought they (Knight-Ridder) would send something about not releasing the column until Sunday, but nothing came, so I changed the tenses," Overfelt told reporter Chuck Woodling of the *Lawrence Journal-World* (Kansas) (Woodling 2005).

On CNN's *Reliable Sources*, a program hosted by *Washington Post* media critic Howard Kurtz, even Albom's friends had a hard time justifying Albom's playing fast and loose with the sacred ethic of truth. Albom, Kurtz noted, declined an invitation to be on the show, but Kurtz did quote Albom's *Free Press* apology, where Albom wrote, "You can't write that something happened, that didn't." Kurtz's guest were friends of Albom's, Tony Kornheiser of the *Washington Post*—who has a TV show on ESPN on weekdays and is a commentator on *Monday Night Football*—and another multimedia star, John Feinstein, an award-winning former newspaper columnist who has written a string of best-selling books, including *A Season on the Brink*, which was adapted to film. Feinstein, a regular on National Public Radio, also appears on ESPN's *The Sports Reporters* along with Albom, but Feinstein also was fired by ESPN (before being rehired more than a year later) for criticizing ESPN. On *Reliable Sources*, Kurtz— a colleague of Kornheiser at the *Post*—lit into Kornheiser in this exchange:

Kurtz: Are you willing to tell your friend he screwed up?

Kornheiser: Well, I think that he knows he screwed up, in the sense that what he wrote did not turn out to be true. But I don't think there was any malice in it.

Kurtz: Not turned out to be true. He wrote "they sat in the stands in their Michigan State clothing and rooted on their alma mater."

Kornheiser: I understand. Right, I understand. When they ask somebody on Friday to write a column for Sunday about something that happens on Saturday, there's got to be a better back-stop method than that. But I don't think his intent was to defraud people. The people he talked to, the Michigan State players, have not said he didn't talk to them, have not said that they were misquoted. I mean, yes, it is a mistake, but I don't think he has to be killed over the mistake. And he is being killed by the people in journalism who like to eat their young.

Feinstein was not willing to let Albom off the hook as fast as Kornheiser.

" . . . I agree with Tony that I don't think there was malice involved," Feinstein said. "That having been said, this isn't a misdemeanor. This isn't a speeding ticket, journalistically speaking. He did, in fact, make something up. It could not have happened.

"And the excuse that he had a Friday night deadline, he knew he had a Friday night deadline when he wrote the column. He easily could have said that they said they're going to the game. They're planning to go to the game. They're looking forward to the game because of all these things he wrote about without writing that he saw something that didn't happen."

Kornheiser said the whole concept of writing "P.M." sidebars has to be reviewed.

"When you are asked to write in advance like that, I think that's mistake No. 1, to write on Friday for Sunday about an event that didn't happen yet," Kornheiser said. "But I think there is some shared responsibility here. Mitch—I think Mitch's major crime, as I read these stories, is that he's rich, famous and successful, and a lot of people want to bring him down. An editor has to say, when the column is handed in on Friday, 'Whoa, hold it. This didn't exactly happen yet.' There has to be a backstop."

Feinstein interrupted.

"I'm sorry, you can't blame it on the editor," Feinstein said. Kornheiser said he was not blaming it on the editor, but Feinstein called Kornheiser out.

" . . . You said, 'An editor has to.' That's blaming it on the editor, just as in his first apology, which I thought was the second part of the problem, Mitch tried to throw the editors under the bus with him," Feinstein said. "You've got to realize the climate those editors are working in. This is a newspaper where the managing editor killed a review of his last book because it was negative."

Indeed, that review sparked controversy. Ironically, Albom had gone from being a hugely successful first-time book author, working in the nonfiction genre with *Tuesdays with Morrie*, to *The Five People You Meet in Heaven*, where Albom was dipping his toe in fiction. Some critics might argue that is a parallel arc he took—only this time he started making up stuff in his newspaper column. Albom has been shielded from in-house and public criticism, something some (Voas 2005) credits, including Detroit's *MetroTimes*, claim is unethical. In an effort to avoid conflict of interest by having someone on the newspaper staff review it, the Freep hired an independent voice, Carlo Wolff, to review Albom's *The Five People You Meet in Heaven*. While Wolff praises Albom's narrative as it relates to readability in what could be called an overall favorable review, Wolff did chide Albom's "sugary" style and said the story just "didn't work" for him (Wolff).

The review never saw print: Carole Hutton, executive editor, decided not to run Wolff's piece: "In the end, it came down to a decision about how I want the *Free Press* to treat its employees," she wrote, adding that the *Free Press* has "an unwritten policy of not reviewing the work of a colleague" (Voas 2005).

The *MetroTimes* notes that "Somebody might want to remind Hutton that Albom wrote *Heaven* for Hyperion, not the *Free Press*... and he received $5 million—according to the Freep—to do so" (Voas 2005). Hutton did not explain why Wolff was contracted in the first place. Further, just months earlier, the *Free Press* sent its own theater critic, Martin Kohn, to New York to review the stage production of *Tuesdays with Morrie*, based on Albom's book (Albom also co-wrote the script). Kohn called the play "magnificent work" and noted that "any emotional response the play gets from its audience is honestly earned"—so much for "not reviewing the work of a colleague."

Lest anyone think the *Boston Globe*—which seems to surface when any hot-air ethical balloon is floated—escaped notoriety on this issue, think again. The same week that the fallout hit from Albom's Final Four column, the *Boston Globe* admitted it ran a piece about a seal hunt that had not taken place. The freelancer who wrote it was cut loose by the paper, and the *Globe* ran a correction.

Referring to Hutton's choice to spike *The Five People You Meet in Heaven* review: The Cleveland-based Wolff said that *Free Press* assistant managing editor for features, Sharon Wilmore, asked him for a 1,000-word review of *The Five People You Meet in Heaven*. Wolff beat his deadline by a week, and was told it would run in the paper as the lead book review. Then he was called back and told that Hutton had pulled the review but rescheduled it for a week later. Another call informed him the review was "permanently unrescheduled." Wolff, 60, has written reviews for the *Christian Science Monitor*, *Atlanta Journal-Constitution*, *San Francisco Chronicle*, and *Boston Globe*.

Wolff claims Wilmore apologized to him, saying, "We thought we were doing the right thing, and I'm really, really sorry you got caught in the middle of it." Wolff said he felt "intellectually insulted" and called it "puzzling that a paper that celebrates the quality of its star columnist does not have enough confidence in him to roll with the punches that come with his being a public figure."

BOK'S SCORE

Sissela Bok, who has spent a good part of her academic career writing about how truth is discovered and what it really is, believes that the "moral question of whether you are lying or not is not settled by establishing the truth or falsity of what you say. The key: Whether you intend your statement to mislead" (Bok 1999, 1).

Albom says he actually did not intend to mislead, and even in his so-called apology to readers claims that had the players been at the game, the whole controversy would have never occurred—yet that does not change that, even if the players had been at the game, he wrote it before the game so he was not writing the truth as he knew it at the time he wrote his column. As events unfolded, what he reported was false. However, he had talked to the players involved, and they told them—with intended truth—that they planned on going to the game. One had chartered a private plane, and the other said he had in hand a commercial airline ticket. Both players told Albom they had tickets to the game and would sit together.

John Stuart Mill (2007) would note that Albom had to write a column for his readers for Sunday. Utilitarian brethren would point out that if Albom waited until game time, or post game, to write the column, the "bulldog" edition could not be printed in advance, as planned, and many readers in outlying areas of Detroit would not get a Sunday edition of the *Detroit Free Press*. Albom's column, one of the most read in the newspaper—or in any newspaper—is something readers enjoy and look for in each newspaper. Bok would have been concerned that one of Albom's lies would have led to another—and in this sense, she was right, because the subsequent investigation of Albom's columns revealed that he had been using quotations in his column from other newspapers and broadcast sources without attribution, in clear violation of the Freep's ethics policy as it relates to attribution.

Immanuel Kant (and George Serles and I. F. Stone for that matter) would have wanted Albom's head on a platter (granted, it would have had to have been a *big* platter). He wrote something that was not true and had not happened—knew it and wrote it anyway—so since it was not truth based on facts it did not belong in print. Kant would have nailed this one right on the money because Kant believes "when a person starts thinking about possible consequences, he or she begins to compromise ethics and falls into a trap of expediency . . . One should not lie, simply because lying is unethical, not because lying might lead to good or bad consequences" (1).

Kant's "Categorical Imperative" further hammers home the point—and would have put the final nail in Albom's professional journalism coffin—because it says, "in essence, that a person should do only those things which he or she is willing to see everybody else do" (2)—Albom never defends the practice of his, or any other journalist's, doing what he did. The only loophole Albom and his editors could have slithered through is Kant's "deontological" ethics—that Albom's reverence of duty led him to sacrifice facts to deliver to his readers the manna of their Sunday newspaper, his feel-good column.

This is what this author believes was Albom's thought process to the letter: His readers expected his column, and they expected the kind of detail and personality that defines Albom's writing. The fact that he was not at the game, in Albom's mind, had zero part in whatever ethics he has. To write a column that ran alongside the game story—but was annotated as having been written before the game—would not have met with Albom's standard of always being there, being "in" with the athletes, and being "at the scene" of whatever was being most talked about that day—and Michigan State's game was the story du jour, even as Albom flew to New York during the game to be on ESPN's Sunday morning television show *The Sports Reporters*, which is aired live from New York City.

Greek philosophy would apply a similar vein of reason to Bok's, but with different justification. Aristotle would weigh in with this author's point of view: Albom could write the column in advance, but he should not have written it as though it had already happened—write it as a feature story, because it is relevant and timely, and anyone who is a Michigan State fan would want to read what the players have to say, regardless of whether they ended up going to the game. Albom should have written it as a straight feature, which is to say he should have written it and been forthright that he spoke to the players earlier in the week, and that while they had planned to attend the game, the story should not have indicated that they were actually at the game together—because at that point they had not been (and never would be, as events unfolded). Yet the readers would have still gotten the feel-good column they expect and enjoy from their favorite sports columnist, Albom.

CONCLUSION

In another irony, Albom's controversial column ran on April 1, 2005—April Fool's Day. Maybe Mitch Albom was just joking—of course, he has not told us that, so I cannot write it and present it as having happened.

The internal investigation by the *Free Press* did blame Albom and his editors, and also revealed that Albom was using quotes from other news papers and broadcasters without attributing those to the proper media outlet. Once again, Albom said he was not doing anything that was not done at other newspapers. "I have never presented a non-attributed quote as something said personally to me—or something exclusive to me—and never would," Albom said as part of his response to the investigation (Albom 2005).

But if Albom does not attribute his quotes, does that mean he got them on his own, or they came from another media outlet—how are readers to know the difference? Or his editors, for that matter? Once again Hutton, the editor, said the problem showed Albom did not know the Freep's rules regarding attribution, and that she would address the problem.

The entire affair brings to the forefront three very important issues:

1. Whether deadlines for Sunday editions should be moved so that readers do not have to be "fooled" into believing they are reading something "fresh" that in reality was printed 48 hours earlier.

2. Discussion should take place about whether ethics have deteriorated so deeply that a reporter—standout or just out of journalism school—never has to admit wrongdoing and be accountable for what is an obvious, very black-and-white (not gray as Albom paints it) journalistic sin.

3. When a journalist becomes a multimedia celebrity, what are her or his obligations to the newspaper, and should the workload stay the same—or can it even reasonably be expected to stay the same with so many other projects going at once? Maybe Albom has simply outgrown his metro newspaper column.

Addressing the first point, the "bulldog" edition is a unique beast. To get the newspaper to out-of-city subscribers, a thick Sunday paper is printed in advance. This edition will not include late games from Sunday night—maybe not even anything past Friday night—because it runs Friday or Saturday, before the regular midnight or so Saturday night press run for the late-edition Sunday paper, which would include Saturday night sports scores (the exception being a late starting or delayed game on the West Coast). The "bulldog" is a valuable product for readers—and newspapers—and there is certainly no reason to do away with it. However, the same ethics should apply. If the Detroit Pistons are beating the Boston Celtics at halftime of a Friday game at 8 PM, and the bulldog has to go to press, neither Albom nor anyone else can write a column saying "The Pistons beat the Celtics last night" because that has not happened yet—and it might not.

Second, Albom's apology and follow-up comments indicate either a basic lack of understanding of ethics or a lack of accountability that comes from Albom himself, and each choice is equally troubling. How does one become so accomplished if one does not understand the simple rights and wrongs of journalism? Or how can he look in the mirror and claim he really did not do anything that wrong after being confronted with facts?

Finally, the multimedia star is such a double-edged sword that it is going to cut the newspaper either way. Papers need their reporters to be in other media on some level because it gives them more exposure, and thus draws in more readers to that reporter's column—in other words, multimedia exposure has tangible financial effects. However, when the line between fact and fiction is blurred, we can hardly expect that someone will step over wherever the line had been drawn before it was erased. Albom's case is unique in that he has so much success in so many dramas, conquering radio (a highly rated talk show), TV (ESPN is the sports-broadcast leader hands down), newspapers (he is a regular Associated Press Sports Editors [APSE] winner), music (songs he has written have been recorded), live theater (plays), movies (two of his three books have been adapted, and the third is under a movie option), and, of course, books, where his run on the best-seller list is as impressive as anyone not named J. K. Rowling or Stephen King.

With his schedule of flying from Detroit to New York to be on ESPN's Sunday morning *The Sports Reporters* show, his travel for Detroit sports, his radio commitment each weekday, his book appearances—and the time he has to set aside to write books—some wonder if Albom, as well as he does many things, has not stretched himself too thin and thus cannot give himself to any individual pursuit fully. Writing several newspaper columns a week is, for most writers, a full-time endeavor in itself. Cutting corners—and one could argue that writing about things happening in advance is just that—will lead to lapses, be it in quality, proficiency, or ethics.

Most journalists agree on one thing, that before the "celebrity journalist" and new media news cycle, Albom would have lost his job over the incident. No matter what the punishment, he should have had to explain himself better, take full responsibility, and map out both how this incident happened and how and why it would not happen in the future. The readers would not have been best served to lose their favorite columnist, and the Freep would have lost revenue losing its multimedia star. The only way I could have seen firing Albom was post-facto, after his apology and accountability dodges were deemed enough to begin his column again—to me, his conduct post-lying was more reprehensible than the lie itself.

As the Internet and real time continue to redefine journalism, no one can assess where ethics stands—or will fall. Whether the *Free Press* gave a free pass to Mitch Albom can be debated ad nauseam, but the truth is, another big paper—or newspaper—would have hired him in a heartbeat. And the competing *Detroit News* would have been at the front of that line.

READER FEEDBACK—WHEN, HOW MUCH, AND WHAT RESTRICTIONS

In addition to claiming the new media journalists of tomorrow must be masters of all trades rather than specialize in one over the others—it is the contention of this book that students aspiring to be journalists should master one and develop a working knowledge and competent skills in the other multimedia applications—textbooks also claim that journalists no longer decide and report what the news is: In fact, textbooks are calling it a "conversation."

These ideas have merit and some practicality. But go back to the beginning of time, and conversations with readers—we called it having your fingers on the pulse of your community—have always been a necessity for journalists. However, while many textbook authors—most of whom never worked in the media since the advent of the media—want to believe that reporters can respond to every email, read every blog, and give out their cell phone number to every single reader, the simple fact is that such a romantic idea of new media is not logistically possible. Absolutely yes, journalists should be scanning blogs, reading emails, and seeking out story tips through social media, message boards, and following up on the few most credible comments at the end of news stories. But for reporters to respond to every single one is simply not realistic, and textbook authors trying to push this upon student journalists really do not have a clue how the news business has worked since they left the field for academia.

Cultivating a source and following a news tip means knowing the source, whether in person or by electronic means. Reporters could be fed a thousand bad news tips if they had to follow up on every single one. They would have to defend every story to each and every side of the political spectrum if they have to give long, well crafted essays in response to every email or message board post directed at their story. What they should do, and do in most cases, is look for trends from several emails or posts indicating something new or something the reporter had not figured out. If the source can provide good information—rather than the all familiar (and often profane) rant—about a topic, that person could be a news source worth communicating with, or reading their blog, well into the future, at least on that topic.

As mentioned, one of the more important, immediate developments of the online news story or even blog is the comments that can be made at the end of stories.

This is a dilemma that mainstream media especially faced with reader comments at the end of the story. This was seen as a new breakthrough in the exchange of information, with readers—rather than write letters to the editor as in the past—able to post their comments directly at the end of stories. The theory was that this was another great democratizing aspect of the Internet, that everyone would have a voice, and in this heretofore unseen marketplace of ideas and exchange of information, people would become more educated than ever. That would round out the story, offer additional facts and perspective, and enhance the experience for all involved, included those who published the story online. However, the actual result was far from what had been hypothesized by both schools of dreamers, those who foresaw community building and collaboration and those who romanticized that giving everyone the forum for their opinions would create a better and more educated form of democracy. That is because the reality has been that while the well-thought out, concisely and clearly crafted comments were few and far between, invariably a lot of the messages turned to political rants that may or may not have anything to do with the story, and anyone with a contradictory opinion would turn the forum into their own personal rant Web site. This, in turn, left readers turning away from vulgar and occasionally profane rants and personal attacks.

A lot of readers did not want to leave their names, and leaving that kind of anonymous posting format caused a lot more grief than gratuity for the publisher of the news Web site. Readers could—and in some cases still do—post libelous and slanderous comments that often had no basis in fact, and readers untrained to reporter ethics and talents did not see the need to cite, or perform, any research to back up their rants.

The result was that people had to register to post comments, which steered away a lot of potential clients, whether it was either those who did not want to attach their name to their opinion so they could say what they want or those who did not want to suffer the stalkers and hate-filled rant posters who wanted to come after those who expressed a differing point of view.

The original position of newspapers originally—again, with nothing on which to base policy—was that the Web site would police itself and comments would balance out each other; in other words, the democratic ideal of giving a voice to the people that would in itself be a self-righting mechanism never manifested itself into a working model. So the forums ended up needing to be moderated—constantly—and in many cases that meant adding employee hours, this at a time when the publications were slashing jobs. Some newspaper and magazine Web sites instituted a policy that comments would have to be examined and then approved before being posted; that did not go over well with readers who had liked hitting "Post" and seeing their comment appear instantaneously, and then rolling up their sleeves for the online-verbal brawl that followed. Newspapers had been afraid that putting controls on the people who were posting would drive them away to other Web sites, but they also realized that as the publishers of the Web site, they had some liability for what was posted. This remains a great unresolved issue.

ELECTRONIC INTERVIEWS

Electronic interviews are the wave of the present and future. Once you have the email of a news source, it is a relatively easy way to conduct an interview. You still need to constantly be aware that the person you think you are interviewing is the person answering the question; to that end, you will find that some people, despite the email format's convenience for you, do not enjoy typing out answers to a long list of questions. In some cases, I have instead emailed questions and had people digitally record their answers and just email me back the audio, which I transcribe and use for my story, whether for a book or a newspaper.

There are drawbacks to doing such a format, however. First of all, the interviewee is far less likely to say something spontaneous; indeed, this format, though it lends itself to more reflective and thought-out answers, often takes away the off-the-cuff comments that journalists are looking for. On the other hand, it is even more transparent to do it this way because it allows the subject not to feel ambushed or set up, or to have to answer a question that he/she does not have an answer to. Being able to respond in the asynchronous format allows sources to find the information they need if they do not have it off the top of their head and give more complete answers.

Some journalists bemoan the idea of even using a computer to take notes rather than writing by hand with a pen in a reporter's notebook, claiming it makes the person being interviewed more aware that the interview is going on. However, one of the tenets of good journalism is transparency, and the fact that you are taking notes should always be very apparent to the person being interviewed, whether it is the scribbling in a notebook or tapping on a keyboard. Another consideration to constantly keep in mind, especially in the real-time news cycles where denials can be issued as fast as the stories are written and posted, is recording all interviews—with the subject's consent, of course. This is a good habit from a practical standpoint because whether you are typing or handwriting notes, you could miss or mishear a word or sentence; having the tape or digital recording as a backup allows you to revisit the interview. From a legal standpoint, it is also a good practice because you have documentation of what the person said, so any charges of misquotes or a source claiming to have never said something can be solved through saving the recording. For enterprise projects that take longer and go more in depth, making transcripts from such interviews, while a time-consuming process, has great value if multiple stories all of significant length are being written.

Consider these tenets if you are doing an electronic interview:

1. Send an email asking for an interview, whether they would prefer to do it by email, and when they can return it.

2. Send a follow-up email with two or, at most, three questions. If sources see five or six questions and have to keep scrolling down, they will think they need hours to answer, and will postpone it until they have a lot of free time—if they ever come back to it. One or two well phrased questions will make them think they can knock out the answers really quick.

3. Ask for complete sentence answers in that first set of questions. This means you will have to phrase the questions as open-ended. Think about how you would answer the question, because if you send a leading question, the answer might just build off the tail end of your question, and while that is good for you to understand the subject, it is not a full quote or complete sentence.

4. Once you get back that first set of two or three questions, send thanks and ask one follow-up question at a time, two at the most. Point out that you just want to understand the comment or issue completely and that you want to make sure you get the facts right for both yourself and the source. That kind of commitment to quality control will get you a response, probably relatively quickly.

5. Tone is difficult in email, so phrase controversial questions carefully. If you must ask about a problem the company has, do not ask about a "problem"—ask about a "challenge" it is facing. That makes it seem less negative and shows your source that you are amenable to "hear" his/her side of the story and that you do not have biases.

6. Ask early for a cell phone number. Promise that you will not use it unless it is urgent, and use it to fact check if needed on deadline—which in the 24/7 news cycle is a revolving deadline. Double-checking on someone's name or a particular year or other date is very easy to do via text, and it is an easy way to respond. Always send an email first, but if you do not get an answer and you are on deadline, follow up with a text—that is why it is so important to get a cell phone number.

7. Do your homework. Read or view other media the source has done. This gives you context for what he/she might say, and it also lets you off the hook if you have to ask about a past issue and you can cite something you read online—like a lot of blogs, the controversy could be from someone misinformed or a disgruntled former employee or a competitor. Being able to say "I read where . . . " shows you care enough to be prepared for the interview.

8. No matter whether the source is good or bad, helpful or not, save the information in a database for you and others in your new media company. Note the best times to reach the source, how he/she responds to email interviews (short answers, long answers, responding quickly or delayed, whether he/she is more prone to answer one question at a time), if he/she does phone

interviews, if he/she minds the "drop-in" interview in person, and so on. It is also good, if possible, to post a transcript of your interview, notes, or at the very least the story you wrote which included that source.

9. When you talk to the source the first time on the cell phone (a good practice before sending an email interview question), ask for two or three additional sources, getting their names, titles, numbers, and email addresses. That way, if the person cannot or will not talk about certain issues, you can go to someone else. If he/she gives you good information but was not in charge of a project or someone else simply has more info, you can continue to build contacts. Again, as per Number 8, you want to save all these sources in a master database. As these employees move on to bigger companies or other branches of the same company, you now have a source in those places.

10. No matter what you get—good or bad information, a lot or little time— there is absolutely no reason for failing to give your respect. The days of telling someone off or losing your temper are gone. That spreads like wildfire with the Internet. You burn one source, and you have scorched the earth of everyone in their world. That does not mean you always write positive stories, but it does mean you treat people with respect, write fair stories, and get comments from both sides of the issues. It means following up when a company that has made mistakes that you reported is doing something about the problems now. It is the Golden Rule: Treat others the way you want to be treated. As you get older and end up dealing with people much younger than yourself, remember this: Do not ask someone a question in a way that you would not want someone asking your own kid. Be fair, be professional, and be courteous. It is a small world, and if you make yours too small, you will have painted yourself into a journalistic corner where people will not talk to you—or read what you write or watch what you report.

ONLINE RESEARCH

Researching stories and doing interviews online is both a gold mine and a mine field. Credible information is harder to find than meets the eye, especially for the person who is looking only to back up an opinion he/she has and is not concerned with either the other side of the story or simply facts that conflict with that point of view.

Where are good places to look for information? The library, for one, is a vital source of often good, solid, well-supported information. This is not your parents' library, however. Libraries today have most of their catalogs online. University libraries are a particularly rich source of online material, from academic journals with the latest research to trade periodicals and archived newspapers that have a lot of information ripe for journalistic picking. Another place to look is government records.

This would, of course, include the cyber-gargantuan Library of Congress Web site, which has all the information you could ever want (and a million times more that you will not need) and which makes knowing how and where to look and search online a premium skill for anyone writing online.

This is an area in which journalist I. F. Stone made a name—and actually created his own relatively successful newspaper—long before the Internet was even an idea, much less a reality. Stone was a "Gonzo" journalist—a term Hunter S. Thompson later was labeled with for his own unique style—before the term existed. Stone was a journalist for the *New York Post* and later for *The Nation*. His own weekly—considered a newsletter more than a newspaper—is something he founded more than a decade after he left mainstream journalist, was named *I. F. Stone's Weekly*, and peaked at a circulation of about 70,000. Stone dug deeply into obscure government documents, which were the official records of how government did business. It was then, as it is largely regarded now, as time-intensive work that those, especially now, in the real-time news cycle would have neither the time nor interest in exploring. Stone would dig for hours, weeks, and months through the Congressional Record.

The value of exploring electronic databases cannot be overstated. News stories exist within the written, official record of public business. The problem is, it takes a lot of work to sift through, and by the time it is recorded and posted, it is days, even weeks, old. The journalists of today are more concerned—for reasons that are both their own and their bosses' who sign their paychecks—with stories that are more immediate, usually whatever is happening "now." This is one of the reasons for pack journalism as it exists in 2009 and points beyond: It is not only "there," but also there "now." How else to explain all of the major news outlets, network and print, following the search for white, blond American Natalee Holloway into the oceans of Aruba? The sensational element of news coverage—and the pack-journalism mentality that hounds it rather than follow the stories that better affect the day-to-day life of news consumers—is certainly nothing new. But it does not explain the battalion of satellite trucks at O. J. Simpson's trial, the aforementioned Aruba search, or the latest missing child in Anywhere, U.S.A.

At the same time, it is a legitimate question, and we now know where all these reporters were when Bernard Madoff was swindling $65 billion from investors, or while the alleged Weapons of Mass Destruction during the Iraq War buildup went largely unchallenged. Ironically, in the case of Madoff, at least two news organizations had gone so far as to call Madoff's company a "Ponzi scheme" for six years leading up to his eventual guilty plea in 2009. All of the U.S. Allies were cautioning the United States against invading Iraq in 2002, and the result, rather than a U.S. investigative report about how Iraq had not only no Weapons of Mass Destruction but also nothing to do with the Afghanistan-supported 9/11 terrorism attacks on New York City's Twin Towers, was nothing but the endless reports of press briefings and the White House's official stance that Saddam Hussein was a terrorist support. Ironically, had investigate journalism survived the move to the real-time news cycle, it is certainly possible that the 120,000 troops bound for Iraq could have been placed in Afghanistan, giving the United States a chance to catch Osama bin Laden, or at least a much better chance than the 20,000 U.S. troops put in Afghanistan while the search for Saddam Hussein became the nation's focus for the better part of 2002.

The rush for more news faster has led to, in other words, a question for less-important, even irrelevant news, at the expense of news that truly does affect the lives of not only Americans but citizens around the world.

Where does that leave the new media writers of today?

For starters, anyone can be a "citizen journalist" or reporter. But the difference—the intellectual gap, if you will—between blogging with a rant about a particular political belief and the carefully crafted, well-researched, informative news item, on a blog or otherwise, is significant.

But it is important to find credible stories. If your neighbor, in the middle of his blog on how he hates waiting in lines, mentioned he heard a woman say a local grocery store is going out of business, and you repeat that in your blog or column, you might be libeling or slandering that business. While it feels good to complain to the average person, a reporter should be wary of such scurrilous reporting, and if you report that yourself, for legal purposes you will be accountable. Find credible information sources—you have better access to them than ever before—and track down these news tips. Do not mistake a blog for anything more than it is. But do pay attention as a source of potential news tips. For every success story that has come from blogs—the Drudge Report was miles ahead of the mainstream media on the Clinton-Lewinsky scandal—there are exponentially more examples of bad information spreading like the plague (including a couple from the Drudge Report). Do not let clicking make you lazy: you should still be rolling up your sleeves and tracking things down, even if to simply verify something from someone on the record.

Archives for newspapers and broadcast outlets are better than they have been in the history of time, and are getting better every day. If you have access to a public or university library, you could write all the blogs, stories, and even books your heart desired from the seat of your home office. There is great value in getting out, meeting people, and paying attention to the sights and sounds of the world around you, and those should always be a part of your day-to-day life, as well as your reporting. But for tracking down information, there is no reason you should ever bypass the library, especially now since it means you can visit it in your pajamas and with your morning coffee without ever leaving the house.

Chapter 5

Media and Digital Literacy

INTRODUCTION

Previous definitions of media literacy were set forth when the media was not a constant presence in people's lives. The Internet has changed that, with news and information in all forms of media available to most users all the time. However, what this means to media literacy rates has not yet been determined, and the technology that brought on this change in media access has created a hybrid media literacy/technology discipline of study called digital literacy. Turning on and off a computer, or visiting favorite Web sites and playing video games, does not increase one's digital literacy. Rather, digital literacy involves being able to use the technology to gain more knowledge and understanding.

Technological determinism asserts that technology, especially that which is pervasive and powerful, shapes a society and can even determine its values and alter culture. Understanding how these parallel or intersect is important to understand how society is changing because of this technology, and how media/digital literacy rates are changing, and for whom. The theory of technological determinism plays a significant part in understanding media/digital literacy (McLuhan 1964). If technology is going to be changing the values and culture of the world, digital and media literacy must be measured and understood to see if the members of the dot-com generation are just pointers and clickers or actually better critical thinkers and problem solvers than previous generations who did not have access to such technology. If technology is neutral, then in theory that answer is up to the user. If, however, technology itself shapes the way people behave, such as driving while text messaging or spending days in front of the computer surfing entertainment Web sites and playing video games, researchers are left to dissect this intellectual maze and find out who is where, how they got there, and what it means. And perhaps more importantly, what can be expected from technology in the future?

Before a definition of digital literacy can be developed, it is necessary to understand media literacy, not unlike media theory begat new media theory in this age of multiplatform media. And it must be noted that people still go to libraries, read hard copies of magazines and newspapers, and have other sources of information that are not online, though information from all of the aforementioned sources is largely available online.

MEDIA LITERACY

Digital literacy has become a new area of research and conversation for researchers, legislative bodies, and public school educators.

The defining of media literacy skills differs among scholars slightly, though there are several key elements (Potter 2001). Basic media literacy is seen through the maturation of such rudimentary or "component skills" (36) as having exposure, recognizing symbols, recognizing patterns, and matching meaning. Exposure is often thought of in a sense of just experiencing the technology. However, for example, if one wanted to see whether a favorite football team won a game, that person could turn on the television or just look up the score online. However, that person would have to know which channel to turn to, what Web site on which to find the game, and even when the game was played. Just knowing how to turn on a computer and log on is not sufficient; this involves structures of knowledge (Potter 2004). The level of access technology is no longer always significantly different between "children and adults" (40), but the more experienced and aggressive thinkers are going to be able to locate the information they seek. Think of it as finding the capital of a state on a map for an upcoming vacation: Pointing to it is not that hard once the map is found and the proper state is located, but getting there involves a lot more critical thinking and planning. Recognizing symbols is another significant area of knowledge building and meaning making, and since some symbols are words, they have to be recognized and understood (Potter 2004). To recognize symbols and make meaning of them, elements must be extracted from items on a screen or page and then processed. An example of this is opening the newspaper; both the illiterate and highly literate will see the same things, but only the more literate users will be able to "extract elements" (40) to make sense of it. Recognizing patterns is done on a number of levels, increasing with literacy. Understanding the letters themselves is part of rudimentary literacy levels, but then learning and understanding words, and putting them together in sentences to understand that the letters are not simply thrown together randomly is an important part of building literacy. As an assortment of symbols or letters grows, so does the level of interpretation required to understand how it fits together and what it means. Knitting is an activity that begins with understanding the process of how to knit two simple stitches, knit and purl, and then following instructions to produce a specific item displaying a pattern, whether planned or random. In the same way, understanding how the patterns of symbols fit together is critical for coherency and making sense in the final component skill of basic media literacy. This involves taking a symbol that one has already learned, interpreting it, and matching it with another that has already been learned. Watching the news is one example. The music comes on, indicating the news is starting, and an oftentimes familiar voice is heard. The person on television begins speaking about a story, and graphics or footage that match or extend the meaning of the lead-in are added. Connecting all of these symbols with meaning is crucial to developing media literacy.

ADVANCED MEDIA LITERACY

Advanced media literacy involves the "message-focused sense making" (Potter 2004, 36) to interpret meaning. These skills are analysis, comparing/contrasting, evaluation, and abstraction (which could be described as advanced critical thinking). Analysis involves breaking down messages into understandable elements. Think about seeing just parts of a movie as it is shown multiple times over a weekend on cable television. Understanding each part, if it can be understood under isolated terms, is hard enough, but understanding what it means to the other parts as well as the rest of the movie is difficult without seeing the entire film. The message has to be put together with all the other parts so that meaning can be made and so it can be understood on more than just a "surface level" (45). Analytical skill requires an advanced knowledge structure, which in turn allows for more context, and it allows users to explain why they did or did not like something, and how and why they were able to understand it. Those with highly developed analytical skills are also better able to understand the usefulness of messages. To illustrate this, think of the adage that if something sounds too good to be true, it probably is. That message is far more likely to come from a wise, older sage than a child on a playground (Potter 2001). Analysis is also critical for understanding percentages, especially in the digital era of constant polling.

Comparing and contrasting involves breaking down a "media message to its component parts" (Potter 2001, 47). These elements are compared to those already in the user's knowledge structure, and if the new information is different, as long as it is true it can be added to the knowledge structure. This reinforcement adds strength to knowledge already accrued, which in turn makes these structures less likely to change down the road. However, contrasting is just as important and requires greater literacy because it presents our current structure with cognitive dissonance (Baran & Davis 2009). The important factor is realizing that comparing is important, and that even if elements of new information contrast with existing knowledge structures, it does not mean such structures are completely invalid and must completely be torn down (Potter 2001). Indeed, comparing and contrasting is something done by only the most media-literate individuals and as such is not a "rudimentary" (Potter 2001, 47) skill. An example would be showing someone the price of gas, the fall of stock market value, and the costs for the war in Iraq. Only an advanced user would be able to connect all three to each other, yet in media reports around election time, polls showed that Americans were no longer as concerned with the war in Iraq as they were with the economy, when in fact those were connected logically and literally. Another example would be when a favorite character in a television show, who had been completely likeable, does something that makes viewers no longer like the character. What the character did contrasted so heavily with the way the character had been developed that it broke viewers' knowledge structures. To use this advanced skill people must actively seek a broader understanding and set of meaning in messages, and then apply the derived skills to make sense of messages on an even higher level.

Evaluation is making "an assessment of the worth of an element" (Potter 2001, 47). This involves taking information and comparing it to criteria the user understands and has a working knowledge of. If the new information does not make sense, the user has to either build an additional knowledge structure to account for the new information or access and develop structures to disprove it. For the evaluative mind, it is critical to include all sorts of knowledge structures that include information empirically based in addition to cognitive, emotional, aesthetic, and moral information. The evaluative mind will not only see the ambiguities in the questions that allowed the survey designers to produce the at-first-glance eye-popping numbers, but also see what company did the poll and which organization financed the poll, which might also explain not just the questions but the results. The final advanced media literacy skill according to Potter is abstraction, which is "the ability to assemble a brief, clear, accurate description of something" (Potter 2001, 49). An abstraction is a summary of key parts that give, in far fewer words than the text itself, a clear picture and context. This involves analyzing a text or other media message, breaking it down to its component parts, evaluating what are most important and how these each contribute to the message, and then succinctly summarizing, for example, a journal article, a movie, or a 300-page book with nothing more than a paragraph.

As one moves along in adulthood, media literacy should continue to develop and increase, though it increases at a slower rate at a certain point (Sternberg & Berg 1987). This will vary from person to person depending on one's cognitive style or approach to how each person first organizes and then processes information (Hashway & Duke 1992). For maturing adults, the web of knowledge development becomes more complex (Bruner, Goodnow, & Austin 1956). These supra-advanced stages include field independency, tolerance for ambiguity, conceptual differentiation, and reflectivity-impulsivity (Witkin & Goodenough 1977).

Field independency means being able to separate signal and noise in messages, with noise being the "chaos of symbols and images" and signal being the actual information that is filtered from the noise. People stuck in field dependency hear or see all the information, but are not able to make sense of it. Those who are field independent are able to process and sort all the chaos and make sense of it, understand where it fits together or not, and come to some context and making meaning out of the signals (Potter 2001). An example of this would be the director of an orchestra, or perhaps a referee during an important football game in a crowded and loud stadium. Having a tolerance for ambiguity means being able to break down information inconsistent with current knowledge structures, yet being able to reason and make sense of it; confusion does not stop the person with a tolerance for ambiguity. Instead, it "motivates them to search harder for clarity" (Potter 2001, 27). Conceptual differentiation involves being able to categorize a message by how it is similar to or different from currently held concepts. Reflectivity-impulsivity is defined as how people use their cognitive styles to make a decision about a message, and "how accurate that decision is" (Potter 2001, 27).

DIGITAL LITERACY

Defining digital literacy has as much to do with understanding and how to use technology as it does with meaning making. That means digital literacy's definition must outline not just how to turn on the technology and find something with it but also make meaning of what is found (Tyner 1998). The technical information infrastructure is made up of the physical properties and raw materials of literacy, including the "tools, technical personnel, systems design, and distribution mechanisms" (Tyner 1998, 5). Since Tyner provided such a definition, it has been further extended to include the following:

The ability to make independent choices about the selection and interpretation of the content; an understanding of the emerging structure of the Internet and its impact on content; an awareness of the impact of the Internet on the individual and society; the development of strategies with which to analyze and discuss media messages conveyed over the Internet; an awareness of interactive content as a "text" that provides insight into our contemporary culture and ourselves; and the cultivation of an enhanced enjoyment, understanding, and appreciation of media content conveyed through interactive media. (Silverblatt, 2001, 321)

The proliferation of Internet access has made the media not only a bigger part of our daily lives, but literally a constant presence (Potter 2004). The era of going days without picking up a newspaper at a newsstand or twisting a knob to turn on a television are gone; people have access to breaking news, and years-old media, once they are logged on.

One of the issues that still plagues scholarship in the area of this study is understanding what people do online. The debate over whether the Internet is creating globalization or creating a worldwide democracy is neither supported nor contradicted—yet. Researchers are still seeking ways to measure the impact of the Internet on society and individuals (Tyner 1998).

Understanding digital literacy also includes acknowledging the digital divide (Baran & Davis 2009). This involves groups of people who do not have access to the technology, primarily "people of color, the poor, the disabled, and those in rural communities" (Baran & Davis 2009, 264). While that is a just concern, there is another reality, and that is of getting these people on the other side of the digital divide to first acquire the proper equipment, and then providing them the instruction and education on how to use it. Indeed, a stack of boxed computers in a poverty-stricken school district is not going to bridge the digital divide if there is no one there to orchestrate the access, which includes installing it, teaching how to use it, and repairing or maintaining it.

The technology itself continues to evolve; more news and information is being exchanged globally at a faster rate than ever before (Tyner 1998). However, with the 24-hour news cycle unfolding in real time, even people who step away from their computers can still get text messages and calls from cell phone technology that includes emails and news updates, as well as the capability to search the World Wide Web from phones and laptops. People are so information saturated that they can suffer from what has come to be known as information overload (Silverblatt, Ferry & Finan, 1999). Eventually part of the definition of digital literacy may include people's ability to filter out information so that they can make sense of, and find context for, the information that is most relevant to their lives and interests them the most. This has also come to include the term "interactivity," and though it has been a term of considerable weight both before and after the introduction of the Internet, it must also be included in the explication of digital literacy since interactivity is such a crucial part of the user's online experience and a key to meaning making, particularly in the digital era.

DEFINING "INTERACTIVE"

A key to understanding and framing digital literacy goes far beyond just turning on a computer or clicking on a link to a Web site, though both certainly have a place under the banner of digital literacy. Terms, however, must be clearly defined so that areas can be understood and be broken down so they can also be studied as elements.

"Interactive media" is one of those terms that is being used often in educational circles (Silverblatt 2001). Yet interactive is a word often over-used or misused, much like the term "integrated marketing communications" is tossed around in trendy technological conversations about advertising and public relations (Bedbury & Fenichell 2002).

Interactive media takes the principles from media literacy and uses them to understand and enhance the digital media world (Silverblatt 2001). Interactive media refers to the communication between an initiator and receiver, using a "combination of established media to emulate humans' patterns of thought and expression through a transparent machine" (Silverblatt 2001, 322). People's lives are literally constantly technologically interactive now with the Internet and cell phones being part of their minute-to-minute waking existence in a lot of cases. The idea behind this is the literal definition of interactive. This involves communication between an initiator and receiver, and it is done using a combination of already existing and established technology, which for the purposes of digital media is the multiplatform world of the Internet. Interactive media engages users' thoughts and expressions, and what they seek in terms of uses and gratifications (Baran & Davis 2009). These various platforms, whether it is a YouTube video or even a textual email message or notification from a message board, allow users, be it announced or anonymously, to access the Web sites they want when they want, and to retrieve the information they seek. This has caused the "movement" for information, and meaning, to be nonlinear. Paul Levinson (1999) notes that media analyst Marshall McLuhan's work from nearly a half century ago has new life breathed back into it by the nonlinear, vertical, and even spherical new media platforms that are part of not only our daily routines but our minute-to-minute lives in many cases.

TECHNOLOGICAL DETERMINISM

Technological determinism is a theory stating that the technology determines a society's cultural values and social structure (Postman 1992). Certainly, media literacy, more specifically, digital literacy, is much more related to uses and gratifications than the advent of cable TV or the penny press, especially since people often believe they only want the skills they need to use the media for whatever they want it for. And for many, that has very little to do with continuing education or joining public debate about society and the world's more serious issues (Lanham 2007). In fact, with selective retention and exposure, issues like global warming or the need to downsize the SUVs that Detroit continues to produce in the face of environmental and economic realities points to a scary truth: Some very educated people are compiling a lot of the same facts and coming to polar-opposite truths. Is this partially attributable to media-digital literacy or the technology?

While media literacy was an area of considerable research since the beginning of information travel, the Internet, with its multiplatform dissemination properties, has brought to life the academic term of "digital literacy." This new discipline can be connected to technological determinism, as the technology itself has allowed far more people access to information made possible by the Internet. The question as to whether technology is neutral is still being debated (Christians 1989). Indeed, thinking that technology is "merely a tool which can be used rightly or wrongly" (Christians 1989, 123) answers no questions and provides no direction.

Communicating through technology has created an open space that while creating its own cliques and groups has also broken down walls to the world (Meyrowitz, 1985). Yet, the entire belief or lightly grounded previous theory that technology is neutral is based on the idea that technology was far more linear, even as a mode of information exchange, than it turned into with the Internet (Christians 1989). Christians's two faces of the technological process, the first phase (design) and the second phase (fabrication) are stages in which rapid technological advancement, which have been in development and evolution for decades, are driven by the need to make what the public decides it needs (also called technological appropriation). The making of these programs, software applications, and hardware products allows us repeatable maneuvers for finding, disseminating, and storing information, which was the same goal of the printing press. In fact, type has been since its conception a repeatable commodity that puts a visual stress on the reader and requires the writer to assemble a narrative or coherent body of information that the user can process and contextualize (McLuhan 1962).

Postman cites McLuhan's famous phrase that "the medium is the message," and extends it to "the medium is the monopoly" on the technology, finances, and even knowledge. It can be a never-ending intellectual tax of sorts, from buying the hardware and then all the software, and then hiring by phone or in person "tech support" for even more money to make this costly engine you have purchased start running correctly. These financial concerns are another less talked about barrier to digital literacy, especially those with poverty-level or below means. "Private learning and individual problem solving" (Postman 1992, 17) are beneficial for those who can afford, and make sense of, the Internet opportunities. Perhaps the ceiling for digital IQ is unlimited, for those who have the means. Pushing these largely public educational achievement places into personal and private environments takes away the group-learning aspects that orality and pencil-and-paper scholarship brought forth, and the social responsibility that came with such a setting and group-oriented approach.

In another work on the subject, Postman notes how the media itself is a metaphor in the communication process:

The printing press, the computer, and television are not therefore simply machines which convey information. They are metaphors through which we conceptualize reality in one way or another. They will classify the world for us, sequence it, frame it, enlarge it, reduce it, argue a case for what it is like. Through these media metaphors, we do not see the world as it is. We see it as our coding systems are. Such is the power of the form of information. (1985, 39)

Technology shapes culture in ways society is aware of, and ways that it either does not imagine or is incapable of imagining (McLuhan, 1964). It can be as simple as the media platform we access or as complex as how the information is contextualized (Postman 1992). Sholle (2002) moves one more step along the technological determination path, referring to technology as tools we use in our everyday lives. He claims we are still asking questions about old technologies as well as the new ones, and if technology is an "agent of freedom or instrument of control" (Sholle 2002, 2). Technology has brought change to our lives whether we know it or not, and has, Sholle claims, become a part of a progression that will alter not just our society and economy but our consciousness as well.

Measuring media or digital literacy is hard to do; no such scales exist. Access can hardly be the meterstick (going global means going metric, even in clichés) by which all are measured. Meaning making must involve context (Postman 1985). In his work predating "Technolopy," Postman saw where the Victorian Internet itself, the telegraph, "made relevance irrelevant. The abundant flow of information had very little or nothing to do with those to whom it was addressed: that is, with any social or intellectual context in which their lives were embedded" (67). Writing almost a decade before deafening dial-up modems occasionally silenced oral exchanges, Postman saw a "sea of information with very little of it to use" (67), noting that while the telegraph created the first real-time global village, no one knows anything except "the most superficial facts about each other" (67).

Chapter 6

Narrative Theory

Samuel D. Bradley

TELLING STORIES

Storytelling is among the most fundamental human activities. From drawings on cave walls, to etchings on stones, to oral tales of the Trojan War, to iambic pentameter presented on stage, to the novel, to the silver screen, and to multimedia Flash presentation, we have always told stories. Stories define us. One story—like Jack Kerouac's *On the Road*—can even define an entire generation. Put two people together, and it is almost impossible to keep them from telling stories. When native speakers of different languages are thrust together, they will invent a new language, a pidgin, to communicate and tell stories. Indeed, even the athletic event named the marathon dates from the Greek messenger Pheidippides's run from Marathon to Athens to tell the story of how the Persians had been conquered.

The online writer has at his/her disposal the most versatile storytelling platform ever. The Internet allows the seamless integration of the written word, sound, vision, and motion. When all of these storytelling features converge, the creative and information-conveying potential is virtually limitless. Despite the potential, however, good storytelling tools do not ensure that good storytelling will occur. Instead, good storytelling begins with a proper understanding of the art and the science of narrative. There is also a fundamental difference between being a writer and being a good writer. Sight, sound, and motion added to bad writing might entertain some readers, but it will not translate into effective storytelling.

STORY BUILDING BLOCKS

If someone were to say to you, "Tell me a story," what would that mean to you? What does it take for something to be a story? At the most basic level, a narrative story consists of two elements linked to one another in time (Labov 1972). Obviously, most stories are more complex that this. However, this allows for exceedingly short stories, such as a haiku poem, which typically contains 17 or fewer syllables. This 11 word haiku by J. Lent, an award-winning poet from the Haiku Society of America, tells a vivid story: "driving lesson done; father and daughter run; fingers through their hair."

Typically, however, stories are more than two elements connected chronologically. Instead, stories often begin with an orientation of the time setting, location, characters involved, and their circumstances (Labov 1972). Also according to Labov, a fully formed story outlines what happened, a resolution of the events, some evaluation of the outcome (i.e., the moral of the story), and some signal that the story has come to an end. Thus a story can range from just a few-word poem to Tolstoy's epic tome, *War and Peace*.

THE PRIMACY OF NARRATIVE

How pervasive is storytelling to human thought and culture? Consider this elegant experiment from 1944. Two psychologists, Fritz Heider and Mary-Ann Simmel, showed participants a 2.5 minute film of three geometric figures moving around a two-dimensional plane, which was empty except for a rectangle with a hinged portion similar to a door. The first group of participants was simply asked to "write down what happened in the picture" (Heider & Simmel 1944, 245). Only one of the 34 participants failed to describe the shapes as animated beings, and the majority used narrative to describe the action. This excerpt from one participant's description illustrates the human drive to attach narrative to action, "Triangle number-one shuts his door (or should we say line) and the two innocent young things walk in. Lovers in the two-dimensional world, no doubt; little triangle number-two and sweet circle. Triangle-one (hereinafter known as the villain) spies the young love" (Heider & Simmel

1944, 247). That is a vivid narrative constructed from abstract shapes. If people watching three shapes move about construct this rich a narrative in their heads, the possibilities are vast indeed for the online writer.

A narrative then is not merely another form of human communication. Instead, it represents the very way that information is represented in the brain. Language evolved, it appears, so that humans could convey more elaborate stories. As the only creature capable of language, humans can tell stories vastly more complicated than any other type of animal can communicate. Honeybees can signal the location of nectar-bearing flowers through elaborate dances, and chimpanzees can learn rudimentary hand signals. But only humans have the power to tell complicated tales about the past, present, and future. And only humans have the power to pass these tales on from one generation to the next.

Current biological theory assumes that humans evolved through natural selection, a theory originally proposed by Charles Darwin (1859). In the theory of natural selection, information is passed from one generation to the next through genetic material, which we now know to be DNA. For every species other than humans, almost no information can be passed from one generation to the next other than DNA. Long before Darwin, science ruled out Lamarckian evolution, or the idea that acquired characteristics could be passed from one generation to the next. For most animals, then, the nature versus nurturer debate is rather one-sided. A baby chimpanzee can learn how to eat from its mother, or a sea otter may learn to roll onto its back and use a stone to crack open a mollusk. But neither chimps nor otters can talk about what it means to be a chimp (or an otter). And even in the exceedingly rare event that a single sea otter had a single such sentient moment, it would have no way to tell this story to friends, family, or future generations. Instead that story of otter humanity, if you will, would be lost as soon as it was created.

Humans alone have language—whether it was evolved or endowed. And research suggests that language is built around narrative. Our propensity to record these stories on cave walls, papyrus, and Weblogs allows narratives to take on lives of their own. Once a story is out there, it cannot be taken back. Galileo could be imprisoned, and his tales of a sun-centered universe could be banned. But once the heliocentric story had been told, it could not easily be killed. It persisted as it took on a life of its own, separate from any individual creature. Biologist Richard Dawkins (1976) calls these self-perpetuating ideas *memes*, a loose take on the word "genes." The meme allows ideas to be transmitted through story for hundreds or thousands of years. What would the average person know of the Trojan War if it were not for Homer's epic poems? His *Iliad* is credited as the first work of Western literature, and depending upon which scholar you believe, that narrative is in its twenty-ninth century of existence. There is no other way that information could be passed down through so many other generations than through narrative. Through these stories we pass along ideas of morality, codes of conduct, and normative guidelines for society. Much of religious thought takes the form of narrative, first in the oral tradition then as written scripture. Rather than a simple recitation of facts, most religious texts are a compilation of prescriptive narratives.

In addition to passing down stories across thousands of years, narratives add considerable muscle to the human cognitive arsenal. There can be no questioning that language has a profound effect on the way the human mind works, but complicated language and storytelling have an even farther reaching effect. Philosopher of cognitive science Andy Clark (1997) calls this extended cognition. The human mind is capable of extraordinary things, but it suffers from a severe limit in the short term: you just cannot hold very many thoughts in mind at a given time. For most things, the number of distinct units you can keep in mind at once is about seven (Miller 1956). For more complicated objects, you can think of about five, and for simpler objects, that number is closer to nine. For example, most people have a very difficult time keeping a 10 digit telephone number (seven digits plus the area code) in mind. That is, unless they know the area code. Then the three digit area code—such as 212 for New York City—really counts as just one object. To test this, come up with 10 random digits that have no semantic structure. Then recite the 10 digits to a friend, and ask the friend to rehearse them in mind for a minute or so. This should be an extremely challenging task, which may even be impossible for some people if there is no meaning between digits. Ten random digits are exceedingly difficult to keep in mind. Fifteen is surely impossible for all but a savant. But put a story behind the numbers, and it becomes easy. Any elementary school student could remember 1 through 10. There is a structure to the numbers. Few would be challenged to remember 2 through 20 counting by 2s. Technically there are still 10 numbers to remember, but instead you simply remember three rules: (1) start at 2; (2) count by 2s; (3) stop at 20. And three things are exceedingly easy to remember. It is a story about numbers.

You can think of stories as Post-it® notes for your mind. Once you learn the structure of a story and have that committed to memory, then the chunks of an actual story can fit more easily in mind. There is a reason that the simple image of *Peanuts* cartoon character Snoopy sitting atop his doghouse typing "It was a dark and stormy night" conveys so much information. Not only does it fit into a narrative structure, it fits into a clichéd narrative structure. We can use this external structure to support cognition that otherwise would not be possible. This is sometimes called scaffolding. Consider this book. You can pick it up at your convenience and read as much or as little as you like. You can mark in the margins, underline certain passages, and highlight others. As you read these words, your story is intertwining with the story being told by the book. By marking it up (hopefully not if it is a borrowed or library copy), you are providing access points to come back to the story. As you reflect upon notes that you left to yourself, such as "think more about this," you are refreshing your memory about what went through your mind when you read the passage the first time. And you are not merely remembering isolated, disembodied facts. Instead, you are remembering the facts in the temporal sequence in which they occurred. You are remembering the story. Very little of this would be possible without the presence of a narrative structure and the use of extended cognition, or scaffolding.

Imagine sitting down with a fiction author and asking her to tell you a book's story from memory. Even though she penned every word on every page, how much of the story would you reasonably expect her to be able to recite from memory? Chances are that she would omit entire chapters of the book without any external memory cues. Now consider taking the case back one level of abstraction. Imagine asking the author to recite arbitrary facts about a character from the book without any narrative structure. What percentage do you think that she would be able to freely recall? If she is like most people, the answer is very few. And once she did recall a fact, the narrative structure tied to that fact would likely activate other thoughts from memory. For example, one primary character might be allergic to peanut butter. Thinking of this fact in isolation is likely to activate other thoughts in memory—like the fact that field trips always made him sad because other kids got to eat peanut butter sandwiches in their sack lunches.

THE INTENSIFYING EFFECT OF NARRATIVE

Given the power of narrative, it is not surprising that the addition of narrative appears to intensify emotional experience. A great deal has been learned about the structure and function of human emotion by studying reactions to a set of emotionally charged photographs known as the International Affective Picture System (Lang, Bradley, & Cuthbert 1999). Most people have never considered what happens in their brains and bodies when they see a photograph of a snake or a cockroach walking across a piece of pizza. Despite the fact that a photograph is a still, two-dimensional image, your body reacts much as it would if the snake were actually present: it gets your attention. This is especially true for phobics, many of whom cannot even stay in the room where a photograph of a snake (or spider) is being shown. When the image is displayed, your heart slows momentarily (unless you are a phobic) as your brain allocates cognitive resources to figure out what is shown in the picture, the facial muscles used in frowning begin to contract, and the palms of your hands begin to sweat as your sympathetic nervous system prepares to flee from the danger (Bradley, Codispoti, Cuthbert, & Lang 2001). All of this occurs from just a few seconds of looking at a picture. When the photograph is swapped for a few seconds of video of the same object, the cognitive and physiological reactions intensify (Detenber, Simons, & Bennett 1998). When the same emotional objects are accompanied by a narrative—such as a television drama—the emotional response is of another magnitude altogether (Bradley, Maxian, Wise, & Freeman 2008). This accords with what we know about narrative.

When a story unfolds, we quickly identify with the characters. It becomes clear who is the hero and who is the protagonist—just as it was clear to participants in 1944 which triangle deserved our sympathy and which one was the villain. As we root for the "good guy" and fear the intervention of the villain, we also pick up on foreshadowing. The music to *Jaws* sends chills up the spines of former viewers three and a half decades after the film first hit the big screen. Why is *Jaws* so much more terrifying that a still photograph of a shark? There is nothing frightening about the music in isolation. But we do not experience the music in isolation. Instead, we have come to learn about a vengeful, plotting, murderous shark that attacks, unseen and unannounced, from below. The *Jaws* viewer has learned the shark's narrative, and the viewer comes to anticipate the shark's attack. The movie's direction and score serve to intensify that suspense. That is the emotional power of narrative.

KNOWING YOUR STORYTELLING PURPOSE

As an online writer, it is important to understand your goals for your writing. Are you writing to inform, entertain, or persuade? Is it sufficient simply to capture the reader's attention, or are you hoping to leave them with something? Narrative can be used differently to achieve these different goals. A large body of research shows that a well-attended narrative will not necessarily be a well-remembered narrative. Traditional newswriting perhaps serves as the best example of this discrepancy. News stories are rarely written in chronological order. Instead, they are written with the most interesting aspects at the top of the story, a format known as the inverted pyramid. Some claim that the inverted pyramid originated with unreliable telegraph lines. No matter the origins, the practice of putting the most important facts at the top lends efficiency. When stories need to be cut, there is an explicit understanding that the bottom paragraphs represent the low-hanging fruit. "If the 10 inches of available space suddenly shrinks to 8 and the 40 seconds of air time to 20, no problem. The story structure makes it possible to cut the bottom two paragraphs without losing key information" (Mencher 2000, 131).

The news reader's attention is fleeting. It is a busy world with many demands upon a reader's time. There is no time to read merely hoping that a payoff awaits. Chronological stories rarely begin with the most interesting details. Instead, a story told chronologically often begins with background minutia that is relatively uninteresting. Unless a reader is especially committed to a story, these boring background details are likely to lose attention and lead the reader to turn the page or navigate away from a story.

A newswriter's goal must be with gaining and maintaining a reader's interest. No matter how good the underlying journalism, the story will have no impact if it is never read. And readers are unlikely to stay with a boring story long enough to find out the exciting end. This is not to suggest that journalists unnecessarily sensationalize their stories, but bored readers are bad for business. However, life happens chronologically rather than in inverted pyramid style, and our brains have evolved to best understand the real world (Reeves & Nass 1996). This begs the question: does storytelling format make a difference?

Due in part to the fast-developing pace of online media, relatively research exists on the processing of online narrative. However, research data suggest that the cognitive processing of a television news story is strongly affected by the presentation format. When shown broadcast news stories both in chronological form and in traditional broadcast form, viewers recalled slightly more information from the chronological stories; however, perhaps more importantly, their memories were significantly more accurate for news they had seen chronologically (A. Lang 1989).

MEMORY

This finding fits well with models of human memory generally. Broadly we distinguish between two types of memory, declarative and nondeclarative. The second type, nondeclarative, involves things such as muscle memory that cannot readily be verbalized. This type of memory is less interesting for the online writer. Declarative memory, however, involves the things that we talk about: facts, lists, and episodes of our lives.

Furthermore, we can separate declarative memory into semantic and episodic memory (e.g., Tulving & Thomson 1973). Semantic memory includes the many isolated facts that reside somewhere in your brain, whereas episodic memory is tied to specific events. If you are like most people, you can probably remember that George Washington was the first president of the United States, but you probably cannot remember the actual event of learning that fact. That is, you cannot remember what you were doing before and after that fact was introduced and where you were when you learned it. Using complex reasoning, you might be able to estimate approximately when you learned about Washington (i.e., it was probably in preschool or elementary school rather than last week). Unless you have a photographic memory, you cannot recall the exact episode.

Contrast this with your high school prom. You likely have a very detailed memory of the event. You know what came first, second, and so on. You can remember picking out the formal wear, selecting a date, and the pre-event planning. If the night was especially memorable, you might even be able to recall which songs were played in which order. Finally, you can likely remember how the evening wound down and finally came to an end. You can do all of this rather effortlessly and in relatively precise temporal order. This is the power of episodic memory—a story is an entire episode not just as a series of disconnected facts but rather as a narrative woven together in time. In this sense, each isolated memory serves as a cue to every other memory from the event. Think of the memory as a snowball gaining momentum as it rolls downhill. When you think of the prom, it triggers a memory, which is likely to trigger another memory. Although it is possible for these memories to trigger one another in haphazard arbitrary fashion, it is more likely that a given memory (e.g., giving of the corsage) will trigger the next related memory (e.g., posing for photos) because that is the order in which the memories were learned (see Elman 1990). Indeed, data show that once you retrieve a memory from a given source, you are likely to continue drawing memories from that same source (Shapiro 1991).

When tested experimentally, narrative exerts its strong grip on human cognition. In another study of television news, researchers varied the narrative content of both the audio and the visual channels. Visual—but not audio—narrative structure increased subsequent memory for the news (Lang, Sias, Chantrill & Burek, 1995). However, the most interesting finding is that participants tended to recall the news stories in a narrative structure even for stories presented with minimal narrative. This suggests that viewers invest the cognitive effort to reorganize a story into a narrative format even when it is not presented that way. If this is indeed the case, then presenting stories out of narrative order places an additional cognitive burden on the viewer. This would explain, in part, why memory suffers for nonnarrative messages. Narrative's superiority on memory is not constrained to adults. Even preschool children showed more detailed and more accurate memory for stories with a cohesive narrative (Kulko-fasky, Wang, & Ceci 2008). For people of all ages, the data are consistent: If you want your message to be well remembered, it needs to include a narrative component.

PROCESSING CAPACITY AND NARRATIVE

Why should the lack of narrative structure *decrease* subsequent memory for the information? The answer is that we have long known that human processing capacity is limited (Kahneman 1973; Lang 2000). There are only so many cognitive resources to accomplish mental tasks, and when that capacity is reached, mental processes begin to break down. Luckily for us, we are not usually aware of this breakdown. We go on perceiving the world around us, but later we may find that our memory of an event—such as studying for a test—is not what we had hoped. This is likely due to the fact that some other mental process, such as text messaging or thinking about weekend plans, prevented resources from being allocated to store information about the test. In short, we reached cognitive overload.

This cognitive overload is especially relevant to the Internet writer, who often will be writing multimedia content. And once again the online writer must carefully consider the goals for a message. Many people—especially young people—enjoy messages that are fast-paced, colorful, and exciting. When it comes to multimedia, preferences usually dictate the more animated toys, the better. If getting and keeping eyes on screen is your only goal, then keep adding plug-ins. However, two decades of research suggest that these well-liked messages will be poorly remembered.

As you may have figured out by now, narrative is one tool to help make messages easier to encode. There is increasing evidence that the process-ing of narrative structure is relatively automatic (see A. Lang et al., 1995). Some parts of the worlds are processed rather easily, or automati-cally, and they require very few cognitive resources (see Schneider & Shiffrin 1977). Conversely, some parts of the world require controlled processing, which requires a great deal of resource allocation. When you hear someone say your name, this is generally thought to be an automatic process. Even if you are busy with another conversation, your brain automatically picks out your name being said in a nearby conversation.

For most people, long division is a controlled process that requires time and concentration. Thus, some tasks are by nature automatic while others are controlled. And sometimes the circumstances dictate the processing mode. Driving on a sparsely travelled interstate on a bright, sunny day is a relatively automatic process for most people. Sometimes you can drive for miles at a time, and it is so effortless that you can think back and have almost no memory of the intervening miles. All this changes when you hit traffic. This previously automatic process becomes very controlled as brakes slam on and other drivers dart between lanes. Curiously, most drivers will reflexively reach for the radio to turn down the volume. All of a sudden, the background noise of the radio is too distracting as it competes for preciously limited cognitive resources.

The data suggest that narrative acts like the wide-open spaces of the deserted interstate. It is an automatic processing mechanism that creates slots for information. These cognitive "slots," if you will, wait for information from the story to fill them and automatically move on to the next position like moving to the next chapter in a book. When you tell a story out of order, the brain must shift into effortful, controlled processing. The story fills one slot at the end, then jumps to the beginning, and then heads to the middle. All of this searching for slots takes time.

The exact relationship between narrative and processing capacity, however, is not always clear. Data from memory tests suggest that narrative structure leads to automatic processing as information is more easily digested. At the same time, however, easier processing could likely lead to more in-depth processing. That is, you are more likely to become immersed in a story that is easy to understand. A. Lang and colleagues (1995) used a measure known as secondary task reaction time (STRT) to study the effects of narrative on processing capacity. The idea is simple enough: participants are given a primary task, such as watching television or reading a Web page. It is stressed that the primary task is the most important thing that they will do. At the same time, however, participants are told that they will hear a tone from time to time. When they hear the tone, they are instructed to push a button. This is the secondary task. The idea behind STRT is that as the primary task requires greater cognitive resources, there will be fewer resources remaining for the secondary task, which translates into slower reaction times. That is, it would take you longer to push the button during heavy traffic than easy highway driving. This begs the question: does narrative slow down or speed up the STRT? When the narrative structure was audio, news messages with a greater degree of narrative structure actually led to *slower* STRTs. Video narrative made no difference on STRT. This suggests that the presence of audio narrative—the channel through which stories were told in the oral tradition for centuries—caused greater cognitive resources to be allocated to message processing. Narrative actually pulls the reader or listener into the message. Once the reader is invested in the message, it is easier for the narrative structure to maintain attention because each new component of the message is semantically related to the previous component, which makes the message easier to comprehend (A. Lang, Bradley, Park, Shin, & Chung 2006). Taken together, several studies looking at different message aspects show that narrative leads to easier and more in-depth processing, and better memory for the underlying message.

PERCEIVING REALITY ONLINE

Cognitively speaking, narrative structure is well justified. However, this discussion has overlooked the fact that there are two broad categories of narrative, fiction and nonfiction. The fact that readers can go back and forth between the real and the made-up so seamlessly is an interesting component of human psychology. It seems highly unlikely that a message's truth value would not matter at least somewhat in the processing of a narrative. If you have ever taken an introductory theater class, chances are that you have learned about the so-called "willing suspension of disbelief." That is, when you sit in a seat of a live theater or a movie theater, you are aware that what you are about to see is a work of fiction. It is made-up, so you leave your truth-expecting hat at the door. Under this approach, your natural tendency is to disbelieve, and you have to disengage this predisposition in order to enjoy the work of fiction. At some level, of course, this must be true. You obviously *do know* that it is a work of fiction, and at some level you are likely not sitting in the theater actively rehearsing that thought in mind. However, research shows the underlying psychological processes to be almost the opposite. Instead, it appears that readers quickly get pulled into stories whether they are fiction or nonfiction (Shapiro & Chock 2003). You must actively engage disbelief to avoid being consumed by the message.

Most fiction messages are not like our everyday lives. If they were, they would be boring, and you would not want to invest your time with them. Your real life *is* real life, so why would you want to watch real life on YouTube? Unless you are incredibly dull, the answer is that you want fiction that is somehow bigger, brighter, or bolder than everyday life. Take, for example, an earthquake. Most readers have never experienced an earthquake (sorry, Pacific Rim readers). Everything you know about what happens in an earthquake is mediated, either through another person or the mass media or the Internet. Most people have no idea what *really* happens during an earthquake. Despite this relative ignorance of what actually happens during an earthquake, readers can make split-second decisions about the likelihood of an event happening during an earthquake (Shapiro & Fox 2002). When asked if it is plausible that the walls shake during an earthquake in a TV drama, for instance, almost everyone will readily agree that it is highly likely. Conversely, when asked if family members would climb onto the kitchen table and begin dancing during an earthquake, hardly anyone will think it is plausible. Many people will even laugh at the thought. How do we make these distinctions between what is typical and what is atypical when we have never been in most of the situations described in mediated communication?

It appears that we use a vast body of knowledge about the world we know through direct experiences, interpersonal sources, and mediated communication (Shapiro 1991). If something we read is too discrepant with our lifetime of experience, it immediately stands out (Shapiro & Chock, 2003). This also has a profound effect upon our memories. When a narrative is very typical—when it is like so many other narratives we have heard before—the new narrative gets intertwined with the lifetime of memories. Even a half an hour later it is difficult to separate the story we just heard from a lifetime of similar stories. This is why it is so difficult for people to remember whether they took their medicine in the morning. That memory blends in with hundreds just like it. In this case, the smaller narrative is subsumed by the narrative that is your life. Rare events—such as graduations, weddings, and childbirths—are unlikely to be forgotten, however. In order for parts of a narrative to be well remembered, then it appears that they have to have a dramatic, unusual element. Drama is important, but overly sensationalized writing will quickly engage mechanisms of disbelief as the story fails to resonate with the reader. When a writer understands how rare and common events are represented in memory, then stories (both fiction and nonfiction) can be crafted in a way that makes them stand out in memory.

IMPLICATIONS FOR INTERNET WRITING

Narrative structure is a fundamental building block of human writing. If the online writer fails to provide a narrative structure for the reader, then a body of research suggests that the reader will invent her own narrative—even with something so simple as geometric shapes. Taken together the data on attention and memory make different recommendations based upon the goals of the Internet writer. Chronological narratives are easier to understand, but a message is more likely to garner attention when it leads with the "good stuff." However, if learning is the goal of the online writer, then chronological formats with well-formed, coherent narrative structure will lead to greater memory. It is important to understand the balance between getting attention and remembering the story. Different online writing tactics will accomplish different goals. Finally, readers are constantly assessing the perceived reality of what they read, hear, and watch. Commonplace details and routine events are easily lost into the abyss of memory that is a lifetime of experience. Dramatic stories are more likely to stand out in memory.

Section Three

Internet Writing and Technologies

Chapter 7

Web 2.0 Technologies

CHARACTERISTICS OF WEB 2.0 TECHNOLOGIES

When you think of the wide range of technologies found on the Internet today, and the variety of tools and software programs used to view and develop Web site content, you will most likely hear the term "Web 2.0" associated with them. Web 2.0 is not an individual technology or single software program that drives the Web. Web 2.0 describes a collection of Web-related technologies that enhance the usability, accessibility, and interactive quality of online content, using the latest capabilities of applets, scripts, and software. Web 2.0 represents a fundamental shift in user interaction with Web content to create personalized and customized products. Some technologies considered to be part of Web 2.0 include content management systems (wiki, blog, social networking sites), scripting languages (AJAX, PHP, RSS, XML), and new media technologies (podcasts, instructional video). Web 2.0 technologies provide platform flexibility by running many applications client-side through the use of a standard Web browser.

While a number of diverse tools and technologies comprise Web 2.0, specific underlying characteristics best define it. Web 2.0 technologies are highly collaborative, encouraging a convergence of authors, texts, media, and viewpoints. Blogs, wikis, and social networking are examples of tools that encourage multiple authors, fostering a sense of communal knowledge and commentary on any given topic. These electronic texts often rely on the feedback and user posts as much as their primary content. Web 2.0 tools are also highly structured, integrating methods for easily categorizing and organizing content. Content management systems (CMS) and wikis provide templates, user search tools, and hierarchical structures that make it easy for developers to import and organize content. Languages such as Extensible Markup Language (XML) have built-in capabilities, allowing users to define and customize unique document structures and templates. Web 2.0 tools are also hypertextual, in that individual content units, or chunks, can be deposited into the system used and interlinked however the developer sees fit. This accommodates both layering and reuse of the same content unit, as it can be linked and displayed with others to comprise a complete page. For example, a single product description can be linked to a product specification sheet, marketing brochures, a technical support page, and a user knowledge base. Another important trait is that Web 2.0 tools are increasingly interactive and immersive for its users (Heim 1998). Beyond contributing comments to a blog, these tools are interactive in the sense that users have some control over the speed, direction, order, rate, and configuration of how content is displayed on their screen. Media controls, customized searches, hyperlinks, and other types of user preference settings can help users customize the content on their screens. Based on user input, the system reacts and adapts, and in some cases can learn from the user by building a library of user preferences and offering customized suggestions, links, and supplemental content. Bookseller Web sites are a good example of this, which base recommended purchases to users on their buying history, wish lists, and past searches. Much Web 2.0 content can function like common desktop applications, with much of the back-end coding seeming almost invisible, and creating a seamless user experience. As interfaces and systems become more visual and interactive, they create more immersive and compelling environments for users, as well. Virtual reality scholar Michael Heim argues, "the wide degrees of involvement that different media deliver in terms of sensory detail and amount of interactivity" is essential in considering the effect these environments have on users (Heim 1998, 19). What is usable to one person may not be as user-friendly to another, so part of seamless experience seems to suggest a degree of adaptability, where the system provides choices or permits the user to customize their experience to some degree. Peter Morville (2005) recognizes this as an iterative process by which users learn and confront the complex tasks of information seeking, arguing that information findability is essential for creating optimal user experiences.

In addition to the overlapping characteristics that underlie Web 2.0 technologies, Tim O'Reilly (2005) identifies some important principal features of Web 2.0 technologies that include using the World Wide

Web as the primary platform for publication, harnessing collective knowledge, networking robust data sources, recasting users as co-developers of information, and creating rich user experiences. Each of these characteristics are discussed below:

- *Using the World Wide Web as the primary platform.* Multisystem, multi-browser, multiapplet, multilanguge, multi-interface capability that maximizes usability, accessibility, and compatibility well beyond the capabilities of a single software program.

- *Harnessing collective knowledge.* Hyperlinking, cross-references, collaborative authoring, search portals that track analytics, CMS, and social networking software all serve this common function. Collectively, they provide the tools to create the Web infrastructure that interlinks knowledge, relates and customizes that knowledge, and is founded upon the vast knowledge of its users and collective content published on the Web.

- *Creating robust, networked data sources.* Shared (and interlinked) databases, proprietary freeware, data libraries, syndicated content, and single-sourcing data are significant characteristics many Web 2.0 technologies have at their core. The ability for users to repurpose or "remix" content, templates, scripts, applets, etc., is significant, as well. This also raises important control issues and questions of who owns and has rights to reproduce data, which have yet to be answered.

- *Recasting users as co-developers.* Collaborative authoring and development of open-source products that support user involvement in the evolution of content, data sources, and information databases. As mentioned before, the ability to repurpose and various forms of meta-discourse support this feature. User feedback, beta testing, knowledge bases, and support forms are examples of how users become involved on a development level. Blogs, wikis, and social networking sites provide the infrastructure for users to contribute content in these multiauthored spaces.

- *Creating rich user experiences.* The capabilities of advanced markup and scripting languages provide the means to create client-side content that is scalable, customizable, highly interactive, and easily single-sourced. Examples include Flash-based content, Geographic Information Systems (GIS), email applications, interactive games, and RSS feeds.

At their core, Web 2.0 technologies are designed to address various information needs and problems that older Web-based and software-based platforms created. One significant problem is that digital technologies can accommodate extremely large volumes of information. Some of the difficulties include how to structure, network, control, and organize it into usable interfaces and systems. While many CMSs and related tools provide existing hierarchical structures for developers, they often require some customization to address the unique information problems each site or project brings. The use of mixed media also presents a significant challenge for developers and users. In its early days, because of reduced bandwidth, storage capacity, and access, the Web presented many problems in delivering high quality and mixed forms of media. Web 2.0 addressed these problems by providing media players, static and streaming capabilities, and more standardized media formats to improve both access and quality. As a result, it has become commonplace to access pages with mixed media forms including interactive text, images, audio content, video content, and other forms of blended and layered media. Web 2.0 also addressed the need of users to interact with one another and to greater degrees with Web content. Another problem was that much early interaction was done asynchronously, where there was an expected delay among the sending, receiving, and replying to a message or a discussion board post. Web 2.0 technologies include both asynchronous and synchronous, or real-time, interactive capabilities. Blogs, social networking sites, and even some CMSs allow users to have real-time chat sessions as well as other asynchronous means such as message boards, email, and forums. Another problem with early Web technologies was the lack of personalization and customization of content. One vast improvement with Web 2.0 is that users can interact with site content and customize how it is filtered and displayed, and can even convert content to more viewable forms. Advances in Web browsing and searching tools have accounted for these changes. Many search engines can convert text from one language to another, and some content can be converted to Hypertext Markup Language (HTML)-equivalent or Portable Document Format (PDF)-equivalent formats for optimal viewing and printing. HTML is a markup language used in writing Web-based content. PDF is a portable document format used for document exchange, created by Adobe, Inc. Web 2.0 technologies such as XML and CMS help to homogenize multiple data sources, which can then be searched or modified by user input to create a unique individualized data product. This single-sourcing of data also partially addresses the information volume problem, giving content a recyclability, where it can be authored once and then reused or repurposed. This type of content remixability extends beyond simple reuse and has become a cornerstone of many blogs and social networking sites, where user commentary is an essential part of the user experience.

Despite the significant changes in Web 2.0 technologies, many problems still persist and have created new challenges for Internet writers and developers. The issues of control and ownership are still a significant problem and advances in technologies have only contributed to the issue.

Questions of who controls what and who owns what apply to intellectual property, freeware, content libraries, and even meta-content, such as user posts or comments. Another significant problem is accessibility. While Web content accessibility standards have been developed by both the U.S. government and the World Wide Web Consortium (W3C), there is no formal mandate to use them, save the U.S. government's publicly accessible Internet content. The primary purpose of these guidelines is to ensure Web content is accessible to people with disabilities, including a wide range of auditory, visual, vocal, cognitive, and other perceptual limitations (W3C 2009). In addition, despite the multiplatform compatibility of many markup and scripting languages, there are often differences on how that content displays on individual Web browsers. This is still one particular challenge with some of the more recent Cascading Style Sheets (CSS) specifications. And finally, one major problem perpetuated by Web 2.0 is the ever-steepening technology curve required to stay abreast of new tools. With the creation of new technologies, methods, and tools, there has also been a need for some degree of skill specialization. Put simply, no single person can master the range of Web 2.0 software, languages, and technologies. This requires not only continual learning but also increased resources, including time and money. While freeware, open-source technologies, and content libraries help provide users with cost-free solutions, mastering a smattering of Web 2.0 technologies requires a great amount of research to maintain proficiency over time. As technologies continue to develop and improve, the next major evolution of Web technologies may be built on these core ideals to address these continuing problems.

CONTENT MANAGEMENT SYSTEMS

Content management is Web 2.0's solution to the information volume problem created by computer technology and perpetuated by the Internet. Content management is a highly structured approach to organizing, reusing, and delivering adaptable sources of information to fit a variety of purposes and users. As a modular approach to information design, content management involves the use of smaller content chunks, types, and patterns, which are stored, reused, and reconfigured into a wide range of displays. It encompasses the creation, storage, retrieval, display, delivery, and archiving of content throughout the life cycle of a product. In an electronic publishing medium, such as the Internet, content management is handled by software and/or Web-enabled systems that can be tailored to fit the unique requirements of an organization. Blogs, wikis, knowledge bases, and online help systems are all examples of fully functional content management solutions, which automate many organizational and functional aspects of data-driven Web sites.

CMSs are fully developed and data-driven software systems that provide an organized framework, structure, and built-in templates to create out-of-the-box Web site solutions. Most content can be entered into a CMS using a forms-based interface, allowing users with limited Web development experience to import and publish Web-based content. CMSs provide basic document management functions, which provide built-in tools for search, retrieval, level of access, metadata, and archiving (Rockley 2003). Most CMSs also have predefined stylesheets, page templates, structured databases, and image libraries that provide varying levels of customization to specify both the functionality and display of a site. As a result, one significant advantage is a high level of usability and, subsequently, consistency for users. Content can be cut and pasted from other sources and external files, such as videos or documents, can be embedded into CMS pages for rapid publication. From a security standpoint, CMSs typically have varying levels of access, which accommodate collaborative authoring and roles, such as content provider, reviewer, and site manager. As far as accessibility and usability, most CMSs tend to be fully browser compliant, unless significantly modified from their original state, and many adhere to the Web Content Accessibility Guidelines set forth by the W3C. Some examples of out-of-the-box CMS products include wikis, blogs, groupware, knowledge bases, help systems, and content portals. Some CMS products have more restricted functions, focusing solely on document management, Web site content management, or instructional learning.

CMS accommodate a separation of content (texts) from presentation (visual and structural characteristics). In most systems, content is standardized through a series of information templates that define single data fields (units), a group of data fields on a single page (types), or a group of multiple pages in an entire Web site (models) (Hackos 2002). Presentational aspects, including visual design, page layout, navigation, and structure are also specified through templates and stylesheets that ensure internal consistency. One advantage of the separation is it allows different functions of a product to be developed simultaneously by different members of a development team. Another benefit is that as modular components, individual content units and stylesheets can be extracted, replaced, and reused to create different displays based on user input or other specifications. Despite this functional separation, content and presentation always end up working together in the final product (Clark 2008). Content units and pages merge with stylesheets, templates, and scripts to create the whole effect.

There are a wide range of uses for CMS and an equally wide range of products available. Blogs, wikis, and social networking sites are all widely used CMS types used to publish and share personal information, serve as specialized topic references, foster online communities, and more. The business sector is also increasingly making use of such systems to capture tacit knowledge, improve processes, and create a more formal internal networking structure for employees. Some of the systems used include help systems, knowledge bases, and fully developed Web sites. Corporations and news organizations use content management solutions to help organize, structure, and rapidly publish Internet-ready content. Businesses have also invested in the use of enterprise content management systems (ECMS), which manage a wide range of content that includes Internet publications, financial and human resources, company records, internal communication, and the corporate Web presence. Educational institutions have adapted and used many varieties of CMS, such as learning management systems (LMS), which help instructors organize online course materials, and provide built-in features such as assignment uploading, synchronous chat, message boards, and so forth. These systems are used to manage everything from individual courses to entire training programs in an online setting.

SELECTING THE RIGHT CONTENT MANAGEMENT SYSTEM

Ten Questions to Consider

1. What purposes will the system satisfy (learning, knowledge gathering, help, data clearinghouse, social networking, etc.)?
2. What core functions should the system have?
3. What are the existing technical limitations or compatibility requirements?
4. What are the existing resources available?
5. Which product(s) will be used: an open source or a commercial product?
6. What customization options and features are available?
7. Does the product have any accessibility issues or problems?
8. What are the long-term implications of using those products (licensing fees, product longevity)?
9. How will the system be maintained long-term (resources, personnel, updating, archiving)?
10. What support mechanisms are available for the product(s)?

Selecting the right CMS product to use can be difficult for a number of reasons, including cost, built-in features, customization options, compatibility issues, scalability, product support and longevity, and the range of products available. In some cases, the product may require a larger perspective—it may not be simply a matter of selecting a single CMS, but rather, a few products that support a larger content management solution. For example, a corporate technical support site might require a knowledge base to contain technical support articles and include a blogging system for developers to network or share ideas and knowledge with each other, or even with customers. Some additional technical issues to consider include formal training, customization, structure, and overall accessibility. As highly structured systems, many CMSs may use default layouts that are simply incompatible with an organization's needs and may require a significant level of technical knowledge to customize. For example, knowledge of the base scripting and programming languages may be required to significantly modify the built-in templates, data tables, and forms used. While many CMSs are highly usable out of the box, the usability and accessibility of these systems may be challenged as the product is modified and customized from its original state. Thoroughly researching the available options is essential in ensuring the product can meet expectations, serve as a sustainable solution over time, and minimize contingencies that could result in costly mistakes.

ADVANCED MARKUP AND SCRIPTING LANGUAGES

Web 2.0 technologies, including CMSs, incorporate a variety of markup and scripting technologies to develop content, which contributes to the interactivity, accessibility, findability, and overall usability of Internet writing. Some of the more commonly used technologies from organizational to news reporting Web sites include XML, RSS, AJAX, and PHP. As part of understanding the basics of how these technologies function, it is important to recognize the difference between markup and scripting. Markup languages specify where specific content elements are placed in a document and how each element on a page will be displayed. Scripting languages add functionality to a markup content, including advanced layouts, interactive styles, processed form data, and other interactive features. A variety of markup and scripting languages are used together to create interactive and well-designed Internet content. Both types of languages are used in Web 2.0 technologies to create stability and cross-browser compatibility, which makes them highly accessible and usable for a wide variety of users and browser or operating systems. They also provide cross-browser and cross-platform capabilities, which make many Web 2.0 technology-driven sites highly accessible. The good news for Internet writers who are not experts with these languages is that many software programs used to develop Web-based content generates the coding for the writer. However, it is important to have a working knowledge of some basic coding skills and technologies to help understand the range of capabilities each language has and to solve minor editing problems that may arise. What follows, is a discussion of some of the most commonly used markup and scripting languages, essential to Web 2.0 technologies.

Content Markup

Hypertext Markup Language (HTML) and Extensible Hypertext Markup Language (XHTML) are the basic markup languages used for the publishing of Web-based content. HTML is a Web markup language used to outline and markup content so it can be read by a Web browser. It specifies both the basic structure of individual Web pages and the basic markup of individual content elements, such as paragraphs, images, and hyperlinks. XHTML is an evolved version of HTML using a stricter syntax that conforms and works more seamlessly with XML. Both HTML and XHTML use markup tags and attributes that specify the format of internal content elements and inclusion of external content, such as stylesheets, interactive scripts, and other files.

XML is one of the most versatile and widely compatible markup languages used in developing Web 2.0 content. XML was introduced by the W3C in the mid-1990s as a reformulation of Standard General Markup Language (SGML) to better meet the demands of online publishing. XML is different from HTML and XHTML in that it provides developers greater control over the document structure and customized markup of content elements on a page. While HTML and XHTML both have defined tags to mark up content, XML allows authors to develop and define their own content tag rules. This capability makes XML ideal for creating highly structured documents and data sources with a high degree of versatility. XML can also be used with a wide range of other markup and scripting languages to add Web-browser friendly formatting (HTML, XHTML, CSS), to translate content into different document types (XSLT, XPath—a query language used to select data from nodes in an XML document or database), to add interactive scripts (AJAX, JavaScript, PHP), and to create searchable content from a data file or database (XPath, DOM [Document Object Model, which is used to define the structure of objects within document markup]). And XML has also been used to develop other applications and scripting technologies, which use the core XML markup language.

Stylesheets and Formatting

Extensible Stylesheet Language Transformation (XSLT) translates native XML documents into other Web-friendly, readable formats, such as HTML, XHTML, and even PDF. XSLT is a type of XML stylesheet, but can also be used with other stylesheets developed for Web pages, such as CSS. XSLT is highly useful creating different formatted templates that can translate XML document data into a variety of different displays. For example, a single XML document that contains biographical data such as name, position title, photo, writing experience, and so forth can be converted into different page displays, such as one formatted for public release on a Web site and another created for publishing on an organization's internal Web portal.

CSS is a scripting language used to specify styles and position of markup content in Web pages. CSS allows authors to create electronic stylesheets for Web pages, which address stylistic elements such as fonts, colors, margins, and text alignment, as well as positional, media, and visual formatting. Through CSS, a single stylesheet can be created and applied locally to markup tags on a single page, on multiple pages, or even globally to all pages throughout an entire Web site. As such, CSS helps developers create consistency in the use of styles and design elements throughout an entire Web site. When combined with other scripting languages, such as JavaScript, document styles can be made interactive, changing based on specific user actions (mouseover, click, hover) and other forms of user input.

Interactive and Syndicated Content

Really Simple Syndication (RSS) describes a set of scripting technologies used to create synchronous (and syndicated) content from other data sources and Web sites, generated in real time. This format addresses the needs of rapid updates and time-sensitive content, which eliminates the need for other types of asynchronous content distribution subscription services. RSS content, also known as feeds, is read by RSS reader software plug-ins and requires active subscription to an active RSS feed. RSS content markup is XML based and typically uses a .xml or .rss file extension. Some examples of RSS feeds include news headline tickers, podcasts, weather reports, stock information, real-time event calendars, and many other time-sensitive content objects. RSS allows Internet writers to create and publish real-time syndicated content for readers. Once a user subscribes to an RSS feed, he/she receives new content as it is pushed to users automatically, as long as the subscription is valid.

Asynchronous JavaScript and XML (AJAX) comprises a combination of markup and scripting languages, including the client-side scripting language JavaScript with the highly structured markup language XML to create seamless and interactive Web content, which resembles many common desktop applications. AJAX's unique combination of languages can be used to store and retrieve data, handle data, and apply and transform styles into highly customized page layouts. AJAX also works with other markup and scripting languages, including CSS, HTML, XHTML, and XSLT.

Hypertext Preprocessor (PHP) is a server-side scripting language used to handle and process form data in Web sites. Its initial use was to assist in tracking Web site users and later became used in interpreting form data. PHP can be used with other markup languages, such as HTML, XHTML, and XML, as well as database query languages, such as MySQL and MSSQL, to handle and process data, and scripting languages, such as JavaScript, to create interactive forms. Over time, developers have contributed to the development of PHP, adding support for XML, command-line scripting, desktop and mobile computing applications, and object-oriented programming. Its cross-browser and cross-platform compatibility gives it a high degree of accessibility and usability.

These core languages are used to develop Web 2.0 content and related technologies, but are by no means the entire list of what is available. As existing languages evolve in their data sharing and interactive capabilities, and new languages are created, it becomes increasingly important for Internet writers to be familiar with the latest languages and technologies used. A basic understanding of these technologies provides writers with a wider range of tools from which to produce high quality Internet content. Although many software programs can automate the markup and scripting for Internet writers, through the various toolbar and drag-and-drop interfaces, more advanced customization requires some knowledge of these technologies. A wide range of books, courses, Web sites, and instructional applications are available that are useful in building a working knowledge of these tools. Online libraries with tutorials, references, and downloadable free scripts are available to help beginners get started, as well.

NEW MEDIA TECHNOLOGIES

New media technologies, including interactive applets, streaming and static video, and serialized media, are also important components of many Web 2.0 technologies. Much Web 2.0 content is composed of mixed media forms, and it is the Internet writer's challenge to make them work together seamlessly. Web pages often contain multiple content types, formats, and media forms, providing users with multiple forms of media. Web users have become increasingly savvy in their electronic literacy and have adapted to switching back and forth between these different content types and forms in their searching and browsing. Depending on the user's interest, mood, or need, he or she may begin a search with a text-based search term, browse pages for textual or static visual content, move on to video clips, read a handful of blogs on the subject, and possibly subscribe to or download supplemental documents or podcasts.

Web 2.0 technologies have greatly influenced the development of new media, particularly evident through some of their shared characteristics. One important characteristic is modularity, which describes how different components are assembled to create new media objects (Manovich 2001). Any media object might be composed of text, raster images, interactive scripts, and video and audio components, which makes them composed of different modular media content. In addition, these content forms might be composed of a number of different layers that comprise the media object. Some examples include applets, learning objects, interactive movies, and instructional videos. Modularity is also an extension of convergence of media forms, since it focuses on how individual media objects or content forms can be layered, combined, and reused in different products and situations. Media convergence describes the resilient quality of media forms, which no longer have a separate delivery mode or method, but rather allow the same content to have different and multiple forms of delivery (Jenkins 2006). New media need not be created for every new product; rather existing content can be remediated, or refashioned into new forms and combined into new structures (Bolter & Grusin, 1999). This other characteristic, remediation, involves the repurposing and reuse of existing media in new contexts and forms for distribution. New media objects also have multimodality, which describes the ability to move interchangeably between interactive media forms, such as visual, vocal, tactile, and so forth. Mobile computing devices such as global positioning system (GPS) units, BlackBerries, and cellular telephones engage users with multimodal media forms that require more than one mode of interaction.

There are many examples of Web 2.0 new media forms widely used in online publishing. Serialized media content, such as podcasts and RSS feeds, provide a constant stream of asynchronous content to which the user subscribes, downloads, or simply waits for the next edition to be transmitted to them. Formal training programs, colleges, and universities are using syndicated content as course supplements, where students download the week's material for study. News organizations also use syndicated content that allows users to have a synchronous monitor of the latest headlines, stock market information, and even downloadable reporter commentary. Mixed media is increasingly common in highly modular forms of blogs and wikis, which allow users to contribute commentary and metacommentary, which includes static visuals, hyperlinks, and audio and video content. Many business are modular in their approach to developing content, using a variety of forms and formats for its users. News sites provide a good example of both modular and remediated content, combining text, graphics, media, and user commentary, some of which may be reused, as a part of reporting the whole story. Instructional media forms are also prevalent in formal and informal training. Essentially everything from the classroom to the workplace to the home has access to a wide range of learning objects on a variety of subjects. Learning media demonstrate a high degree of convergence, in that they are distributed and remediated through a variety of different means including software, syndicated content, content libraries on the Web, and the Internet. These objects may include simple games, tutorials, reference guides, forms-based quizzes, interactive applets or models, and animated sequences. Learning objects may also be used in an organizational context to illustrate complex processes, procedures, or working models. Collectively, Web 2.0 media technologies demonstrate a high degree of versatility and reusability that maximize their usefulness and value to Internet writers and users.

IMPLICATIONS FOR TODAY'S INTERNET WRITERS

In addition to their many benefits, Web 2.0 technologies suggest a number of important implications for Internet writers. With the rapid evolution and convergence of technologies, writers must keep abreast of the latest tools and technologies. One important question in the mind of every Internet writer may be: *How do I keep up?* With any technology, it is important to continue training, individual study, research, and practice to achieve a consistent level of mastery. Courses, seminars, reference books, informational Web sites, online scripting libraries, technical support forums, journals, magazines, and networking with other professionals are all ways of keeping abreast of the latest technology trends. Get involved, stay involved, and practice. While impossible to keep up with every possible technology, selecting the right tools, languages, and techniques for the job at hand is essential. Equally important is the need to expand the breadth of knowledge of software and languages readily available. While it is important to specialize in skills to some extent, a surface awareness of the latest technologies is required to identify new trends and tools that may improve the quality of written products. In addition, familiarity with a variety of tools is also necessary. Investing resources in a single tool or software program will eventually lead to a dead-end when that product is discontinued by the manufacturer or discarded by the organization. A wider variety of tools will also provide writers and developers with some choices when selecting which solution is best for a project or task. Finally, it is essential for Internet writers to integrate knowledge of structure and content management into the writing process. Developing Internet content involves skill in planning and developing much more, including the structure, design, interactivity, usability, and functionality of the product. As such, Internet writers must familiarize themselves with the entire range of skills required of online publishing, which, largely due to Web 2.0 technologies, extends well beyond the task of writing and editing content.

Chapter 8

Chunking and Hyperlinking

CHARACTERISTICS OF INTERNET WRITING

Writing effective content for the Internet involves two important but somewhat complex tasks, chunking and linking. Content chunking involves writing and adapting content that follows specific templates, structures, as well as specific design and content specifications. Linking content involves determining the relationships between content units and pages, selecting relevant content and following specific naming and structural guidelines the site may have. Together, these important Internet writing skills have a tremendous impact on the readability and usability of online content. Content must be structured to create consistency and optimized in its length to maximize its usefulness to readers. Equally important, using descriptive link names and providing relevant and useful links is necessary to produce content that is easily accessible in the shortest amount of time possible. Longer, unstructured content can create usability problems and affect the credibility and length of time required to read online. Since users tend to prefer shorter passages and skim online content, it is important to write online content to accommodate these needs.

Internet-based content has unique characteristics, which are important to understand in order to write usable content. Internet content is modular, single-sourced, highly structured, and hyperlinked, and it can be user customized. Modular content is multifunctional in that it can stand alone as a single unit or be used in a variety of different pages and information types throughout a site. Examples of content units include a definition, product description, disclaimer statement, or basic instructions, which can be written, stored, and then used (or linked) on pages where the information is relevant. Another related characteristic of Internet content is that it can be single-sourced, or in other words, written once and reused multiple times, often for different purposes. For example, a disclaimer statement can be reused on pages throughout a site where information is proprietary or requires a legal disclaimer and on product information pages. Product descriptions on e-commerce sites can be used on sales pages or technical support pages. Internet content is often highly structured in that it can be developed using templates, content model specifications, schema, document type definitions (as in XML-based content), stored and retrieved in structured content management systems, and even arranged into hierarchical structures, such as Web sites and topic architectures. Most content units and types adhere to specific structural guidelines, such as the types of information they contain (such as title, description, reference links, and price) as well as their style, length, language, arrangement, and size. And on a larger level, content units and complete Web pages are interlinked into a larger structure such as a content management system or fully developed Web site, which has very specific content arrangements that allow users to search and browse through. One major advantage of Internet content is its ability to link based on association, relevance, order, user preference, or even keyword search. One fundamental characteristic of Internet content is its use of hyperlinks, which allow content to interconnect and reference other relevant content. Linking provides users with supplemental content, references, and serendipitous search results, which are often useful complements to Internet content. And finally, content can be highly customized, often based on user input and preference. The use of forms, tracking cookies, site use statistics, usability tests, and user search data are all methods that allow user preference to control (or influence) the presentation and delivery of content. Some methods allow users to specifically input preferences or settings, which customize the page layout, styles, visibility of content, presentation, and so forth. Other methods collect user preference data for Internet writers to review in creating more user-friendly and customized content.

An understanding of the basic methods and characteristics of content chunking and linking is important in producing quality Internet writing. It is important to distinguish between the granularity, or size, of different content units and types and how they are combined in a modular fashion to create large-scale information structures and complete Web sites. Knowledge of both structured and unstructured authoring and content development is also important to the writing process, since much Internet-based content is highly structured and involves adapting semi-structured content to fit online templates and information models. Understanding single-sourcing methods that allow writers to create content once and reuse it many times is an important characteristic of the Internet content, as well. Learning linking strategies for producing relational and usable content is also an essential task. And finally, an awareness of issues of remediating content into different, usable forms and highly compatible formats is necessary in promoting the accessibility of Internet-based content.

ONLINE READING HABITS

An understanding of user reading habits can be beneficial in understanding the complex task of Internet writing. Research in online reading reveals some interesting reading and interactive habits users have when reading Internet-based content. Users tend to skim content pages in an F-shaped pattern and focus on headers and subheads as their eyes move across a page (Nielsen 2008). They focus on navigation tools and other visual cues to learn how content is arranged and to find relevant information (Baehr 2007). Users rely on visual information to help them discern structure, organization, layout, function, and relevance of content and other visuals on the page. Users are also somewhat skeptical about the usefulness of overly stylized content and tend to ignore graphic banners and advertisements (Nielsen 2008). This underscores the importance of user experience, as they will learn and adapt based on reading and examining online content. Users also develop expectations based on their experiences and on conventions they observe. And perceptual research reveals that users engage in nonlinear problem solving as they explore online content (Barry 1998).

With these trends and habits in mind, there are some characteristics users have come to expect in reading online content. First, users expect context sensitivity, or rather content written within the appropriate context or constraints for the medium. A great deal of frustration can occur when a keyword search or hyperlink leads to content that is not relevant to material the user expected to find. Often, database-driven Web sites and search portals have context sensitivity problems because content is not tagged or linked properly. Improper page titles, keyword lists, meta descriptions, or indexing problems can all contribute to this problem. Internet writers must ensure that these important concerns are addressed on a page level to help avoid frustrating users. Single-sourcing strategies can be used to produce content that is multifunctional, that can stand alone, or that can be combined with other content based on users' needs. On a database level, improper indexing might be a problem for the site administrator to address. Another characteristic users have come to expect is information findability, which is the degree to which content is accessible and easy to locate through searching, scanning, and browsing (Morville 2005). Although Internet writers and developers cannot completely control the experience for the user, there are a number of ways they can improve information findability. Beyond basic usability, content must be written to ensure credibility, accessibility, and usefulness, as well as to have specific value (Morville 2005, 109). Plenty of Internet content lacks credibility because of inaccuracies, lack of research, poor design, and poor usability. Making content accessible might include providing alternate formats and versions as searchable text. Making content useful and valuable is rooted in knowing the information needs of users during the writing process, not simply waiting for feedback after something is published. Developing content that is highly structured and consistent in its organization throughout a site can contribute to both usability and findability. Content customizability is another aspect of online content users have come to expect. Content can be customized based on user selection, search parameters, and user controls for everything from search returns to navigation to the display of visual content. And finally, users have come to expect online content to have some degree of interactivity. Examples of interactive content found on many Web sites include media clips, applets, user customization controls, interactive forms, and multiple navigation tools.

CONTENT MANAGEMENT AND STRUCTURED AUTHORING

Content management is important to Internet writing because it provides guidelines and tools to help organize content and provides improved usability of online products. Content management describes the ongoing process of managing and structuring the online content of an information deliverable (such as a Web site), while the content management system is the actual container (software, system, and specific structure) that houses the content itself and delivers it through a series of templates and databases (Clark 2008, 38–39). Content management is important to Internet writers for a variety of reasons. They help writers organize content into coherent structures, which are easier to search and browse. These structures provide consistency and a higher degree of usability for online content. Content management also encourages writers to develop templates for content units and types, which also ensures consistency across content types. Many content management systems provide built-in search tools, which help users browse through content inventories and databases. They can also deliver customized content, based on their search preferences.

One important aspect of content management is structuring content in ways that it can be modular, be reusable, and demonstrate a high degree of usability. Internet writing involves working with structured and somewhat unstructured legacy content and adapting it to fit the specific structure of the Web site or product. Structured authoring is a writing approach that supports effective content management, helping writers develop organized and consistent standards. Structured authoring involves the development of organized frameworks used to categorize and structure information resources so they can be used and reused most effectively. Developing specifications for information models, types, units, metadata, templates, prototypes, and separation of presentation from content are all part of structured authoring. For example, creating a specification for an information type, such as a book entry for a bookselling Web site, might include specific content units (title, author, description, ISBN, price, format) and other guidelines that dictate the styles, length, order, and display of each. As such they can serve as content templates, for which additional entries can be added and have the same set of specifications applied. Content management systems (such as wikis, blogs, and other database-driven systems) and markup and scripting languages (such as XML and CSS) are examples of the kinds of technologies that support structured authoring and content management. Many provide built-in or fully customizable templates and structures that have their own content specifications. Unstructured or semistructured authoring approaches are more free-form in their arrangement and structure. Some examples might include email, short descriptions, blog entries, drafts, and notes. Often, writing Internet content involves remediating and adapting less structured legacy content into more structured units and types.

Structuring content is essential for a variety of reasons. First, set structures provide greater internal consistency across pages, content units, and types in the site. Using consistent structures promotes good usability, navigation, and searching. When users learn the structure of content and see patterns in how content is organized and accessed, they become more proficient in their searching and browsing of a site. Structure also provides an organized framework around which the entire information product or site is built. The use of indices, hierarchical navigation, and site maps can further reinforce the organization to users and contribute to more effective use of the site. And finally, since Internet content can be read out of sequence, and in nonlinear fashions, structure helps provide a framework or road map that users can rely on to help navigate and locate information.

CONTENT CHUNKING, TYPES, AND STRUCTURE

Content chunking is the process of writing modular units of content that are reusable and appropriate for Internet-based media and for highly structured content systems such as Web sites. Internet content is produced through a series of information templates that define single data fields (units), a group of content units with a specific purpose (types), or a structural group of multiple pages, types, and units that comprise an entire Web site (models) (Hackos 2002). Content units (or chunks) are the most basic type of content, such as single titles, short descriptions, abstracts, lists, author background, or link descriptions. While they can serve as stand-alone content on sites, they are often combined into content types, which are composed of multiple content units that adhere to a specific structure or template. An example of a content type would be a complete product information sheet, including its name, price, description, rating, and reference links.

Entire information structures, such as catalogs, inventories, references, or partial or entire Web sites are examples of structural models, which serve as macrolevel organizational templates for content. Topic architectures are one example of commonly used structures. They are often hierarchical structures, similar to a topic-based table of contents, which outline the arrangement of specific content within the information structure (Hackos 2007, 412). Developing and customizing an information structure is essential for high-volume Internet writing, particularly for sites with large content inventories. Content must be organized in ways that make sense to users and maximize the usability of the product. In addition to topic architectures, as one method of providing structure, there are others to consider. Content management systems and out-of-the-box Web site development software can provide customizable templates and structures to help Internet writers organize and deliver content. Writers can also develop their own information structures that follow specific organizational guidelines or schemes the product or site require. Some specific types of structures used to organize site content include linear, hierarchical, hypertextual, and custom (Baehr 2007).

- Linear structures organize pages in a specific sequence to be followed in a specific order. These structures are used for processes, such as training modules, online shopping checkout, registration, and filling out surveys and forms.

- Hierarchical structures organize pages based on topic and subtopics, similar to a table of contents or outline. These structures are used to organize more than a few pages by topic, category, or section, such as products, forums, libraries, or news sites.

- Hypertextual structures organize pages based on relevance or relational aspects. Ideally, any single page can be linked to any other number of pages in the same document. These structures are often used in sites that customize content based on search parameters or construct pages from databases or content libraries.

- Custom structures organize pages based on a specific purpose, often determined by the nature of content or the product itself. As such, they may vary widely in their organizational scheme, but may also make use of elements from other structure types. These structures may use multiple structural types or follow a customized pattern created by the developers. Custom structures may also be the result of user-generated content, as the result of information searches.

Most sites will not follow a single structural pattern throughout, but rather may make use of multiple types or slightly customized versions of a single structural type. For example, a bookselling Web site may use a linear structure for online checkout and entering customer information and a hierarchical structure for the overall arrangement of products by topic and subtopic.

There are a number of advantages and benefits from a well-planned content structure. Well-organized content contributes to good usability and assists writers in maintaining a long-term document. Chunking content and organizing it into consistent structures helps users learn how to navigate and search a site more easily. Structures also provide a scalable framework that can accommodate future content additions and changes. They also serve as a set of consistent standards that can be used across a multiauthored project or team. This is particularly useful in products with multiple writers or ones in which the users can contribute content of their own. Organized structures also help manage large volume content projects over time.

SINGLE-SOURCING CONTENT

Single-sourcing is an essential part of Internet writing because online content must be written for reuse across a variety of Internet-based products and sites. Single-sourcing describes the set of skills related to the converting, updating, remediating, and reusing of content across multiple platforms, products, media, and projects (Rockley 2003). Put simply, single-sourcing is an essential method of writing for the Internet that allows the writer to write a content unit once and reuse it many times, based on purpose, function, or need. Reuse is not restricted to online media; rather it can be applied across a wide range of print-based media as well, including marketing brochures, literature, and advertisements. Technology has had a significant impact on single-sourcing methods, more recently focusing on context sensitivity, personalization, content management, and both collaborative and structured authoring. Single-sourcing has many benefits, the most tangible perhaps that it can save time, effort, and resources in developing content. Content reuse also supports multiple purposes and uses for the same content. It also supports a modular writing process, which allows content to be stored and reused multiple times in creating customized pages and content. Database-driven Web sites and content management systems use content libraries that retrieve content and customize its arrangement to create dynamic pages. Content can be stored, retrieved, and reused based on a specific information search or need. In addition, single-sourced content is written with versatility and scalability in mind, so it can be reused to fit different purposes. As such, single-sourced content supports hyperlinking stand-alone content units with minimal rewriting necessary. And finally, a content library of single-sourced content is an excellent source of references and supplemental content, which Internet writers can draw from to provide additional material on a given subject in their writing.

Some authoring strategies for writing single-sourced content include considering user knowledge, working with a coherent structure, establishing metadata, developing style guidelines, normalizing content, adopting writing strategies across multiple media, and working with a sustainable, object-oriented content development process (Rockley 2003; Winston 1998). To begin with, a knowledge of the user's need to know and specifically how they will make use of the content, including their reading preferences, are important to keep in mind during developmental writing. One method of doing this is through use scenarios, which are descriptions that describe typical workflow processes and tasks a specific type of user follows in using a product. User scenarios are developed from audience analysis research (and user profiles) that describe the characteristics, roles, background, and information needs of each specific user group (Hackos 2007). User scenarios are an important part of the writing process, enabling project developers to develop user-centered information models and types to provide structure. Writing single-sourced content involves working within these set structures for the overall product, for the individual content types, and down to the individual content units, including their presentation. Writers must adhere to or create templates based on specific structural and stylistic guidelines. For example, when writing a short article or news story, each content unit that comprises the full article should have specific guidelines for its length, styles, links, and so forth. Following these important guidelines throughout each content unit and information type will ensure content can be reused properly throughout the site. When possible, writers must develop fully accessible content, which is text-based and uses standard markup languages (HTML, XHTML, XML) or methods (as specified by the content management system or database). Ensuring compliance across browsers and systems is also essential for single-sourcing content. This can easily be tested by viewing the content in one or more Web browsers to ensure it displays properly, regardless of the browser or system. Keeping these important single-sourcing methods in mind when writing Internet content is important, and it will accommodate reuse across a wide range of products and will save valuable time and resources.

REMEDIATION

Another related single-sourcing methodology is remediation, which describes the process of adapting content designed for one medium to another. This might suggest remediation is restricted to some form of audio or video content, but this is not always the case. Online might include hypertext, hybrid content forms, interactive media, and audiovisual content. Remediation, in digital space, strives for immediacy and transparency, creating an experience perceived by the user as real (Bolter & Grusin 1999, 53). Online content can be remediated and reused by providing multiple versions of the same media type, for usability purposes. This might include single-sourcing content from one media type into other types (textual, graphic, media) or even possibly mixed media types, such as interactive audio-video with links and text notes, such as Viddler. Providing accessible equivalents of media types and converting content from one media type into others are two other methods of remediating content. Adapting or updating one form into a more up-to-date version or media type also qualifies.

Remediated forms often carry with them some remnant of their previous form, and sometimes as content hybrids. Communication forms, media, and related technologies have influenced cultural shifts in the ways in which we think, interact, transmit, and create knowledge from oral, to written, to print, and now to digital (or electronic) forms (Heim 1999). Transformation theory describes this process of change, where each new form evolves and extends from the previous (Heim 1999, 66–67). Internet writing, no doubt, carries with it a foundation of print-based publishing, writing, and editing methods. During the process of transforming from print-based publishing to online or digital publishing, some hybridization of content forms has occurred. Some examples include printable online content, digital content forms that resemble print, interactive video, and collaborative knowledge bases. Hybrids suggest this overlap between dominant forms of communication and remediation has become even more necessary now, in adapting previous forms into Internet-ready ones. Some hybrid forms spring from remediated versions, or even from convergences of technologies. For example, Adobe's Portable Document Format, which fairly recently was adopted as an industry standard for electronic documents, is a hybrid form that accommodates both print and electronic content to be converted into a single hybrid form, which can be distributed online or printed on paper. Increasingly, our daily communication relies on a mix of print and electronic content, which underscores the degree to which remediation has become an adopted strategy in creating digital and Internet content.

Remediation is an important method in Internet writing for a variety of reasons. First, remediation helps to maximize the overall usability of content, by providing online-friendly equivalents that can be accessed from a standard Web browser or downloadable viewer. By providing fully accessible versions, it ensures all users have access to the same content regardless of system limitations or settings. Since the same content can vary from one form or media type to another, it is important to provide the necessary conversion or format appropriate for online viewing. Content specifications and structures may require some remediation of legacy content to fit the site structure. On a larger scale, limitations of the platform, content management system, or site structure may require remediated forms in order for online content to be fully accessible and browser compliant. Additional technical issues might include compatibility issues with media and browser types, which might require providing multiple media forms. Differences in the ways in which users search, access, and view content may exist that might also affect the media types and controls used. And finally, mixed-media forms in the content inventory might require downgraded or separated versions to accommodate various user preferences or limitations. With a wide range of purposes, remediation is often a necessary task for Internet writers in developing online content.

HYPERLINKING

One fundamental characteristic of Internet content is its ability to be linked to other content units, internally or externally. This often contributes to the usability of content, providing users with informa-tional supplements that are related to the specific content they are view-ing. The task of linking content units within the overall information structure of a product is hyperlinking. Hyperlinks are found throughout Web content, in text, image maps, navigation toolbars, and interactive media. They also serve as important cognitive aids for users when brows-ing Web content in that they outline content, show relationships between content units, suggest concepts, and can indicate a specific function (Baehr 2007). Hyperlinks are also a form of communicating visually to users, since they often have added emphasis on a page, either in their standard blue underlined text format or in highly stylized navigation menus and buttons. Users also rely on hyperlinks as their primary method of navigating Internet content and in their information searches.

User perception research addresses how users respond to visual and textual content, including hyperlinks, and how they use them to solve information problems. Gestalt perceptual theorist Rudolf Arnheim states that one of the principles of user perception, fixation solves a problem, describes users' predisposition to examine and fixate on visual content that they believe will help them solve problems (Arnheim 1969). An important part of user perception is visual focus, or selecting with our eyes, what to examine. In this process of examination, humans evalu-ate the various objects in their visual field to determine which will help them solve a specific problem, such as how to perform a keyword search or download a form. Often, this perceptual process is a form of nonlinear problem solving (Barry 1998, 11). Online content is interconnected by hyperlinks often associatively, the way humans think and perceive. This suggests the important cognitive value that hyperlinks and visual content share communicating with and directing user responses, particularly in online environments.

There are some important guidelines with regard to hyperlinking to con-sider. First, linking suggests a relational aspect between content units, which should be made clear to users. With few exceptions, linked content should demonstrate relevance between the items. Next, linked content units should be stand-alone. Sometimes users will arrive at a specific page of content, out of sequence, from a keyword search, and it is equally important to provide links to related content to avoid confusion. Link names should also suggest the function or topic of the linked content, by using descriptive text and/or images. Link names such as "click here" fail to describe the function or topic of the content that will be displayed by following that specific link. Link names should use familiar terminology, alternate text equivalents for visual and/or textual links, for accessibility, and for proper understanding. Users with specific visual impairments may require text-based equivalents for links instead of images, since screen-reading software cannot verbally interpret visual content. When using a specific naming convention, link names should be internally consistent in their terminology or naming scheme (Baehr 2007). For example, when repeating links, providing terms, or using a navigation menu or index, using consistent terms throughout a site will aid user comprehension. When using visual icons or graphics, it is important for the symbol or picture to be used consistently and for its meaning to be clear to users. If it is not, text labels or tags can be used to suggest their specific meaning. In addition, the linking order should be consistent when using lists or navigation menus of consecutive links. Users will learn the order of links in a menu and remember their spatial location as a guide to recall where to locate the same link. When using navigation menus, it is also important to place them in consistent locations throughout a site to help users quickly locate these important tools. And finally, links should demonstrate good usability and accessibility, and the best way to determine this is to user test linked content and solicit user feedback.

IMPLICATIONS FOR INTERNET WRITING

Content chunking and hyperlinking are two essential skills Internet writers must master in order to write successful content. Understanding unique

GUIDELINES FOR WRITING EFFECTIVE HYPERLINKS

1. Demonstrate relevance between linked content by selecting meaningful link names.
2. When possible, use link names that suggest the function or the topic of the linked content.
3. Use familiar terms and alternative text-based equivalents to maximize comprehension and accessibility.
4. When using naming conventions, ensure links are internally consistent to those conventions.
5. Use familiar icons or graphics when linking them to other content or provide text labels along with them to help readers comprehend their function.
6. When single-sourcing a list of links or a menu, place them in consistent locations and use a consistent order for the list.
7. Test links and solicit user feedback to ensure proper functionality and to maximize usability.

content characteristics is important in Internet writing to accommodate the difference between online content and writing for copy. Online content is modular, single-sourced, highly structured, linked, and customizable. Equally important, knowledge of user reading preferences can help writers produce more usable information products. Internet content has different granularities as well, including links, units, types, and complete structures. Content management principles and systems can assist Internet writers in creating consistent and highly usable structures to help manage large content inventories. Knowledge of structured authoring technologies and methods can also assist writers in adapting and writing content for these systems, as well. Single-sourcing content is a hallmark of the Internet, and learning how to optimize and adapt content so it can be written once and used in multiple documents and products is an important skill for Internet writers. Understanding the complex issues involved in remediating content into Internet-viewable media and forms is necessary to provide access for the widest range of possible users. And finally, creating meaningful and relevant hyperlinks between individual content units is essential in developing robust and highly usable content.

Chapter 9

Ownership and Copyright of Digital Content

INTRODUCTION

The issue of digital content ownership and copyright is highly complex, where rules vary widely and enforcing intellectual property rights can be difficult with the vast number of Web sites accessible on the Internet. Authors still carry over the desire to own and control their work, mostly from print-based ownership rights. Conventional print-based content still carries a greater ethos to its digital varieties, particularly in terms of research value in the academy. Online content often supplements or serves as a companion for printed books, failing to produce the same fully bound equivalent when online content is printed. However, despite the lingering value of printed content, print-based models of ownership are insufficient in terms of determining ownership of digital content. Because of differences in digital versions, ease of distribution, format differences, and use of interactive features and multimedia, authors and publishers are rethinking their approaches to acquiring permissions. And simply, printed publications lack many of these characteristics, and as a result, their intellectual property protections fail to cover all the necessary components of digital content.

Since ownership and economic factors relate, it would stand to reason that economic models for digital content use, sale, and distribution lack consistent standards and vary widely. Digital music sells for different unit costs, depending on the seller, and often varies in how a user can download the track (based on limited number of downloads or limited number of days) before their access expires. Digital content sharing also varies from unlimited to highly regulated (requiring a specific player or a limited number of shares). Software programs can even restrict the number product activation keys, which are registered online, to limit installation sharing. This process can require deactivation of a key to install the product on another system, but in the case of hardware failure or theft, a user may be unable to comply with this restriction. Web content tends to be regulated by password protection, which might require a purchase to obtain, such as a recurring subscription, or simply allow unlimited access with a single password. For authors and publishers, it is difficult and often more costly to determine if digital ownership rights are being violated. It may require thorough and regular searches of Internet search portals and sites. Smaller companies and organizations simply lack the resources to research and pursue legal action to protect basic intellectual property rights. However, in some cases, media and entertainment conglomerates such as Disney have demonstrated vigilance in protection of their intellectual property rights and interests. Variations in distribution, format, access, and regulation underscore the different economic models that must be considered in the sale and protection of digital content.

Publishers still want to make money, but seem confused about which models to use. Companion and advertising Web sites for products provide a limited amount of free content for the public. Some publishers of textbooks have moved to a custom publishing model, where shoppers can select what chapters they want in the book and have them distributed in print or digital versions. Some digital versions, including Web site content, require proof of purchase or login credentials to access supplemental digital content. Illegal distribution and hacking still have authors and publishers worried, too. This may be in part due to limitations in protection technologies, lack of resources, and overall hackability of content, or extent to which content can be compromised. Some may argue this is symptomatic of digital technology itself, where the latest measure to protect is met with an almost instant countermeasure or hack. The Apple iPhone was designed with a number of limitations, including authorized use with a single cellular phone service, limitations in background and viewer settings, yet quickly after its launch and subsequent updates, users found ways to customize other features of the device. Digital content archives both formal, such as the nonprofit Internet Archive (http://www.archive.org), and informal, including personal archives of online content stored in Web browser caches or on hard drives, exist as mostly unregulated sources of legacy content from the World Wide Web. Authors have little to no control over the use of these archived content sources, and no royalties are paid for content with prolonged publication online. Another publication issue is that no standards for linking to on-line content exist. Normally, linking to other online documents is common for personal pages, but in the case of linking to organizations and businesses, acquiring permission is considered the polite standard. Requests to remove links are often accommodated, if the owner of the linked-to content sends a request in writing. In the age of sharing and downloading, many individuals are still somewhat confused about digital citation and copyright. Copying a digital image without any disclaimer or permissions statement may seem like fair use to some and a violation to others. Individual Web sites typically provide a statement describing the terms of use, but these also vary widely and are sometimes very complex. The wide variation in free and limited use permissions for digital content creates additional confusion. Digital content permissions can permit free use, implied permissions without any notice, limited use, use with cita-tion, or use with payment, or can require formal permission in writing.

DIGITAL COPYRIGHT AND OWNERSHIP FUNDAMENTALS

The Digital Millennium Copyright Act (DMCA) of 1998, as an exten-sion of U.S. copyright law, was passed to prevent unlawful distribution of digital and multimedia content, including the use of technologies to circumvent technological prevention mechanisms, such as digital rights management (DRM) technologies (Litman 2006, 136). A variety of these technologies are used by corporations such as Apple, Microsoft, Real Media, and Sony to prevent users from downloading, copying, and con-verting digital content into formats compatible with other devices not intended for use with the content (Lewis 2008). These technologies pro-tect textual content and static imagery as well as multimedia content, including audio, video, and interactive content, including games. Some corporations are making the move toward DRM-free digital content, such as Amazon and Apple, and this may be a move consistent with the technology convergence of mobile computing devices. Bottom line, con-sumers want a portable media library they can use on computers, cellular telephones, and other mobile devices. Another important aspect of the DMCA is its limitations of liability for Internet Service Providers (ISPs), which absolves them of liability simply because infringing material may have been hosted or passed through their systems (Litman 2006, 143). Critics have argued that social networking sites, such as Facebook and MySpace, cross the boundaries of violating user data protection rights, by creating loopholes for crimes such as identity fraud and unauthorized disclosure of information (World Wide Web Consortium 2008). In addition, no standard international protection laws exist to protect the digital rights of individuals, which further complicate digital copyright.

One tension in defining the boundaries of digital ownership is the notion of democratization, in other words, providing equal and open access to digital content for all users. This debate underscores the tensions between corporate entities and consumers in defining rights of use for purchased or licensed digital content. The open source movement may have created some confusion about what is freeware in the public mind. Open source content is characterized by free redistribution, licensing, and access to software source code (Open Source Initiative 2006). Although a vast amount of digital content on the Web may not have explicit terms for use, the tendency may be to use freely without acquiring permission. On the other hand, accessing digital content through work-arounds and hacks can be a violation of fair use and intellectual property rights, in accordance with the DMCA. With regard to the hackability of digital content, Diana Saco presents the notion that hacking some aspect of cyberspace, is ultimately the hacking of society (2002, 197), or in the case of altering or copying digital content from social networking sites, we may be hacking ourselves.

The most crucial issue with regard to digital ownership has still largely been an economic one. Ted Nelson's project Xanadu, conceived in the 1960s, was the first conceivable prototype digital hypertextual publication system with an economic model that included automatic rights and version management. Every time digital content was accessed, cited, linked, or downloaded, the author's bank account was automatically paid a permissions or use fee (Nelson 1993). Some current digital distribution models are based on the notion that an electronic account acts as a conduit for the user, by which he can click on content and pay manually or automatically through an electronic account, such as PayPal. Online vendors such as Apple iTunes, Beatport, and eBay function on this model. Online booksellers incorporate a modified version where the electronic account can be set up for a single click purchase if the user desires. Even advertising banners when clicked can result in automatic payments to a vendor. While Nelson's early model failed to serve as a template for future digital content management, elements have been preserved and integrated into existing economic models.

THE IMPACT OF DIGITAL TECHNOLOGIES

A number of characteristics of digital technologies have affected the ways in which rights and ownership are determined for digital content.

Digital content makes it easy to obtain a quick, identical copy through download or content sharing. A copy of a digital product is virtually identical to its original, whereas a copy of a print product is not always exact or similar in quality. This is one aspect of digital products that makes them superior to print-based equivalents. It is also easier to distribute digital content online and in more than a single purchased copy in its original form. For example, an individual can loan a single digital copy to an unlimited number of friends by using email or uploading it to a networked server. Publication or transmission via email or Internet download can also greatly accelerate the speed of distribution. The hackability of digital content, or degree to which it can be compromised, is another major factor. Digital content can more easily be modified, converted, redistributed, and shared by users with less time and cost, compared to print content. The relative ease of editing and modification of digital content, or content remixability, has changed the nature of ownership. Users can download, modify, excerpt, append, and publish a version entirely unique, yet somewhat reminiscent of the original. The key issue seems to be, when does digital content become sufficiently modified to become intellectual property of another author? In the case of Content Management Systems (CMS), which support collaborative authorship, the notion of digital ownership is changed in a variety of ways. First, with multiple authors and different levels of authorship (i.e., primary authors, contributing authors, content providers, user contributions, etc.), the distribution of rights becomes more complex. This facilitates a greater number of contributing authors and users. Second, these content systems can be updated, published, and archived much more quickly, making version control a difficult task, while easing the task of distribution. Third, access levels vary from system to system, permitting a tiered approach for level of access and publication.

Digital technologies have enabled customized products, such as academic textbooks that can be compiled from a content inventory of chapters and features and published in print or digital form. Downloadable multimedia content is sold by episode or individual song, allowing users to customize their collections and purchase only the content units they want. Users can manage multiple syndicated subscriptions of podcasts and feeds that suit their needs and compile a playlist or compact disc (CD) that is a mélange of various forms of digital media content. This creates the notion that every copy is not standardized, which might create additional problems when it comes to citation, payment, distribution, and reselling.

MODELS FOR LIMITED SUCCESS

Despite early setbacks, the distribution of multimedia content such as audio files has found some successful economic models, such as those for Apple iTunes and Rhapsody. However, the problems with these models are mostly the user's in terms of synchronization and distribution across multiple computers and mobile devices owned by the same user. Additionally, technology convergence has created a content distribution problem between multiple devices. For example, a user can download an audio file but, due to technology limitations, is unable to download that file to a computer, phone, and audio player, even if they are all supported or manufactured by the same entity. Other problems still exist with the distribution of media content, despite the spike in availability of downloadable digital content. Not everything is available online at the same level of quality. Additionally, proprietary content formats create problems for users, although they somewhat protect distribution. Amazon's eBook downloads require a specific mobile device for viewing—the Kindle—yet other downloadable media content may be available in other formats, viewable by a wider range of media devices.

Citation format for digital sources has quickly become standardized to accommodate and recognize digital works in publication. Generally, anything that is published online can be cited using its site title, page title, date accessed or date of last update, uniform resource locator (URL), and authoring entities if known. This type of citation is appropriate for publications with bibliographies or published research found in journals or books. However, there still remains some confusion about how and when to cite digital content used or cited within digital sources. And the issue of fair use of some digital content types is also somewhat unclear, except for textual content, which can use the carryover guidelines for works in print.

Syndicated content subscriptions, which are generally free or paid for with a small fee, work the same as subscribing to a magazine or newspaper, which can be borrowed or loaned. Podcasts and videocasts are two examples of sharable syndicated content. However, the issue becomes more problematic with the ability to distribute multiple identical copies to an entire address book. With no specified limit under the terms of use, an individual could potentially loan their single copy to a much larger number of friends. At some point, it might be construed as unlawful or unfair distribution, rather than a simple loan. Syndicated content such as Really Simple Syndication (RSS) feeds are typically designed as no-cost mass distribution models, which require no limitations of use or sharing. Users can embed syndicated feeds in individual Web pages, making them a feature of another published Web site. These permission-free content sources generally have few permission restrictions; however, when a feed embeds graphic content or links to other sites, the issue becomes a bit more complicated. This is particularly true when the embedded content is a video clip, song, graphic, or link to a corporate site.

Technologies and formats that limit use, limit distribution, and require specialized players or devices for access seem to create problems of their own, particularly when it comes to the consumer. Limited use models and formats, such as Digital Video Express (DIVx) or downloadable rentals that expire after a limited number of uses, may seem a less attractive investment to users. Although the nature of digital content may make it seem disposable in a sense, building a library of downloaded content seems to be an important consumer trend. The popularity of high capacity storage in mobile devices such as phones, hard disks, and thumb drives support this notion. Colleges and universities have tried offering free download libraries of software, music, and other content; however, these efforts have met with very limited success mainly because of the restrictions placed on them and, most notably, because such content must be surrendered upon graduation (Timiraos 2006). It may be simply a matter of economics to users; they may be more willing to purchase a copy with unlimited use than pay less for a limited use copy. Proprietary formats and technologies may tend to be less successful because they fail to offer the flexibility and versatility consumers desire. For example, downloading songs that can be shared across multiple mobile devices and computers may appeal more than those that require a specific product or player. Users have also found viable work-arounds for proprietary technologies, which some might consider hacks. For example, the shareware utility Handbrake allows users to convert proprietary audio formats to more widely used ones. Perhaps the less versatile or more proprietary the technology, the more isolated that technology is likely to become. And, the greater the financial investment over time, the more users may seek out buying alternatives in making digital content purchases.

CONSUMER AND AUTHOR CONCERNS

Digital ownership is equally important to both author and consumer, and because of the variation in terms of use and distribution, each may be left with many important and unanswered questions. From the consumer perspective, the questions may involve issues of sharing and distribution. If I purchase content, what are my ownership and distribution rights? How can I share it with others? Will I be able to use the content on devices I own, or will I have to purchase others? Is there a onetime cost or a recurring cost? What is the return policy for defects? These questions underscore important issues such as investment cost, content portability, content sharing, and reliability that consumers face when deciding on a purchase. One distribution problem users are often faced with deals with the limitations of use. For example, Apple iTunes permits a download only on a limited number of authorized computers, and synchronization or distribution across multiple mobile devices and portable computers is problematic. Users may prefer a download once, reuse and distribute multiple times model, to one with many restrictions. Other distribution issues may involve fair use over other types of media. For example, does digital content download authorize transmission or copying to other forms of media such as CD or digital video disc (DVD)?

Because of technical issues encountered online, errors in downloading occur and may create additional consumer insecurities. Some vendors require a lengthy process to request a replacement download key, whereas others allow the user additional downloads within a limited period of time after purchase. Another issue might deal with archiving—if users purchase a digital copy and lose it, what are terms of redownloading it under the initial purchasing agreement? Are users required to repurchase at the same cost? Users are often responsible for making their own backup copies after downloading content. No digital return policies seem to be the standard and users cannot simply purchase a digital copy and return it within 30 days to the vendor. Often, this loaned content can be streamed or redownloaded from the vendor until the term expires. However, digital content can be purchased and used for a limited number of times or days, and then expire. This version of a licensed loan might be one solution to address the consumer concerns over product download defects, transmission, and archiving.

Another consumer concern deals with distribution and rights to subsequent versions, updates, or upgrades. With regard to new versions and updates, three dominant models exist: (1) full and free access to updated versions; (2) limited access to updates based on a specific term; and (3) access to updates requiring additional payment. The first model is widely used by open source products, such as freeware and shareware, and syndicated content sources, including RSS feeds and podcasts. The second model is used by many software manufacturers from everything including office productivity software to games. Additionally, this model permits minor updates compatible with the purchased version, but may require subscription fees to update to the next version or for add-on products, updates, or features. The third model is used primarily in the sale of fully licensed multimedia content, where the user must purchase additional episodes, collections, or supplements. Since no universal standards govern digital ownership and copyright, there are a number of grey areas when it comes to dealing with more complex permissions issues. When a user purchases a digital copy, the individual distribution and sharing rights vary widely. DRM-free media permits users greater flexibility in using that content on a wide range of mobile devices. Still others restrict the use to a single player, device, or even limited number of authorized systems. Publishers may also permit a limited number of copies for sharing, make it difficult or altogether impossible, or allow complete and open distribution.

Sometimes users find themselves in the role of author or content provider, rather than solely as content consumer. From the author perspective, the relevant questions may deal with issues of payment and ownership. How will I get paid? How do authors and publishers retain a fee for content sharing? What are my options for copyright? In a contributed authoring environment, at what point does the primary author completely lose control or rights over content? Collaborative knowledge forums and databases allow users to post comments, add related content, and share new ideas. This is one case where a content consumer can also become a content contributor or co-author. One important question with regard to ownership is—what ownership rights do content contributors have? Generally, most sites adopt a policy of *if you contribute, you are consenting to release all rights and ownership to that material.* Depending on what is at stake, users may opt out of contributing ideas or material for which they may later not receive any recognition or royalty. Corporate entities typically allow limited access to marketing materials and online content for a specific product, yet encourage consumer participation only to a certain point before they retaliate with legal action. One example of this is fan Web sites often generated for movies, products, characters, and other cultural icons. While the sites may be considered a means for consumers to participate in the phenomenon, not to mention free advertising and endorsements, corporate entities may consider their enthusiasm as infringement upon ownership rights to the brand or product. The tension between corporate entity and consumer is a result of the unclear line drawn between ownership and legally accepted participation or contribution (Jenkins 2006).

Another unclear issue deals with the fair use of copyright content online, in whole or partial form, such as video content found in media libraries such as YouTube or Google Video. While print-based content has fairly fixed fair use guidelines, in comparison to digital content, it is difficult to apply word count to online media. Significant modification clauses also can be more difficult to interpret when it comes to the use of source code, templates, or media content. Multiauthored digital content also creates some complicated problems with determining ownership rights. For most syndicated content, such as podcasts and RSS feeds, users subscribe (either with or without a fee) and are granted use and distribution rights for each issue or episode until the subscription either expires or is terminated. In more highly structured models, such as wikis, blogs, and CMS, contributed authorship in the form of user comments, message replies, and discussion board posts creates a more complex permissions issue. Often with digital content resources such as Wikipedia, YouTube, and community discussion forums, the question of ownership of user contributions is assumed by the corporate entity. But in terms of longer-term use, permissions may become a future issue to revisit, particularly if new products are developed based on these ideas and profit is earned.

COPYRIGHT IMPLICATIONS FOR NEW MEDIA

While Napster was a breakthrough service that "allowed" users to swap songs at will, it was also the beginning of the death of copyright and started a very dangerous trend. In Chapter 5 we talked about how people were raised and learned knowledge structures, and as additional or "deeper" information come along those structures help accommodate and make sense of that new information. Without such structures, however, that information is never understood, or even properly processed. The generation that came up not knowing that Napster was illegal, or at least the severity that many people viewed copyright and artistic license with, will never know how much those laws allowed writers, artists, singers, and video producers the means through which to make a living with their craft.

After Napster and as YouTube emerged as the most user-friendly—and often fun—platform in the world, people would post videos of anything they wanted: television programs, news reports, and occasionally their own videos. But most of it was from content already made, and since the user had a copy of it handy, he/she saw nothing wrong with uploading it to the world to share. The only problem with this is that it is not his/hers to share with the world. Before this was reigned in, entire programs were posted—even movies were shared—in violation of the oldest copyright law in the world. Again, most users had no idea they had done anything wrong, and those who did, did not really care because "everyone else was doing it"; besides, they wanted the programs, and so did their friends.

Unfortunately, this train left the station long before the law has begun to catch up with it. The music industry sells its songs for about a dollar per song. The CD, promoted at one time as not just the latest but the greatest technology of all time, is now a thing of the past. Users want their content now, and they are not going to pay $15 for one or two or even three songs. This is another example of technological appropriation, and now that there is a financial model that, while far from being ideal or as profitable as before, provides a constant revenue stream for the record companies.

Printed products are taking just as big a hit. Stories are copied and pasted without permission at all hours of the day. When a user is confronted, it does little good. First of all, there is an attitude that spreading someone's work around to more viewers is nothing but a good thing because it widens the audience. However, those hits go to the Web site that stole it and posted it, not to the company or writer who paid for it and created it. Artistic courtesy is not part of the discussion, and since it is so widespread, it is often a useless battle to wage. Additionally, the response of these users when confronted is to enlist their friends and others who want at-use at-will rights into a negative public relations (PR) campaign against the company demanding its copyrights be respected. Frankly, it is not a battle any company can fight. It is too costly, the PR nightmare that comes out of it is a different kind of cost, and people get worn down from chasing these things down.

YouTube was sold to Google for more than $1 billion, with Google knowing full well there are copyright lawsuits headed its way. Viacom has been one of the few to successfully keep its programs off of YouTube, with a lawsuit that will eventually cost Google, experts believe, a lot of money, and perhaps open the door to something of the class-action persuasion that draws in some law and enforcement to copyright infringement. At the same time, the number of visitors to *The Colbert Report* and *The Daily Show*—Viacom distributed products—pales in comparison, though iTunes downloads are now providing a better revenue stream to those show's producers than any of the tiny sums paid by Google based on hits and views on YouTube. Still, it is an uphill battle.

Another area affected is archival resale. Lexis-Nexis, which collects stories that have appeared in publications around the world, and without the permission of those publications or without compensating the authors of the stories, sells those to anyone who wants to buy them, keeping the money for themselves. And who owns the bulk of Lexis-Nexis? A group of lawyers, ironically, who have been unable to reach a settlement with those suing them for selling their stories without either permission or compensation. Again, lawsuits are costly business, and in a couple of near-settlement deals, most authors and freelance writers listed as plaintiffs in the lawsuit against Lexis-Nexis would get a fraction—literally pennies on the dollar—of what Lexis-Nexis gets for selling the authors' stories.

So, like new media theory, new media law has a long way to go in terms of development and application. If new media is a field you have an interest in, there is a lot of room—for everyone. And it will all—be it stories or briefs for new media lawsuits—involve a lot of writing.

Section Four

Visual and Interactive Rhetoric

Chapter 10

Visual Structure
and Information Design

VISUAL INFORMATION DESIGN

Today, the Internet is a highly visual medium, having evolved from its early text-based roots and text-heavy and solid grey backgrounds with blue hyperlinks. Largely, evolutions in technology can be attributed to the increased visual interactivity of Internet content. Affordable design software programs, faster bandwidth, improved computer hardware capabilities, and relatively inexpensive Web hosting services have all helped users become avid content publishers. The Internet itself has become a fairly inexpensive alternative to print-based publishing as well, making it more affordable to deliver visual content across a wider audience, including interactive media. One trend with Internet writing is certain—visual content continues to be an essential part of online publishing. Users have come to expect a certain level of visual sophistication in terms of the overall design and interactive content when browsing the Internet. Visual content has become as important as textual content, yet the two work together in online communication in very important ways. The visual design of pages includes more than graphic images and media clips, but extends to unique textual styling, spacing between page elements, background shading, use of color, and the quality of interactive content. As a result, writing for the Internet involves skill in information design, including page layout, media use, and developing information graphics that work together with written text to produce effective online content.

Internet writers need to have an understanding of the unique design considerations of online visual content and how it may differ from print-based design. Some of these differences include the viewable formats, sizes, resolutions, number of unique colors, and viewers used to display visual content. While many of these differences are technical in nature, many of these design considerations affect usability and user access of Internet content. Successful design is also often grounded in an understanding of some design theory, including use of color, structure and layout, understanding of user perception, design principles, and methods commonly used in information design. An important component of online design is learning about the needs and expectations of users. This can serve as a valuable source of information in creating designs that are usable, accessible, and professional. Usability research and testing can identify problems with designs as well as user preferences, habits, and needs when interacting with visual information. Finally, the best designs are based on specific standards and conventions, many of which are established by the overall design concept and stylesheets used.

DIFFERENCES IN ONLINE VISUAL CONTENT

Designing information online or in digital form can be quite different from producing visual content for a print-based medium. Print-based content is static, fixed, portable, and the methods used to produce it are fairly standardized across media, such as book, newspaper, pamphlet, and so forth. Digital design must account for additional technical differences including user screen resolution settings, software plug-ins, graphic and media file formats, color depth, monitor frame rate, and Internet bandwidth available to users. In order to maximize usability of visual information, using file formats and software plug-ins commonly available and viewable in standard Web browsers is important. Designing content that is viewable on at least two different screen resolutions or resizable based on the size of the browser window is necessary to ensure all users can view content regardless of individual browser or system settings. For example, different browsers will often interpret electronic stylesheet information differently, creating slight to extreme variations in the display of a page. Using templates or testing a stylesheet in at least three different browsers should help minimize these problems, or at least indicate how they should be adjusted so they display properly. While it may be difficult to account for all possible technical issues with design, extensive usability testing can be one important way to identify problems so the designer can best decide how to address them.

There are other technology related accessibility issues and limitations that affect the display of visual content on the Internet. Page and graphic file sizes, Internet bandwidth, user screen resolution, and system settings can affect both speed and quality of visual content. Often, these client-based limits can be accounted for by providing different formats, file sizes, or downloadable alternatives to streaming media, or by offering alternate content for users with disabilities (such as text or audio equivalents).

Another characteristic that makes online visual information different is interactivity. Many Web sites are composed of multiple forms of visual content that can be static or interactive. Some examples of interactive content include navigation tools, applets, media, and interactive forms. Interactive quizzes, games, instructional models, drop-down menus, and video content are all commonly found online. Client security or browser settings may prevent access, requiring alternative content versions or client overrides; explaining how the system works and the means of interaction is essential to avoid confusion

Two other important differences are layering and customization. Online content is also composed of multiple layers of visual information, including background colors or images, navigation tools, selections of text, and media. Structurally, the overall page layout can be composed of multiple layers of stylesheets and individual visual elements on the screen. Often, visual content, such as individual styles, layers, or page layouts, is customizable by the user. Content and browser windows can be resizable and either hidden or visible; users can select style or template preferences; audio and video content can be controlled by the user or even blocked. Designing scalable content, adjustable by users, or providing fixed controls or sizes can solve the problem partially, although this may conflict with user expectations.

One other fundamental difference with the design of online visual content is that no set standards or guidelines exist across all types of Internet content. Conventions for print-based design are based on many years of using print, limitations of book and publication medium size, delivery, and other factors. However, in an online environment, design standards vary widely, depending on the purpose, use, audience, and other contextual factors. While some conventions and similarities in overall design may be observable in some Web sites, there is often a wide range of visual formats, templates, and customized layouts found online. As such, Internet writers must be skilled designers of visual content, selecting appropriate guidelines and standards tailored for the content they create.

DESIGN THEORY FOR INTERNET WRITING

Separating good design from poor design is more than a debate of aesthetic concerns. Creating a successful design is often based in specific design theories and methods, based on years of research. Designing visual information for an online environment, such as the Internet, requires knowledge that explains how users perceive, comprehend, and interact with visual content. The basic elements of graphic design, such as the use of shapes, textures, emphasis, text styles, and so forth, merely scratch the surface of designing online content. There are many technical differences as well—visual content is also interactive, layered, and highly structured. A broader knowledge of design theories can be useful in developing visual content for the Internet, which addresses these unique differences. User perception theory can provide a greater understanding of how users comprehend visual information and interact with it. Principles of user-centered design, which advocate involving user needs throughout design can help maximize the usability of a product. An understanding of the visual structure of online content, from the page level to the site level, is useful in page layout design as well as overall site architecture.

Visual Perception Theories

Our visual perception requires active thinking, in that we seek focal points, drawn on past experiences, and use our visual instincts to solve problems and learn about the world around us (Arnheim 1969; Kostelnick & Roberts 1997). Perceptual theory explores the ways in which humans make meaning from objects in their fields of vision. With respect to perception, cognition, and individual behavior, 40 percent is driven by nature and 60 percent by nurture (LeDoux quoted in Barry 1998). Humans respond similarly to images in their visual fields but, based on experiences and repeated stimuli, may learn to react differently. Gestalt theory asserts that these perceptual activities are a highly developed form of visual thinking, whereby humans examine the disparate visuals encountered in an attempt to create a holistic understanding of their environment (Koffka 1935; Arnheim 1969). Visual thinking (Arnheim 1969) and visual intelligence (Barry 1998) are two theoretical offshoots that describe the integral nature of perception and our cognition of visual content. The act of visual thinking involves how users examine visuals, form concepts about them, comprehend their function, and then act based on their understanding (Baehr 2007, 7). Visual intelligence characterizes user perception as a holistic process as well, where visual and verbal reasoning help users comprehend visual information (Barry 1998, 6).

Perception theory is particularly relevant to Internet writing and design because of the complexity of online content, which is highly visual, interactive, layered, animated, and bound by no set of conventions for arrangement or function. Gestalt and visual thinking theorists outline several key theoretical principles that explain how humans perceive and interpret visual content. These principles are particularly applicable because of the highly visual and interactive nature of online content.

- *Area.* The smaller of two objects occupying the same space is perceived as the figure and the larger as the background.
- *Closure.* Part of an object is perceived as a complete whole, even when it is partially missing or obscured.
- *Continuity.* The tendency to predict the continuation of visual objects and perceived patterns they create.
- *Figure-ground.* Similar elements are grouped with dissimilar elements to create the appearance of a whole. In design, figure is the object (content) and ground is the background (context).
- *Proximity.* Adjacent elements, or those closely arranged, will be seen as visually cohesive, or belonging together.
- *Similarity.* Elements sharing similar characteristics will be seen as grouped or belonging together.
- *Symmetry.* When multiple elements are encountered in close proximity, the whole is perceived in favor of the parts.
- *Synchronicity.* Objects occurring in the same time frame are perceived as grouped and sharing characteristics.

These Gestalt principles (Koffka 1935; Skaalid, 1999) describe specific ways that users perceive visual content they encounter. As such, they can provide a unique understanding of specific ways in which human perception affects design and a user's overall comprehension of it. But equally important to remember is that visual instincts evolve based on user experience, so a deeper understanding of user habits and behaviors is also required to fully understand how design affects user perception, as well. This is where other sources of research and other theories that address usability, structure, interaction, and other elements of design are essential.

User-Centered Design

Not every design can incorporate everything a user wants or prefers; however, some consideration of their needs can be essential in creating a successful design. User-centered design places emphasis on user needs throughout the process of design, including planning, development, and testing (Johnson 1998). Usability involves more than the ability to interact with online content and must include a user's comprehension of product or document. As such, one way of learning about user needs is to query or test them formally and informally about their habits, preferences, and methods of problem solving. Conversely, system-centered design involves creating a product that the user has little or no prior knowledge of and that was developed solely by the design team or individual (Johnson 1998). Not involving user research in the design process can be risky and invite a number of usability problems unforeseen by the design team. For example, a highly complex visual layout, while efficient in its arrangement, might be perceived as overly complex by users and cause frustration. Some news Web sites have the problem of displaying too much content or too many navigation choices on a page, and as a result new or unfamiliar users can become lost in the design. And finally, basic knowledge of color theory can assist designers in developing effective color schemes and design concepts.

Visual Structure

There are two components that comprise the visual structure of an online document, the page layout and the overall site structure. On the page level, visual structure is the arrangement of objects on a single page. This can include text chunks, graphics, media, navigation tools, design elements, and negative space. This structure can be more than two-dimensional, since many Web sites often layer different objects on the screen. For example, many sites with advertising graphics will layer them on top of an area of the screen the user views. Two other examples are drop-down menus and scrolling images used to display photos in succession. On the site level, structure involves the arrangement and linking of content pages throughout a Web site. Sometimes, visual models or site maps are used to illustrate the overall organization of content to users, quite explicitly. Site structure can also be communicated visually to users in more subtle ways, such as through the use of unifying colors, headers and subheads, hierarchical or nested navigation menus, and so forth. It is important to provide these visual cues throughout a site because they are used as signposts or guides to help users navigate and recall previously visited content (Johnson-Sheehan & Baehr 2001).

Page-level visual structure is often set by electronic stylesheets using Cascading Style Sheets (CSS) and sometimes other markup and scripting languages, depending on the complexity of the design. Stylesheets can be used to specify both the styles and the overall structure of visual content in Web sites. They specify the visual styles of nearly every element on a page and throughout a site, including elements such as fonts, spacing, colors, backgrounds, borders, emphasis, graphic size, and so forth. Stylesheets can also be used to specify the positioning of elements on a page by assigning them specific locations, sizes, and styles, or arranging them relative to other elements on a page. This technique of modular design is an essential skill required in developing Internet content, and the stylesheet can be a powerful tool in helping the designer position elements on a page.

One advantage of stylesheets is that the core language used to develop them is compliant across browsers, operating systems, and other Web development software, including content management systems, blogs, wikis, and the like. Multiple stylesheets can be used and they can be applied locally to a single page or even globally, throughout an entire Web site. They can be a powerful single-sourcing tool in ensuring consistency throughout the design of a site or document. And, many Web development software tools can even compose the coding for the writer, based on selections made. One problem that sometimes arises with more complex stylesheets is that they may be interpreted slightly differently by browsers, particularly older versions. The best way to address this problem is to test a stylesheet in a variety of browsers to pinpoint any variations, so it can be modified to be fully compliant.

Site-level structure has important links to visual designers in that it is often communicated to users through the use of visual information in a Web site. While developers create the overall structure of documents in a site or, in some cases, the content management system or the out-of-the-box software used to create a site provides a template, the explicit structure is not always communicated to users in exactly the same way. In some cases, a site map that visually indicates the organization of pages and topics in a site is provided, particularly in larger sites. Users can identify the major site content, as well as links to different sections of content, and plan their own information searches using it as a road map. More often, the user will look for specific visual and textual cues throughout the site to help orient themselves and to understand the overall structure of information. Headers, subheads, use of color, navigation menus, site maps, indices, thematic graphics, and other elements can be used to signal how content is grouped or arranged in a site. These visual cues are essential to Web site usability and help users learn visually the layout and structure of content in a Web site. Internet writers can make use of these visual conventions in developing material that reinforces the same visual cues to users, thereby helping them learn the arrangement of content more easily.

Color Theory

Color use is essential to design because it can be used to create themes, contrast, tone, and branding, and to communicate information. Color theory is important because it explains how variations of color are composed and how different schemes are used to create effective designs. An understanding of color variations and schemes can help a novice designer with little experience create the foundation of a successful design. Color theory is also important to Internet writers, since much online content relies on the use of color to communicate information and to develop styles for their designs.

Colors are produced using combinations or blends of primary colors, which are composed of red, blue, and yellow for subtractive colors and red, blue, green for additive colors. Subtractive color mixing uses shades of red, blue, and yellow to create variations of color and is common in print-base designs that use color pigments. Additive color mixing, also known as RGB, involves mixing shades of red, blue, and green and uses light-based displays, such as computer screens. Variations of color are described using hue (color quality), saturation (intensity), tint (lighter values), and shade (darker values). Some commonly used color schemes in design include monochromatic, complementary, analogous, temperature, and harmonic (Golbeck 2005, 21). Some schemes are based on the location of colors in relation to each other on the color wheel.

Monochromatic schemes use primarily variations of saturation, tint, and shade of a single color. Often, neutral colors such as brown, black, grey, and white are used in monochromatic color schemes to accent the palette. Other schemes use variations in hue, saturation, tint, and shade, as well as specific selections from the color wheel. Complementary schemes involve using colors directly opposite of each other on the color wheel. For example, some common complementary schemes include blue-orange and red-green. Complementary schemes tend to produce a greater contrast of colors in designs. Analogous schemes make use of any set of three to five consecutively adjacent colors on the wheel, which tend to provide more blending and lesser contrast between individual colors in the design. Some examples of analogous schemes might include red-orange-yellow, or yellow-green-blue-indigo. Temperature schemes involve using warm colors (reds, oranges, yellows) or cool colors (greens, blues, violets) to create a specific tone or mood in designs. These schemes are used frequently in information graphics used to communicate data, trends, or specific information based on the use of color. Harmonic schemes are composed of colors equally spaced apart on the color wheel, in dyads or triads. Some examples include green-orange-violet and red-blue-yellow. These schemes typically provide wider variations of colors from the wheel and can produce vibrant designs with plenty of contrast.

Using color in online content involves the use of RGB color, specified color names, and hexadecimal values to render colors on screens. Markup and scripting languages such as HTML and CSS allow Internet developers to use specified color names or their hexadecimal equivalents to specify colors. Some examples of color names include red, orange, yellow, lime, navy, maroon, cyan, silver, and aqua. Light and dark variations can also be used, such as light blue or dark red. More frequently, hexadecimal values (and the specific RGB values) for colors are used instead and are fully compliant across graphic software programs, Web development programs, and browsers. Hexadecimal values are composed of a number sign (#) followed by six characters ranging from 0 to 9 and A to F. Each pair of two characters represents the hexadecimal value corresponding to the value for red, green, and blue, respectively, ranging from 0 to 255. The following color words and corresponding hexadecimal values are examples: black #000000, white #FFFFFF, red #FF0000, green #00FF00, blue #0000FF. Software and many Web sites on the use of color allow users to simply select the shade they want, or enter the RGB values, and the hexadecimal equivalent is provided. Charts of hexadecimal colors are also available online using a keyword search for Web colors.

Some specific guidelines for the use of color in developing effective design for online content can also be helpful to know. First, consider the importance of color contrast when using text and backgrounds of different colors. Some color combinations create readability problems, such as using red text on a blue background, so it is important to use contrasting colors to enhance readability. Next, when using images for backgrounds, consider using minimal contrast between image and background to prevent pixilated edges around the image. Also, be sure to resize images as needed to avoid overlapping problems that can affect readability. Smaller patterns with no seams in background images tend to maximize visual clarity, as well. And finally, when using color to communicate specific information, such as with topographic maps, charts, and graphs, be sure to provide alternative versions or accompanying text for users with visual limitations or impairments, such as partial color blindness.

EYE TRACKING AND USABILITY RESEARCH

Two important research areas that can help Internet writers design effective visual content are eye-tracking and usability studies.

Understanding user expectations and interactive behaviors can be useful in making design decisions in developing Internet content. Both eye tracking and usability research are important to visual information design because they attempt to study how users interact with visual content to learn their preferences, expectations, and habits in hopes of improving both the design and the function of Internet content and Web sites. Both approaches integrate the user in the design process and acknowledge the importance that understanding user habits and expectations can play in information design.

Eye tracking research involves testing the visual perception of users to determine how they interact, select, and act based on their visual perceptual habits and cognitive processes in interacting with content. Eye tracking can be used to help determine user search patterns, what they focus on, what they ignore, and how they make selections or decisions based on their interaction with visual content (User Centric 2009). This research addresses what users focus on with their eyes and the specific actions the process elicits. Recent research in eye tracking (Nielsen 2008) suggests that users read Web content in an F-shaped pattern, focus on numbers, and ignore flashy banners, some video content, and advertisements. These findings reinforce what is known about reading habits of users to skim longer content, search for visual cues, and move quickly from item to item on a page. Other eye tracking research has revealed that users tend to follow a habitually preferred path across the visual display (Josephson & Holmes 2002), and when interacting with multimedia, higher quality frame rates are not necessarily preferred over lower quality equivalents (Gulliver & Ghinea, 2004). Trends in eye tracking research provide some useful guidelines to consider, yet not so far as universal standards that apply to every design.

Usability involves the application of criteria-based heuristics to evaluate the usefulness and rhetorical suitability of a product (Pearrow 2000). Usability research focuses on more practical issues, including how users access, interact, and perform tasks when interacting with products or information, as well as any associated technical limitations. Usability testing can help identify cognitive patterns, perceptual habits, and user expectations. While much research on the usability of different kinds of software products, Web sites, and other online content has been conducted, the best way to test the usability of a design is to test the product itself in the context in which it is used. Some common usability testing methods include the following:

- *Task performance.* Typically measures the accuracy and success rate users have in completing basic tasks or functions the site provides. Can help identify problems with specific tools or functions.

- *Searching and browsing habits.* Measures user preferences, habits, and success rates in browsing Internet content. Can be used to help improve search terms, tools, navigation, and visual cues that help users interact more effectively with the site.

- *Problem solving.* Examines how users interact with content to solve basic information problems or queries. Identifies what links, visuals, and other elements help signal to users how to solve a specific problem.

- *Navigation and understanding of structure.* Identifies what contextual or visual elements or cues users rely on to understand how to navigate a site and comprehend the overall organization or structure. May examine how structure can be communicated visually, through navigation menu structure, use of site maps or indices, page headers, or other elements used in the site.

- *Accessibility.* Measures the degree to which users experience accessibility problems, including successful downloading, relevant search results, successful viewing, and degree to which the site provides alternative content for users with specific impairments or limitations, including visual ones.

While studying the latest trends and most useful methods in these kinds of research can offer valuable insights, it is important to also test each unique product itself, particularly since users, purposes, and contexts vary widely from site to site on the Internet. Eye tracking and usability can also be valuable testing methods as part of user-centered design process, where iterations of a product can be evaluated and revised before publication online. By focusing on the user, these methods help contribute to the overall accessibility of Internet writing as well.

CONSISTENT DESIGN STANDARDS AND PRINCIPLES

One hallmark of successful design is internal consistency. A design that fails to create a unifying visual identity will often compromise the credibility and overall success of the product, whether it is a Web site, Internet portal, business, or organization. The visual identity creates a stable, consistent theme that establishes the tone, individual styles, color scheme, branding, and overall concept of the design (Baehr 2007, 135). Corporations and organization often produce a series of graphic elements and logos around which the entire design concept is executed. Specific colors, symbols, shapes, themes, and objects are then used consistently throughout the design to create a unifying visual identity for the site, for everything from the home page to individual content pages and chunks. Often, electronic stylesheets are developed based on the design concepts established by the selected visual identity. Although specific standards for electronic visual design are not yet established, much of the work in creating consistency is up to the designer. In addition to specific design theories, user knowledge, eye-tracking and usability research, some additional considerations in creating consistency include the following:

- Standards should be guided by perceptual theory, while considering user expectations and specific conventions appropriate within the given context of the work.

- Principles based in specific design theories offer important guidelines but are not always universal in their application. Designers should select principles with users and context in mind.

- Design is a contextual process and designs evolve based on the unique needs, users, purposes, and constraints of the product.

- Electronic stylesheets ensure consistency of specific stylistic elements and can be used locally and globally. Since some usability arises with stylesheet interpretation by different browsers, it is important to develop fully compliant stylesheets and, as needed, different versions or customizable features that are fully tested.

- Color theory can be important to consider in design because Web sites often communicate through the use of color, contrast, tone, unifying theme, or specific visual identity. It is important to recognize the unique characteristics and color schemes and how they are used to create online visual content.

- Technology plays a factor in the publishing and delivery of visual information. Not all client browsers, levels of access, and systems will show visual content the same as others. As a result, extensive usability testing with different settings and user queries may help identify problems and suggest possible solutions.

- Redesign of information should be based on usability concerns or changes in overall visual identity, not frequent or trivial. Part of visual design is teaching the user the visual language the site speaks, enforcing it with consistent standards, and making changes based on user feedback. Frequent changes in the overall design can be confusing or frustrating to frequent users over time, particularly when they must relearn the organization and layout of a site once familiar to them.

IMPLICATIONS FOR INFORMATION DESIGNERS AND INTERNET WRITERS

Internet writers must also be skilled designers of visual information, since a large part of Web content involves the use of visual content. Understanding the unique characteristics of online visual content and how they differ from other forms can be useful in helping Internet writers become better designers. Design theory can help writers understand key principles and concepts that can be used to design effective page layouts, stylesheets, and interactive visual content. Eye tracking and usability research can provide important practical guidelines that help designers understand user preferences and interactive habits online. These important sources of research can also help designers identify and account for accessibility problems as well. And finally, successful design rests on internal consistency and creating a uniform visual identity when creating Internet content. Establishing the right guidelines and following them consistently throughout the design of a Web site contributes to both a product's credibility and usability.

Chapter 11

Interactive Content

INTERACTIVE CONTENT AND PROCESS

The nature of interactive content found on the Internet continues to change dramatically from the days when the hyperlink was literally the sole form of interaction between a Web site and a user. Interactive content found today includes a wide variety of applets, instructional media, streaming audiovisual content, navigation tools, and interactive forms. Users can purchase products, subscribe to live content feeds, participate in online training courses, and navigate Internet content in more complex ways. The level of interaction ranges from low (hyperlinks, email links) to medium (interactive forms, instructional media) to high (interactive applets, customization and personalization features). However, the interactive process is more than a simple transaction between user and system, and can be more complex and sustainable over time. For example, systems can store information about user navigation, system settings, purchasing habits, search results, and other data, and use this to create more personalized content the next time the user returns to the same site.

The most commonly used form of interaction in Internet writing involves the use of navigation tools, such as menus, tabs, hyperlinks, media controls, buttons, and so forth. Navigation tools provide choices for users in planning searches and browsing content. Hyperlinks, in particular, allow users to access content in different orders, allowing them to prioritize what they choose to read as well as the order in which they read it. They also accommodate more complex searching and browsing of Internet content, with interactive forms and advanced search tools. These tools allow users to customize queries and filter them by presetting categories and excluding specific keywords. Navigation tools can signal to users how content is organized, provide the range or scope of content contained in the site, or give an overall picture of the site structure. Navigation also links content units and pages relationally, which helps users find relevant and supplemental information quickly and easily. And finally, navigation tools are the primary means users rely on to solve problems and interact with a site.

The interactive process between user and system involves user input, system processing, and system output, sometimes in an ongoing and continuous cycle (Crawford 2003). The user input phase involves measuring data users enter in fields or the type and location of mouse clicks (or touches) on a screen. Users interact with sites by clicking on navigation tools, selecting items, typing text into form fields, and clicking on hyperlinks. These behaviors can be detected by the system, analyzed, stored, and used to generate system responses. The system processing phase of the interaction process involves all of these activities, often in a matter of seconds. For example, scripting languages, such as JavaScript, can detect the type of mouse click, such as single or double click, or compare the value of a selection of text entry to a set of conditions. In turn, each condition can specify the type of output the system produces. Content management systems and Web development software programs have built-in algorithms that can help automate the process for Internet writers, who may not be as proficient with scripting or programming languages. Often, the overall narrative of the interactive experience is created by a series of algorithms that help determine the user's pathway through a site or application (Manovich 2001, 222). Finally, the system output phase involves some kind of reactive response the system makes based on the user's input (or lack thereof). For example, a new page may load, a system message generated, a cookie stored, data stored, a file download started, and any other number of actions can occur as a result.

Knowledge of interaction theory and methods used can be useful in understanding the interactive process, as well as differences between interface design and interaction design. Understanding the expectations of users and their habits can help create a user experience that is both immersive and purposeful. Since navigation is the primary interactive means by which users interact with a site, knowledge of the types of navigation tools and their uses can be beneficial. And finally, specific guidelines related to developing and using interactive content are important to ensure an optimal experience and to avoid some potential pitfalls in the process.

INTERACTION THEORY AND USER EXPERIENCE

Designing interactive content from the user's perspective is crucial in creating an ideal user experience. While some variables, such as system settings, hardware limitations, and so forth may be beyond the designer's control, the more that is known about the user, the better the end product has a chance of being. User experience with content can be described as a series of choices that define a path or process, or a sort of branching inter-action, where each user selection leads to different content or step (Man-ovich 2001, 128). The user experience involves both the interface and the interaction, which work together to present content and a series of inter-active choices. Their overall experience is shaped by the choices made in browsing Internet content, and it is the actual use of the product that defines user experience (Garrett 2003). Two important fields of related research in interaction theory are human computer interaction (HCI) and virtual reality studies. HCI research addresses how users process and interact with digital content, from software-based systems to fully networked online content (Morville 2005). HCI studies have significant interdisciplinary overlap and involve research from computer science, software engineering, usability studies, human factors, virtual reality, and technical communication, to name a few. Virtual reality describes a simulated user experience with a sense of realism, which also centers the experience from the user's point of view (Bolter & Grusin 1999, 161). These approaches are integral to interaction theory because they provide a foundation for understanding the complex process of interaction between user and system.

On the Internet, two important approaches that help define the user experience are interface design and interaction design. The interface is com-posed of everything a user sees on the screen or page, such as text, graphics, navigation tools, and other elements. Interface design is concerned with the arrangement, presentation, style, and media used to create Internet content. Interaction describes the exchanges between user and system. Interaction design is the process of developing usable objects that allow users to browse and interact with Internet content. Together, the two approaches help define the presentation and delivery of Internet content.

User Expectation

Part of the user experience involves the expectations that users have with regard to interactive content. It places some ambitious expectations on Internet writers to deliver content that both is usable and creates a positive user experience. Research in user reading habits reveal that they skim, scan, and browse content. They are suspect of overstylized content, read following specific patterns (F-shaped), and invest about 15–30 seconds on the average per page before moving on (Baehr 2007; Nielsen 2008). With regard to navigation preferences, not all users prefer the same type of navigation tool. Some prefer keyword searches, while others like site maps or hierarchical menus. Often, preference of navigation type may be determined by the specific problem the user is trying to solve, or based on the nature of site content. Users also expect a high degree of usability and that content functions properly and is easy to use. When it does not, they may look for other sites or sources for the same information or products. Usefulness of a product can be directly attributed to understanding the patterns of user problem solving (Mirel 2003, 33). As with their reading habits, users will invest a limited amount of time in trying to figure out how to work a complex interactive tool that fails to function properly. Users also have come to expect instant access with regard to interactive content. They expect fast downloads, easy access, full compatibility, and ease of functionality. Content should be thoroughly tested and optimized to ensure the best user experience possible. Users also desire a relatively low degree of preparation or setup. Users expect a low investment of time to learn an interactive tool, applet, or feature. As such, interfaces and tools should be fairly intuitive, straightforward, and easy to use. Help systems or instructions should be provided as support. Providing simple, quick instructions that describe the function and controls of an application are essential in providing a positive user experience.

Interface Design

Interface design involves what you see on the screen, including the overall layout as well as any content, tools, or styles found on a page. The interface addresses the presentational aspect of writing, bringing together a variety of elements to form a coherent, organized whole picture for the user. Good interface design is not always intuitive or the matter of finding the right template, but should also be informed by good design principles. Four important interface design principles to consider when developing an organized interface include contrast, grouping, consistency, and usability. Contrast involves using visual styles, such as colors, shading, and patterning, to make elements stand out on a page. This method of visual emphasis is often used to help users visually understand the structure and location of elements on a page. Grouping involves the use of negative space, and to some extent, visual styles, to illustrate relatedness of content on a page. For example, some news reporting sites will often group hyperlinks or related headlines under descriptive headers to indicate different categories. Sites that use multiple navigation tools may also group related tools together, or separate each one using space or shaded boxes to show their distinctiveness or relatedness. Part of the process of user perception involves discerning concepts or relatedness from visual content and how it is arranged and grouped on pages (Baehr 2007). Consistency is an essential guideline for good interface design, and in part, it is because of user expectations. When users learn the layout and function of a site and later return, their learned behaviors become habitual and they expect a similar experience. Interface consistency ensures that elements are placed in the same locations or contexts throughout a site. Consistency extends to the visual styles used, amount of spacing, arrangement of banners, navigation, and so forth. Consistent layouts demonstrate organization and contribute to a high degree of usability as well. And finally, usability ensures the functionality and accessibility of objects in the interface. For a variety of reasons, including browser compatibility, scripting languages, software, system settings, and bandwidth, interface usability may vary from user to user.

FOUR INTERFACE DESIGN PRINCIPLES

Contrast

The difference in hue, shade, or tone between layered objects used to create emphasis or show relation between interface elements.

Grouping

The placement of objects in close proximity and use of space to show relationships between interface elements.

Consistency

The placement of screen elements in consistent locations or contexts throughout interface layouts used in the site.

Usability

Ensuring screen elements that comprise the interface function, display, and can be accessed properly and successfully.

Testing interfaces using a variety of browsers and screen resolution settings is essential to ensure content displays, downloads, and functions consistently for users. User-centered design approaches, such as identifying user needs, preferences, task analysis, and user testing, are all ways of ensuring good interface usability.

Interactive Design

Interactive design involves developing processes of interaction between user and system that serve a specific need, purpose, or function. The level of interactivity can vary, based on what is needed. Lower levels of interaction are typically used for quick, short tasks, such as hyperlinking content or graphic content. A medium level of interaction can be used for some types of interactive forms and instructional media. Moderate levels of interaction are found in applications with more scripted content, requiring only some user input to mediate the flow of content. Web-based training applications are good examples of moderate levels of interactivity. Users may have some control over the media or navigation from page to page, or may have to complete a short exercise or test. Higher levels of interaction are typically found in sites that allow significant user control and customization of content, in online games, and in some interactive applets. Interactive media formats that integrate audio, visual, textual, and contributed content, like 3D models and interactive mixed-media content, create an immersive user experience with a high level of user involvement.

Four interaction design principles based on user expectations include content that is functional, easy to use, immersive, and immediate. Functionality is essential for successful interaction between user and system. Content should be accessible from a standard Web browser and instruction for installing additional viewing software should be provided. In addition, any system limitations, requirements, or restrictions should be made explicit to users. Accessibility and browser compliance is also an essential part of functionality. Since it may not be possible to account for every possible user system configuration, it may be necessary to provide an alternate version or equivalent for users to have access to the interactive content. Content should also demonstrate ease of use and provide intuitive user controls and, when necessary, brief instructions on use. The most successful interactive content is fully usable and can be learned quickly by users. User testing can help identify and correct usability issues with interactive content, throughout the development process. Interactive content should also be immersive and provide some degree of user control over the experience. Immersive content is also relevant, is engaging, and provides a good balance of form and function. Providing ample interactive tools for users can also improve the level of immersion for users. Content should also be immediate, which conforms to user expectations of online content. Content should download quickly and provide a sense of immediacy or near-immediate responses to user input. Perhaps the most important method of ensuring interactive content adheres to design principles, and user expectation is to involve the user during the development process. Conducting user tests and task analyses can provide insight into user processes and common usability problems they might experience. Knowledge in interaction theory and user expectation can provide a balanced background of theory and practice, useful in the development process. And finally, using design principles as heuristics can help maximize usability and usefulness, as well as provide a positive user experience.

Task Analysis

One user-centered approach that can be used to develop interactive content is task analysis. This method is used to outline a specific process,

---

FOUR PRINCIPLES OF INTERACTION DESIGN

Functional

Fully accessible, compatible, browser compliant, and working as intended.

Ease of Use

Fully usable, intuitive controls or brief instructions. Quick learning curve.

Immersive

Simulates an experience that balances form and function, which is engaging, relevant, and useful, and provides ample user control over the experience.

Immediacy

Downloads or reacts quickly, and provides immediate feedback to user input.

function, or act a user performs by identifying specific tasks and background constraints that comprise the activity. Task analysis can be used to map patterns of inquiry for complex problem solving at a practical level (Mirel 2003). Understanding the specific details of the environment, content uses, navigation patterns, and specific steps in performing tasks are all essential pieces of information for a developer. In solving problems, users rely on their past experiences, trial and error strategies, base knowledge of the product, and their perceptual instincts (Arnheim 1969; Baehr 2007). In online environments, problem solving involves dealing with large volumes of data, organizing and wayfinding through data, and making meaning (Mirel 2003, 50–51). Knowledge of user preference and perception is simply not enough; the analysis must involve the working context and user environment details as well. Methods of gathering information about how users solve problems and perform specific tasks must involve the user. Task analysis involves acknowledging the goal, context, working examples, and specific tasks involved in the process (Mirel 2003). Observational studies, focus groups, interviews, and usability testing are all methods that can be used to gather important information on how users perform tasks, including their preferences, habits, navigation choices, and working knowledge and context.

A task analysis can contribute to good usability in a number of ways. It can help identify crucial steps in the process as well as those that might have been left out of an existing product. While highly specialized, a developer's level of knowledge can often miss important detail on a user level. A task analysis also supports a user-centered design process, which can ensure fewer technical issues and errors with the product. Task analysis is an important part of the planning process for any project, providing developers with a valuable resource of information based on user experience and the actual working content in which the product will be used.

Technologies and Tools

A wide range of technologies, including software, programming, and scripting languages, is involved in creating interactive content. It is simply impossible to avoid the use of technologies in developing interactive content, but there are many programs, references, and aids to help Internet writers who are not highly proficient in advanced scripting and programming skills. Many software programs can automate processes and complex scripts that are the foundation of interactive content. Some examples of software used include Adobe's Flash-based programs, 3D modeling software, and interactive video software applications such as Viddler. Also, a wide range of Web development software programs have built-in capabilities, libraries, algorithms, and applets that can be used to produce interactive content. It is also important to have some domain knowledge essential for understanding the basic functionality of interactive content. This includes knowledge of a range of software programs and scripting languages. Some examples of languages and features used include JavaScript, Java, PHP, DHTML, XML, and others. (DHTML stands for Dynamic Hypertext Markup Language, which incorporates the use of HTML and other scripting languages to add interactive qualities to Web pages after they are rendered in the browser.) Scripting libraries and other online references are widely available and provide free, customizable scripts that can be used to develop interactive content. While it may not be necessary or even possible to know every language or software program available, an introduction to the capabilities of a few is useful background in selecting the most useful platforms and tools to use.

A wide range of examples of interactive content can be created using software and scripting tools, which include navigation systems, applets, interactive forms, and multimedia content. Hyperlinks, toolbar menus, drop-down, pull-out, image map, site map, index, graphic, or button-based navigation systems are found throughout many sites and content management systems. Customizing the right tools for users and providing multiple navigation options is essential for good usability. Applets, which are customizable programs that can be embedded in pages, include interactive tutorials, demonstrations, diagrams, games, and puzzles. Content libraries of learning objects and other applets are available online from scripting libraries and sites, which allow users to download and customize applets for display. Many types of interactive forms can be used to collect basic user data, provide feedback, test skills, perform search queries, and navigate content. Forms are highly customizable and a wide range of interactive scripts are available from scripting library sites online, or can be written using a variety of scripting languages, such as JavaScript and PHP. Interactive multimedia content, such as audio and/or visual media, including downloadable and streaming varieties, can also be developed and embedded into online documents and Web pages. Syndicated interactive media, such as RSS feeds, allow users to subscribe to online content that can be embedded into Web pages and updated automatically in real time.

INTERACTIVE NAVIGATION

Navigation tools are the primary interactive tools users rely on to search and browse Internet content. Some of these tools are built-in to the browser, which allow users to move forward or back in browsing history, bookmark pages, block content, reload pages, change browser viewing size, search text on pages, and so forth. However, site-specific navigation tools are far more useful since they are customized for the user experience and content found in Web sites. Site navigation can vary widely in terms of interactive quality and function, from a highly structured toolbar menu down to a series of text-based hyperlinks. Often, they will outline site content, provide keyword search boxes, or perform specific functions, such as submitting form data. Some specific examples of navigation tools include drop-down menus, site maps, image maps, indices, buttons, and interactive applets. Navigation tools, such as menus, tabs, or link lists, are effective in visually grouping related links together, which help users understand those relationships and make navigational choices. Some examples of commonly used navigation tools that enhance the interactive experience include the following:

- *Site maps and site indices.* Provide a macro-level view of the structure, with micro-level access. Good for orientation and problem solving.

- *Hierarchical menus.* Excellent for highly structured site content, organized by topic and subtopic. Also reinforces the organization of site content for users, helping in information findability and overall usability.

- *Keyword search.* Good for generating customized search results based on user input. Also good for sites with large volumes of searchable text-based content. Can be less effective for searching graphic content, unless alternative text descriptors are provided for graphic content.

- *Tabs.* Good for indicating the major content areas and functions of a site. Suggests well-organized content, often visually based, and easy to use, straightforward.

- *Image maps.* Excellent in providing visual search tools that can incorporate familiar images or concepts, which users understand. Thematically, can enforce stylistic rules used throughout the site.

- *Interactive visual tools.* Developed as interactive applets or movies that serve as highly visual-based navigation systems. Examples include: three-dimensional navigation objects, such as a navihedron; Flash-based sites, where the entire site content is essentially an interactive movie; customized interactive applets, such as a vending machine that allows users to select items.

It is important to consider some guidelines in developing usable navigation tools. First, when possible, navigation menus and site maps should reflect the overall site structure or outline the site's content for users. Tools that provide structural clues to users have a high degree of usability, since a user can glance at the selections available to get a quick understanding of the range of options available on the site. Many navigation tools provide explicit information, such as a site map, site index, tabs, or hierarchical menu, which also serve this function. Be sure to minimize accessibility issues, such as download time or viewers required to view content. Navigation tools should be simple, accessible, and easy to use. If users experience problems with the main navigation, it will most likely cause users to abandon the site. It is also important to provide multiple navigation tools to accommodate different learning and problem-solving styles. Users have different preferences for tools based on personal choice, nature of the content, and type of problem they are trying to solve. Position navigation tools in consistent locations throughout the site. Consistency improves user learning of the site and helps users comprehend the overall content structure. Use an appropriate amount of visual emphasis in designing navigation tools. Remove visual clutter, conform to site visual identity guidelines, and avoid gratuitous visual content at all costs. Group related links or functions into menus, shaded regions, or lists. Grouping suggests relational aspects between lists of individual links or functions and aids users in making navigational choices. And finally, conduct usability testing for each tool. Tools should function properly, be fully browser compliant, and be free of any errors. Collectively, these guidelines can assist Internet writers in developing effective and highly usable interactive content for sites.

IMPLICATIONS IN DEVELOPING INTERACTIVE CONTENT

There are some implications for Internet writers to consider when adding interactive content to their work. First, writers should ensure that the interactive content serves a specific purpose or function within the context of the project. Additionally, it should support the main content goals of the project. Any interactive content should also be thoroughly tested and backed by usability test results. Interactive content also is good to use when it automates a task or process for a user and, in such case, should be backed by a comprehensive task analysis. This will ensure it functions properly and supports a working process familiar to users. Interactive content should also be developed with a user-centered process, which integrates their preferences, habits, and expectations, when possible.

It is also important to recognize when too much interactive content has been used, and to scale back appropriately. Too much interactive content can overwhelm users, confuse them, and be a significant drain on system resources, including download and response time. In addition, interactive content that has accessibility problems may need to be repurposed into alternate forms, to ensure all users have the same level of access. In most cases, basic usability testing can help isolate problems so they can be addressed. Another issue with interactive content is that it can create usability problems, particularly if the tool or application is complex and without simple instruction on how to use it. A large number of problems with interactive content come from a system-centered design approach, in which the developers rely only on their own knowledge and isolate the user in the process (Johnson 1998). A developer may have specific inside knowledge of the application, and it may function perfectly for the developer; however, the user may not have the same level of working knowledge or system specifications. As a result, this can create a number of accessibility and usability problems for users. Finally, one additional problem with interactive content is that it often is developed with the primary purpose of showing off the latest flashy technology or software tool. When a fad technology drives the purpose for developing interactive content, it is best to remove it from the site content. While users may be initially impressed by such features, their main interest is typically to find specific content on a site, rather than to play with a novel feature of the site.

Developing interactive content involves understanding the unique characteristics of interactive content. Having knowledge of interaction theory can help writers understand the complexities of human-computer interaction involved in creating interactive content. Understanding user experience theory and user expectations can also assist writers in developing content from a user-centered approach. And perhaps the most important and ubiquitous type of interactive content involves developing navigation tools for users to search, browse, and interact with a site's content.

Section Five

Social Media

Chapter 12

Blogging

Samuel D. Bradley

AN INTRODUCTION TO BLOGGING

Before considering what is different about storytelling in a blog, one should consider what is the same. Storytelling in many ways is the same from Homer to Shakespeare to The Huffington Post. You must choose your words wisely, keep your audience in mind, and make your writing compelling.

Most stories today are told by the mass media. Motion pictures, television dramas, best-selling books, and daily newspapers tell our stories. Increasingly these stories are told online, but the model follows the traditional pattern of one speaker talking to many passive listeners.

Web 2.0 applications—especially blogs—change this model. With comments, readers can *talk back.* This dialogue is a fundamental element of blogging. Without comments, a blog is simply an online diary that other people can read. Comments are conversations, and a blog writer's work is not done when the post is published. Instead, a process of reciprocal writing begins when the blogger elicits comments and responds to those comments. Writing for Weblogs consists of process rather than proclamation.

Weblogs, or blogs, represent one of the most diverse forms of communication created by humans. Cancer survivors chronicle their battles.

Pundits attack those with opposing views. And junior high students detail the agonizing minutia of adolescence. And we call all of these things blogs.

In the upper echelon of bloggers, a precious few writers make a good living with nothing but their blogs. This is the overwhelming minority. A larger group of professionals maintain blogs to drive people to their other businesses, their day jobs. Consultants—especially social media consultants—gain clients when their words resonate with information seekers.

Whether you are going to retire early from your 200,000 unique daily visitors or you are writing for three of your friends and your mom, effective blogging begins with effective writing. Successful blogging, however, combines good blogging with good strategy.

As with most writing, blogging is a form of self-expression. You are saying something about yourself both in the topics you choose and in the way you string words together. Although a handful of bloggers write merely for the joy of writing, most blogs are for someone to actually read. Even if you do not harbor delusions of grandeur, you want people to read your thoughts.

While writing is an art form, attracting traffic to your Weblog is much more a science. If you incorporate that science into your expressive writing, your words will reach many more readers, you will engage those readers, and the readers will return again and again.

140 CHARACTERS OR LESS

In the mid-to-late-2000s, microblogging applications, such as Twitter and Yammer, grew in popularity. Twitter, especially, caught the public's eyes, growing more than 1,000 percent during the first two months of 2009 alone. Microblogging sites restrict users to extremely short posts, just 140 characters (including spaces) in the case of Twitter. During the early growth period, Twitter encouraged users to answer the question "what are you doing?" The idea, the Web site explained, was that Twitter filled in the gaps in life between emails and blog posts. Most people, Twitter argued, would not write a blog post to tell their friends that they were going for coffee. However, there were some friends who wanted to know this information. By posting relatively inconsequential facts about one's life, friends can learn hobbies and passions that might not otherwise come up in daily conversation.

These applications were initially popular with those working in technological industries and young professionals working in densely populated urban areas. Applications such as Twitter made more sense in cities, where an update—or Tweet, as they are called—could be answered by a friend a few blocks away who might join you for coffee.

Originally based on the text message platform, also known as short message service (SMS), Twitter based its limit at 20 characters under the 160 character SMS limitation. This limitation requires writers to use an especially tight vocabulary, and "text speak," such as LOL, or substituting numbers for letters is common. Unfortunately for the sake of effective communication, extreme abbreviations can lead to miscommunication.

These tools have a much broader use than finding out what your friends are doing during their daily routine. Like blogging, these communication tools have permeated both media and corporate sectors. Users can pull content from subscribing (or following) one individual or entity, or push content to their own group of followers. Amateur field reporting and collecting interactive viewer feedback are two methods of pulling content from audiences. These tools also have a promotional aspect for everyone from musical artists to scholars. In the corporate sphere, these tools are used to facilitate workgroup collaboration and rapid communication. This trend of short burst rapid communication has no sign of letting up, and as users appropriate the latest technologies, their uses will continue to broaden in both the private and corporate spheres.

GOOD PLANNING MAKES BETTER BLOGGING

Writing is fun. Planning is less fun. So many eager would-be bloggers bypass planning and skip straight to writing. Multiple sites (e.g., Blogger, WordPress, LiveJournal) offer free hosting. It takes just a few minutes to set up a Weblog. Have an idea for a blog? Five minutes later you can be blogging.

Enticing as this may be, it is an incredibly bad idea. A hasty choice can leave you stuck with an unpalatable name for years. The moment you publish your first post, your blog has a presence on the Web. Search engines will eventually crawl your site, visitors will come, and people will remember your name.

Very few bloggers start the project with the expectation of failure. Like new restaurants, however, many blogs close within the first few months. Inertia is difficult to come by once initial exuberance subsides. Before you create a blog, ask yourself this: what is your end goal? That is, what do you hope to accomplish with this blog? If this question is difficult to answer, you need to seriously rethink your motives. The expectation that you are accomplishing your personal goals is a strong predictor of a blogger's likelihood of continuing to post (Lu & Hsiao 2007). So you have to know what you want to accomplish and believe that you are accomplishing it.

Six months into the blog, maybe you have become bored with "Microbrews of the Pacific Northwest" or "All Things Star Wars Collectibles." Now that you have decided to broaden your horizons, your Weblog has what can be thought of as a brand identity. Readers—and more importantly search engines—know you and what you stand for. Or what you *did* stand for.

Change the name and URL of your blog, and every link to your blog is busted. Every bookmark in a reader's browser no longer works. You might as well have started a new blog, which is fine if you do not care who reads it. But if you have grown accustomed to readers, comments, and conversations, most of that will come to a halt with a new name and URL.

It can take a blogger years to reach 1,000 readers a day. That is persistence! You would not expect a successful restaurant to suddenly move across town, and it is just as ill-advised for bloggers.

The problem can be avoided with even the most modest planning efforts. Think about what you want to say. Think of several names and URLs for your Weblog. Ask several people you trust and who might read the blog to rank the names and addresses. A front-runner will usually emerge.

A related planning point is whether you will host the site on one of the blog host's domains or whether you will pay to host your own Web site. Most new bloggers have not fully committed to the idea. It sounds appealing to try it out for free, which means that your blog will reside on the host's site. You will end up with a URL, such as http://wxyz .wordpress.com.

There's nothing inherently wrong with having your domain stored with a hosting site; however, your fate is tied to that company. If it goes out of business or changes its terms, you have no recourse. Conversely, you can pay for your own domain, such as http://yourname.com, and host the blog yourself. This is a competitive market, and hosting plans cost as little as $6 a month.

Investing in a domain name may sound pretty distant from writing, but this up-front expense gives you maximum control over the future of the words that you will write.

BE A LITTLE GENERAL WITHIN A NICHE

Chances are you are an expert about something. There is something you could write about better than almost anyone alive, even if it is just your own life. But a blog is not a short story, an essay, or even a series of articles. If you post just once a week, you must find 52 things to say about your topic in just the first year.

Can you really find something new to say about Star Wars toys three or four times a week? Jot down some story ideas just to get a feel for how difficult it is to turn over fresh ideas. If you quickly exhaust all of your good ideas, then your idea for a blog probably is too specific.

If you want to keep a blog alive, you need to post regularly. And you cannot simply repeat yourself every 10 posts. You need to ensure that your topic is broad enough that you can find interesting, relevant things to say.

Perhaps you are an American military history aficionado who specializes in the Civil War. Many volumes have been written about the Civil War, and you have probably got a lot to say. Will you still have things to say in two months? Six months? A year?

Consider taking one step back from your topic. Instead of starting a Civil War blog, consider an American military history blog or even a military history blog. With a little wider focus, it is much more difficult to run out of ideas to write about.

If you are a financial journalist, consider a journalism blog rather than strictly business reporting. Even if you are writing about your life, try to consider who you are. You are not just writing about yourself. Maybe you are writing about what it is like to be a college student, a nontraditional student, a single mother, or the youngest representative ever elected in your state.

That is not to say that you should try to be all things to all people. You clearly need to focus. Just be careful about being overly myopic.

KNOW YOUR AUDIENCE

Once you know who you are going to be online—or at least what you are going to talk about—it is time to turn your attention to your readers. Every word you write should be penned with the reader in mind. If you are writing an informal blog about the life of a college student, for example, you will likely use informal tone and shorter sentences.

Audience analysis is another area where it is important to plan. It is most helpful to sketch out the target audience before you begin the first post. To whom are you speaking? Think about how these people speak, how they think, and how they talk. Although you never want prose weighed down by jargon-laden technical language, one would expect a science writer to use a more complicated language than a middle school student.

Are you targeting experts, intermediates, or novices? It is going to matter when you start to write. If you are reaching out to first-time tennis players, for example, you cannot be technical in your descriptions of the game. You probably should not assume that your audience knows for sure what is meant by "love" or "advantage Nadal."

Conversely, if you repetitively explain "peloton" and "time trialing" on a blog targeting cycling enthusiasts, then you will likely quickly alienate your audience by talking down to them.

Knowing one's audience means more than word choice. The audience should influence what you write about. Admittedly, blogging is about the writer more than many writing venues. Nonetheless, few readers frequent blogs that are nothing more than disconnected streams of consciousness.

Your audience will grow more quickly with blog posts that target a rather specific audience. Think about what you would want to read if you were to come across your blog. What would get your attention? If there is breaking news in your area, do not just report the news but interpret it. Provide relevant commentary for your audience. Add some value to the conversation.

Whether your audience is expert or beginner, you should write your blog in a conversational tone. A Weblog is neither a textbook nor a legal document. It should be a conversation. You want comments. So talk to your reader. Target that conversation at the level of your audience, but talk *with* your reader rather than *at* your reader.

STAY FOCUSED

How do you write generally and specifically at the same time? In order to write prolifically, a blogger needs to find the appropriate balance between the proverbial forest and trees. If your topic is too specific, as mentioned above, you will quickly run out of ideas and readers. However, without focus, your ideas will wander across the landscape, and you will find it difficult to develop a regular readership.

This again points to proper planning. Before you invest seven clicks to create a blog on a free site, carefully think about what you want to say. A Weblog unfolds over time. If you have just a few things to say, consider writing a guest post on another blog in your area, or confine yourself to writing comments on related posts. If you are going to spend hours a week on your blog for months and even years, then you require a topic about which you care passionately.

As a blogger focused on a topic, you will develop your own expertise. This practice will make you a better writer, and it will make your blog more interesting for other readers. Expertise and focus also will help you write more quickly and develop better themes in your writing.

WRITE TIGHT

Most offline writers have a page or word limit. In the offline, physical world, writers are writing to fill a space. This concept is largely meaningless for Weblogs. Although longer pieces do, technically, take up more server space, the difference is trivial. Seemingly, the online writer and blogger have a limitless canvas upon which to paint their words. This is a mistake. Almost no one seeks out a blog looking for "everything I could possibly know" about a subject. Instead, large blocks of text can be extremely intimidating online, and extremely lengthy pieces will likely drive would-be readers to navigate quickly away from your blog.

Make every word count. Most people expect blogs to be less formal than other writing venues, so the skilled blogger will write in a relaxed, informal style while still writing efficiently. Do not allow the seemingly endless bounds of cyberspace fool you into endless diatribes. Think about what you want to say, and work to convey those thoughts in as few words as possible.

MONITOR LEVEL OF PERSONAL DETAILS

Most bloggers write less formally than journalists or book authors. This informality often translates into a familiar, conversational tone with the reader, which likely helps the reader identify with the author. This sense of identification generally is an advantage to online writing and blogging, and it is important to the blogger, as many blog readers report that seeking emotional exchanges is a primary goal for reading (Huang, Chou, & Lin 2008). However, the familiar can quickly become overly familiar, and the blogger searching for a post idea can too easily lapse into chronicling the minutia of day-to-day life. Perhaps the most prophetic advice on this topic comes from the book title *No One Cares What You Had for Lunch.* There is no clear delineation between a cold, impersonal blog and boring, off-putting lunch updates. Thus discretion is urged here.

This tendency to talk about oneself is not likely to be altogether absent given the personality profile of most bloggers. Not surprisingly, bloggers tend to be high in openness (Guadagno, Okdie, & Eno 2008). That is, they are open to new ideas and are associated with creativity and artistic expression. Thus, blogging is a logical form of personal expression for many bloggers.

Many bloggers start writing as part of an effort to create, expand, or improve upon a social network. In order to be perceived as a social creature, there must be some socializing, and it is difficult to imagine how this could happen without the sharing of some personal social details. Thus, it is not surprising that extraversion and willingness to self-disclose have shown to be related to bloggers maintaining a larger social network (Stefanone & Jang 2008). Bloggers who scored high on extroversion and self-disclosure reported the highest number of strong ties within their online social network. Thus, for bloggers at least, it seems as if you truly must give a little to get a little.

It is also worth taking a moment for bloggers to consider their personal security. Hopefully every interaction a blogger has will be positive, but sharing personal details online makes it easy for stalkers or other ill-doers to learn your routine. Even a seemingly harmless post about enjoying writing in the mornings at a local coffee shop provides a clue to your whereabouts, and talking about your job or showing a photo of you in front of your house provides clues to your personal life. A study of adolescents' blogs showed, for example, that sexual content and profane language were relatively common (Williams & Merten 2008). This could clearly draw unwanted visitors to the blog, and such activities might negatively impact future employment opportunities. There is no single policy that works for everyone, so bloggers are cautioned to think about the information that they publicly display.

YOU ARE NOT EXCUSED FROM PROOFREADING

Traditional journalism educators browbeat students with the importance of grammar, spelling, and punctuation. The importance of mechanics speaks directly to the credibility of the source. If you cannot get a comma correct, how can the reader trust that you took the time to get the facts right? Given that blogs suffer from a lack of credibility anyway (Sweetser, Porter, Chung, & Kim 2008), sloppy writing is ill-advised. Furthermore, maintaining credibility may keep a blogger in the good graces of her peers, as accuracy, credibility, and etiquette have been identified as key themes to bloggers (Perlmutter & Schoen 2007). A blog is a less formal venue, but it should not represent a stream of consciousness download followed by a click of "Publish."

Weblogs allow writers the opportunity to get it right the second time. Unlike a newspaper, magazine, or book, typos can easily be corrected after publishing. After carefully editing the original posting, bloggers should reread their work for errors, and these errors should quickly be corrected. Additionally, bloggers are encouraged to avoid "text speak" and other abbreviations that are not relevant to the longer form blog post.

KEEP YOUR READER'S ATTENTION

Attention is fleeting, and this is especially true on a Weblog where the reader is always one click away from navigating away from your page. As the daily newspaper metamorphosed to keep up with the graphical influence of *USA Today* (see Utt & Pasternak 1989), a common newsroom rule of thumb developed that no solid block of text should be as big as a dollar bill. That is, one should not be able to place a dollar bill on a newspaper page and cover solely text. There should be a headline, subhead, photograph, graphic, or pull quote to break up the grey of the text.

Although the so-called dollar bill rule is not so easily implemented online, too many bloggers begin their posts with a title and type until they are finished writing. No matter how compelling the prose, this style leaves a visually unappealing page of grey (black text against a white background) broken up by nothing. This is inexcusable in a visually compelling medium such as the Internet. Simple subhead HTML coding, such as <h3>, can be used to insert subheads throughout the text. If nothing more, the larger, bolder font serves to break up the page. Images are easy to add to blog posts, and the use of Creative Commons licenses of photosharing sites, such as Flickr.com, allows bloggers access to thousands of royalty-free photographs. Bloggers wishing to use royalty-free images through Creative Commons licensing are advised to understand the updated licenses. Currently, "Attribution" licenses allow you to use the copyrighted work free of charge (even in a for-profit commercial venue) as long you attribute it to the creator in the manner they wish it to be attributed. These licenses are a powerful tool for the blogger looking to add design elements to the page.

CRAFT POWERFUL HEADLINES

Most blogging software packages refer to a post's headline as a "title," but it functions much the way a newspaper headline functions. Studies show that most readers will invest the few seconds required to read your headline, but the quality of that headline determines whether they will invest any time actually reading your post. Despite the tenuous economic future that they face, newspapers have figured out a number of guidelines that make their headlines more compelling. Most readers do not know that reporters do not actually write the headlines. Although there are few exceptions, reporters generally file their stories and are home for the day before anyone ever thinks about writing a headline for the story. Except for very small papers, copy editors write headlines for stories after a designer has laid out the page and decided how big the headline should be. Then the copy editor reads the story carefully and writes a headline to exactly fill that spot.

There are two takeaway lessons here for the blogger. First, write the headline *after* you have written, edited, and polished the post. Because the title comes at the top of the post, there is a tendency to write the headline first. This is a mistake. If you write the headline before you write the post, you are writing the headline for the post that you *intended* to write. Often this is not the post that you actually end up writing. As you write, ideas coalesce in your mind, and you may think of a better direction for your thoughts. This is not reflected in the title that you quickly belted out before you got down to what you actually wanted to write.

The second thing to learn from copy editors is to think about the space you have to fill and the best way to convey the central idea within that space. Although some will surely disagree, many writers acknowledge that it is far more difficult to convey a complete idea in 10 words than in 1,000 words. If you have a page to fill, you need not be so careful in deciding exactly what you want to say. With only a handful of words, however, every one is precious. There is no room to waste a word, or you will ineffectively convey an idea. With a traditional blog setup, you are limited to approximately 45–50 characters including spaces. That is exceedingly few words to entice a reader to invest in your thoughts. What sells this post? By this, do not be gimmicky or promise something that is not there. Simply find the most compelling way to tell your story in 45 characters. Make it interesting. Use concrete nouns and active verbs. Make it easy for the reader to envision your thoughts. Foremost, make the headline count. The headline, or title, should never be a throwaway afterthought.

Sometimes, however, gimmicks work. For reasons peculiar to the human psyche, blog posts that promise lists are especially well read: "5 Ways to Be a Better Blogger" will likely garner far more readers than it deserves. It is neither creative nor especially well written. But it is appealing. It is finite. And it is effective. There is a certain ease of cognitive processing of these "list" type headlines that make them inviting. They are also easy for readers to email their friends, perhaps the closest most bloggers will ever come to viral communication. So if it has been awhile since you last posted, and you are hungry for readers, consider a list post. In 20 minutes, you can write the entire thing and the headline. And it will likely draw more readers than the post for which you spent all day. In the blogosphere it is a constant trade between quality and quantity. Even the most successful bloggers do not make the best choice every day.

Finally, bloggers have one additional reason to write gripping headlines: search engines. No matter how talented of a writer you are, most people will come across your blog from a search engine such as Google rather than word-of-mouth communication. This means that no matter how much time you spend fussing over the design of your blog, it is really your Google search result that will be the public face of your blog. Blog titles have a strong influence on search engines' algorithms, so it is important to use accurate key words. If you are writing about travel to Cancun, then vague headlines such as "A great day in paradise" will not help interested travelers find your site. Instead, related keywords will help search engines—and the readers that use them—find your blog. Titles disproportionately influence search engine results, and they are likely to be displayed to readers. These are two important reasons unique to the online world for making keywords count.

BEWARE THE ONLINE INTERFACE

Every blogging software platform offers the opportunity—and often makes it more convenient—to write posts through an online interface. Each platform also includes some sort of automatic backup. In the majority of cases, the automatic backup will protect you in case of a power outage or Internet failure, but this is not guaranteed. And for posts that require a lot of coding, such as the insertion of photographs, a great deal of time can be lost if the automatic backup captured the text but not the graphical coding. Thus, many blogging authorities advise bloggers to write offline in a word processing program and then transfer the completed post to the blogging platform.

THE IMPORTANCE OF COMMENTS

Interaction happens in a blog through comments. Without comments, a blog is really nothing more than an online newspaper. What makes blogs unique is the ability for readers to interact with bloggers in a reciprocal conversation. There is a lot of comment spam in the world where some bot (software agent) will key in on some word and then try to sell the reader pornography or personal enhancement medicine, and there is ever a good deal of trolls out there simply looking for a reason to add a viscerally negative comment. Yet the majority of comments initiate meaningful conversations. Bloggers can learn from the readers, and posts can take new directions that the author never envisioned. The most successful bloggers invite—and respond to—comments. In almost every case, a blogger should be the most frequent commenter on his or her own blog. Although this may sound counterintuitive, you should strive to respond to every meaningful comment on your blog. This will help readers feel connected, and it will encourage them to return. These types of interactive relationships appear to be key to forming online social groups using Web 2.0 applications, such as blogs (Lai & Turban 2008). Repeat readership is key to forming relationships and an active community around your blog. Furthermore, research suggests that positive feedback through comments keeps bloggers motivated to keep blogging (Miura & Yamashita 2007).

REREAD WHAT YOU HAVE WRITTEN

A number of successful bloggers encourage taking a meta perspective on one's own blog. Although you likely do not have much time to spend on blog maintenance, it is advantageous to keep track of your topics and themes. What are you writing about? How often do you come back to each particular theme? If you write just four times a week, then you will crank out about 200 posts per year. After the second year, you will have posted 400 times. You are surely not capable of keeping all of those posts in mind, so you run the danger of repeating yourself. Do you just have 20 things to say, and you have repeated those 20 things 20 times each? Unless you keep track of your writing, you run that risk.

BLOGGING IN THE CLASSROOM

As a general rule, instructors tend to be older that their students. It simply takes time to learn enough to lead a classroom, no matter what you may think of any particular instructor. Blogging, as with most electronic media, is more readily embraced by younger generations. A given student is more likely to blog than his/her instructor. And by the time that current students become instructors, there will be some new technology that the next generation has adopted. Thus, blogs are relative newcomers to the classroom setting, and they are still underrepresented. For instance, many journalists are expected to maintain blogs in addition to traditional reporting duties, but blogging is not a central course within most journalism curricula. Indeed, data show that journalism professionals are far more likely to use blogs than journalism educators (Chung, Kim, Trammell, & Porter 2007).

Research into blogging and learning is showing that the medium can be a powerful communication, language, and writing learning tool. One project had college second language (French and German) students read native speaker blogs during the first semester of the intermediate course and write blogs during the second semester (Ducate & Lomicka 2008). Throughout the year, students became immersed in both the blogging culture and the second language. Data suggest that the blogs allowed students new creative avenues and allowed them to experiment with the language in ways that would not otherwise have been available.

Within the field of English composition—perhaps the most pervasive writing course within American universities—scholars are calling for instructors to embrace blogging and social networking in the teaching of writing (Vie 2008). The creativity seen in the second language classroom also has been observed when blogging is incorporated into the composition classroom. Given most students' baseline familiarity with blogs, they have been observed to take more risks with their writing, and the feedback of the medium increased appreciation for audience reactions to their writing (Smith 2008).

Even middle school students are drawn in by the technology, with one young woman observing, "That's online writing, not boring school writing" (Witter 2007, 92). Perhaps most exciting (or frightening) are data that show that students may independently develop new and unexpected learning uses for classroom blogs (Minocha & Roberts 2008).

IMPLICATIONS FOR INTERNET WRITING

Blogging is a distinct genre of Internet writing. Although the Weblog will soon enter its second decade of existence, the number of Weblogs continues to increase, and online writers are increasingly being called upon to author Weblogs. This is true of traditional journalists thrust into the convergent newsroom, public relations professions, and technical writing positions. Interactivity is a key feature of all online media, and this is especially true of Weblogs. Gaining an audience and keeping that audience engaged is key to a Weblog's success. Strong planning helps ensure that the blog is broad enough to generate new posts yet tailored enough to have an identity. Once the blog is well planned, effective writing is key to readership. This begins with well-written headlines and extends to breaking up text with subheadlines and images to make the blog visually appealing. Finally, blogs are proving increasingly popular learning tools, a trend that appears to be continuing.

Chapter 13

Reading Online

INTRODUCTION

Neil Postman wrote a story about how a graduate student used a television as a source of light by which to read, the volume down, the screen-filled static illuminating the room, when a reading lamp went out (Postman 1985). He continued about using an oversized television as a bookshelf. With all due respect to Marshall McLuhan, Postman notes, not all mediums are amplifications of their predated kin. It is hard to believe that Postman, even in his later days, could have imagined reading on something that can be used for watching videos, or not even having to go to a library to get a book or journal article.

While Postman uses McLuhan's extension metaphor for comparing the horse to the car, or the candle to the light bulb, the parallel occasionally comes up short when it comes to media. While this debate is endless, in the case of the book, it is also senseless. New may or may not be better. The way things used to be, in fact, were seldom easier. In the case of the Internet and both personal and mobile computing, the opportunities for reading are literally almost always on the person or at least at the fingertips. But has the small screen taken a page, if not the entire book itself, out of the reader's hands? Are students learning the language better, and more about the world, on these 24-hour accessible screens that provide access to millions of pages of information, including books?

The technologizing of text has transformed the way readers experience the word (Ong 1982). According to the dwindling circulation of newspapers and bottom-line concerns at book publishers, it is logical to explore whether readers are intent on experiencing different media, specifically reading online, or if they are moving away from hard-copy text for other reasons, and understanding what, if any, effects these technological advances are having on reading is an area worthy of study.

READING BEFORE "SCREENS"

The use of the word for meaning making and storytelling goes back to oral culture, in which the sound of words determined thought processes (Carey 1967). Since mnemonics and formulas were such keys to retelling and memory in oral cultures, the advent of such technocentric communication caused transformation of its own in terms of how people told and heard stories.

Culture and social organization are related to communication means and methods (Carey 1967). Harold Innis's phrase "the bias of communication" refers to a pair of distinct variables, time and space. Oral, written, and other forms of communication all have unique time and space elements. These vary within media; even in writing's earliest forms, time and space provided a unique concept for drawings on cave walls. Chirographic storytelling left something to the imagination, just as it left out some verbiage (Ong 1967). Orality certainly had an additive style, something that also might be lacking in the digitizing and "real-timing" of communication (Ong 1982). Perception and conceptual thinking are, to varying degrees, somewhat abstract (Ong 1967). Some scholars believed that the proliferation of electronic media, specific to the era of telephone, radio, and the expansion of television into cable, led to a secondary orality (Crowley & Heyer 2003). Secondary orality was thought to be literally the second coming of orality, with cultures able to communicate at will as long as they had access to a phone. In the pre-Internet phase of secondary orality, the linkage was made back to the wholly oral cultures, where the spoken word was the only communication. In secondary orality, cultures can connect by individuals or groups across large distances by what was, at the start of the theory, the landline telephone and the one-way exchange of cable television. Still, something was lost hearing a story over the phone rather than in person (Czitrom 1982). This blending and overlapping of communication forms has impacted storytelling, and by extension, the stories themselves, and audiences.

McLuhan separated human communication into three distinct periods. First was oral, which went back to the cultures that relied on storytelling and memory, regurgitating everything from essential information to myth and faith, solely through oral means (McLuhan 1964). The second phase McLuhan notes was the written phase. The printing press caused great concern to gatekeepers and those who held court at the head of the table in oral cultures. The spreading of information, history, wild lies, and truths placed less emphasis on speaking and forced anyone who wanted to be out front, or even a gatekeeper, into the newest form of media to be able to write. The final stage—McLuhan was no longer around to postulate and pontificate about the Internet—was the electric stage, with telephone, radio, television, and the computer, the latter then in its infancy, in which culture, McLuhan wrote, would be largely shaped by the media itself, and the messages that travel through it would be altered by the media through which it is dispensed, bringing another intellectual dimension and necessary skill and understanding to media use and meaning making.

TRACING TECHNOLOGY

Though these three categories are often cited in media ecology as the unquestioned properly divided periods, others believe adding one pre- and one post-category to McLuhan's three is more accurate (Logan 2002). Before there was oral culture, there were grunts and gestures. This pre-oral communication had an oral element about it, and certainly chirographic wall painting and scrawlings were a primal form of writing. Logan bookends that by separating electric and electronic communication, following McLuhan's landline telephone, radio, and cable television period with electronic communication, which includes the Internet and mobile/cell phone technology, something Logan notes that McLuhan did not overlook:

Neither Innis nor McLuhan lived long enough to see the two post-1980 revolutions of personal computing brought about by microcomputers and the Internet/ World Wide Web. If they had the opportunity to observe these two phenomena, I believe they would have made a division similar to the one I am suggesting here. (Logan 2002, 14)

Logan notes that while electric and electronic communication have parallels in terms of how the information is distributed, there are significant differences. Electric media users are passive, much like McLuhan described television as a cold medium because news programs, for example, especially in the time of only the big three television networks, were on when they were on, and those who missed the 5 PM news were out of luck until 10 PM. However, with cable and the significant addition of around-the-clock cable news stations and the real-time news cycle online, users can determine use. In fact, because so many channels are in the marketplace, the news is now presented in partisan fashion, so users can get the news they want, presented and slanted the way they want to best align with their beliefs and orientations, and more importantly, for the purposes of Logan, whenever they want it. The Internet changed the landscape once and perhaps for all of time, because the exchange can be two-way at all times; the information highway has no exits for the communicative traveler who wants to stay connected through the day and night, never unplugging from the computer or cell phone to remain constantly connected to whomever or whatever they want (Marshall 2004).

WHAT THIS MEANS TO READING

This "connects" to the concept of interactivity, something the Internet is credited to bringing to, among other media, text. The idea that an audience is active excites scholars and leads to such phantasmagorical, societal confluences as globalization and democratization. Reading, often regarded as a reflective exercise, becomes an active exchange (Logan 2002). The author no longer has the final word on the last page. Instead, readers can comment directly to the publishers or even the author, discuss the book among other readers, and even write and publish their own books.

Thinking of the audience as active means that audience members "work" on media texts. Where we can see this activity most pervasively represented by audiences is in their "intertextual" work on media text . . . The activity of the audience generally with traditional media is at the point of consumption or reception even as the activity begins to change the meanings of these terms into something productive. (Marshall 2004, 13)

This, Marshall argues, leads to the disappearance of the audience, the title he uses for this chapter in his book about new media cultures. Knowledge is no longer imparted, and if it is, its foundations can be questioned or built upon by the audience itself. Rather than take the author's proverbial word for it, the reader can take apart or add to the text, making sense or mincemeat of it. How powerful is this concept of interactivity? One scholar calls it magical (Aarseth 1997). The term itself, however, was developed and used long before technology recoined and issued it as a sort of intellectual currency.

Interactivity can be a useful way to distinguish new media culture. In order to reclaim the term, it is perhaps useful to explore its various incarnations in usage and through that etymological tracing identify some of the unique qualities that have shifted. (Marshall 2004, 14)

Such interactivity depends upon access to computers, be it desktop or laptop. It also depends upon connectivity, be it cable or wireless, which though prevalent in the United States and in most countries, is not available to everyone in all places of the world by any means or assumptions (Sholle 2002). However, for the context of this research, the society being studied is able to be, and actually is, plugged in. This allows the audience to be interactive and to assume a form of control (Marshall 2004). Still, if this audience is always plugged in, and thus retains this control element over media text, is the medium itself being used as the controlling device? Or are these devices controlling the user, who is unable to meet a stranger, hear the sounds and see the sights of daily life, make sense of opinions and form his/her own thoughts after reflecting, and abandon all interactions except those with "family and friends" to which they are continuously connected?

In a world that provides a rhetorical buffet for any unsatiated appetite, the classics are falling to the wayside. Indeed, even a postmodern classical scholar, perhaps an oxymoron of a term, would decry the idea of Shakespeare, or the likes, in an ebook. But it is what it is, and "it" is here, and it is here now. Students are probably reading more than ever, but with social networking Web sites continuing to explode on the cyber landscape and dominate the dream demographic for businesses, many students read user-generated content throughout the day on Facebook and MySpace.

The importance of the reader becoming the controller gives a new context to reading (Marshall 2004). Not being able to find a book or article is less of a concern than in the past as text of all kinds is usually available online. While this takes the book-lugging trips back and forth to the library out of the equation, better access to text certainly should be hailed rather than decried. Books that have electronic versions are no longer checked out, and thus are available to more than one user at a time.

COMPUTER-SCREEN READING

Past experiments have produced data that reading on a computer screen is slower than reading hard-copy text (Plume 1988). Additionally, the idea of a paperless society has actually been contradicted, and research shows the proliferation of computers has brought far greater use of paper for printing as users can find information on their computer, or transfer it from a disk, and print it out (Muter & Maurutto 1991), leading to an increase in printed paper rather than a decrease.

Studies to date have predominantly indicated that reading on a computer takes longer than it does on paper (Haas & Hayes 1986). In what was considered a landmark experiment at the time, readers took 28.5 percent longer reading text on a computer screen than they did for hard-copy text (Muter et al. 1982).

Those experiments from the 1970s and 1980s focused on more than a dozen possible reasons for the poorer performance from computer-screen readers (Muter & Maurutto 1991). Those included:

... distance between the reading material and the reader; angle of the reading material; character shape; resolution; characters per line; lines per page; words per page; inter-line spacing; actual size of characters; visual angle of characters; inter-character spacing; left justification vs. full justification; margins; contrast ratio between characters and background; intermittent vs. continuous light (Wilkins, 1986); polarity (light characters on a dark background vs. the reverse); emissive vs. reflected light; interference from reflections (Reinking, 1987); stability (potential flicker, jitter, shimmer, or swim); chromaticity; posture of the reader; familiarity with the medium; absence vs. presence of incidental location cues (Wright & Lickorish, 1983); aspect ratio; edge sharpness; curvature; distortion in corners; system response time; and method for text advancement. (p. 259)

Reading on a computer screen, to include personal computers and laptop computers, has become more prevalent, especially as the Internet has become more accessible and open to information exchange, particularly with the trend of libraries to provide resources online, as well as the tweaking of e-book format over the past decade to increase usability for readers. While some research, including experiments, has been conducted in this area, it was done decades ago. And while the data gathered from those experiments provides some insight, the fact that computers have improved so much for readability and online text has gotten so clear shows that some might view it as easy to read as text on the hard-copy printed page.

Students are now getting "handouts" in class electronically as often as the stapled hard-copy sheets. This is allowing students more constant access, though it is a responsibility to read such handouts, to get used to reading significantly longer text on their computer screens, should they choose to read it that way rather than print it out.

Chapter 14

Cognitive and Psychological Aspects of Online Writing

Samuel D. Bradley

THE MIND AND THE MESSAGE

The human mind seldom receives the attention it deserves in conversations about writing. What does the brain have to do with the hyperlinked word? In a word, everything. Every word that is written starts as a thought in a mind, and it ends as a thought in the mind of the reader. Every word that is written online will be attended to, or not, by a mind. Some pieces of Internet writing will be brilliant pieces of work that are remembered for years, and links to those works will be emailed around the globe. And many of the factors that decide whether a message will reach millions as a viral masterpiece or end up in the back corner dustbin of the Internet depend upon the cognitive and social psychological effects of that message (Lang, Bradley, Chung, & Lee 2003). That is why writers should care what happens in the minds of the readers and viewers of their work.

The study of communication is about the process of message sending and receiving. Lasswell summarized this in 1948, saying that communication considers "Who says what, in which channel, to whom, with what effects." For the online writer, several components of this equation are fixed. First, the writer represents the "who," and the Internet is the "channel." What is said, to whom it is said, and especially the effects of what is said are variables. There is some irony that scholars spend a great deal of time fussing over effects while writers often ignore them. Aspiring journalists spend a great deal of time learning their trade, and in most programs they spend a great deal of time talking about normative ideals of democracy and journalism as the Fourth Estate. Far less time is spent talking about the purpose of the prose. What *is* the purpose? To inform? Perhaps. But what then? If you ask people why they read news, data show that people engage in a surveillance function. They are, quite simply, surveying the landscape. So they want to be informed. Does it end there? Should the writer care whether the news consumer actually learns anything from the news? Because the data there—especially for broadcast news—are not especially encouraging. Attending to a message and remembering that message often are related, but many times well-attended messages are poorly remembered. Understanding why helps the writer craft more effective messages.

ATTENDING TO THE WORLD WIDE WEB

There are an infinite number of reasons why any given individual chooses to devote his/her attention to a given Web page. And writers should recognize that attention is a precious commodity. Even our everyday language recognizes this fact when we tell people to "pay" attention. This colloquial usage equates attention with money, an apt metaphor given how many online venues clamor for a surfer's precious limited cognitive resources. Looking back to Lasswell's "what" is said, writers have a lot of control over their content. If a writer is self-employed or blogging for personal enjoyment, then the writer has exclusive control over what is said. When the writer is writing for pay, however, there is less freedom. Nonetheless, what is said—the content—has a lot to do with whether readers pay attention to a piece of writing. Simply and rather obviously, good writing is better attended. However, in addition to content features of the message, there are many structural features of mediated messages, including Internet applications, that have a strong and often overlooked effect on cognitive processing of the message. These effects are the final component of Lasswell's model.

The human brain is an efficient information processing device. Despite weighing about 2 percent of the average human's body weight, the brain gets about 15 percent of the blood flow, constantly refreshing hard-working neurons with energy. This energy is difficult to come by, and the brain constantly tries to balance the needs of the environment with being a cognitive miser. In order to accomplish this efficiency, low-level circuits in your brain are always trying to predict what is going to happen next. At the same time, your brain has a built-in set of three preattentive reflexes designed to handle novelty in the world. When something new arrives, you need to know quickly whether it is going to eat you, whether you should try to eat it, or if it is irrelevant to you. And the more brain power you waste answering this question, the less you have left to accomplish meaningful cognitive tasks. Add to this the fact that it is generally advantageous to start avoiding bad things before you have fully had time to ponder just what the bad thing is.

Orienting Reflex

The three preattentive reflexes, the orienting reflex (OR), startle reflex, and defensive reflex, combine with ongoing cognitive appraisals to evaluate novelty in the world before you are even consciously aware that there is something new to evaluate. The startle reflex and defensive reflex are less relevant to online writing due to the fact that they are elicited by suddenly occurring (in the case of the startle reflex) and intense (in the case of the defensive reflex) stimuli. A severe example of the startle reflex is when a child jumps out from behind a corner and yells, "boo!" This reflex serves to empty short-term memory to focus attentional resources on the startling stimulus. The defensive reflex is a protective reflex elicited, for example, when you see a large object approaching quickly in your peripheral vision. Unless the online writer is writing horror movies, then messages are unlikely to elicit these reflexes.

The OR is the least intense of these reflexes, and it was dubbed the investigatory, or "what's that?" reflex by Pavlov (1927). The OR is elicited by novel stimuli that are not especially loud, fast-occurring, or intense. Imagine sitting in a meeting around a conference table. A tardy attendee quietly opens the door to sneak in, and as the door opens, you turn to identify the latecomer. This reorientation of your attention from the meeting to the door likely was triggered by an OR. The OR automatically reallocates cognitive resources away from ongoing mental processes and toward investigation of the novel stimulus in the world. This reallocation is neither especially costly nor long-lasting. In the case of the colleague slinking in the back, as soon as you identify the person as nonthreatening, your attention will quickly return to your primary focus, and most of the time you will have no memory for the OR eliciting stimulus. Because of its nature as a preattentive reflex, the person is unaware of the OR. You do not know they are happening. However, the OR can be easily measured in the psychophysiology lab. For reasons that are not completely understood, your heart slows down for the next several beats following an OR. This cardiac deceleration is easily measured and can be reliably seen after certain structural features of messages.

The real world has a rather low degree of novelty. Although one or two people might show up late to a meeting, there is not someone new coming through the door every few seconds. Given the relatively low degree of novelty and the low probability that someone coming through the door is an armed felon, the cognitive effects of ORs are not especially interesting in the real world. This is not the case with the mediated world. The mediated world is full of OR eliciting stimuli that jostle the audience's cognitive resources wildly, even when the audience is unaware of the jostling.

One of the first structural features found to elicit the OR is the camera change in video (Lang 1990). Although you will never feel it, your brain is temporarily disoriented when you are watching video of two people in a car, for example, and then the next frame shows the same two people at the party to which they were headed. In one-thirtieth of a second (on U.S. televisions and most streaming online video, slower in some animated online applications, such as Flash cartoons), the entire visual world has changed from one place to the next. That simply does not happen in the natural world. But it happens in video, and it happens often. Every time the camera changes, the low-level circuitry screams, "What!?!?!," and cognitive resources are reallocated. The frequency of these changes is known as pacing, and today's style is fast-paced. Camera changes often come at the viewer as fast as every three seconds. Although this fast pacing is enjoyable to viewers (Lang, Shin, & Lee 2005), it can quickly lead to cognitive overload (Lang, Bolls, Potter, & Kawahara 1999).

Web pages increasingly include video content, and it is conceivable that a majority of Web sites will contain video in the near future. Most Web pages on the ESPN.com domain, one of the most popular Web sites in the world, already feature video, and video reports are increasingly common on news sites, such as CNN.com. However, video is making its way across the content spectrum, as today's blogs are quickly giving way to vlogs, or video Weblogs. And for commercial Web sites, the "stickiness" of a page is as important as what is on the page. That is, for-profit Web sites are interested in keeping you on the page as long as possible to expose you to as many advertisements as possible. The "stickier" the page, the better. For the paid writer trying to accomplish this goal, orienting-reflex inducing stimuli are likely to keep bringing attention back to the Web page, and keep the reader's attention. Including camera changes in video is one way to accomplish this.

Audio Structural Features

Following the initial work with video camera changes, a flurry of research was conducted to see what other structural features were likely to elicit ORs, and this line of research has increasingly elicited the interest of Internet researchers. Internet writers are not limited solely to video if they want to include attention-gaining structural features in their Web messages. It turns out that it is fairly easy to elicit ORs in audio content, too. The simple act of a voice change—so natural in actual life and video when you can see that a different person begins talking—elicits an OR in audio content (Potter 2000). Your brain must figure out where the change in sound came from without visual support. The voice change, however, is not the only audio structural feature likely to elicit an OR. The onset of a commercial, production effect (such as a laser sound effect), funny voice, or sexual content all led to evidence of a cardiac OR (Potter, Lang, & Bolls 2008). And in support of the theoretical notion of a reallocation of cognitive resources, recognition memory increases for information following the OR-eliciting stimulus. Thus, the Internet writer or podcast producer has many audio structural features at his/her disposal to help allocate attentional resources back to the message.

Internet Structural Features

Looking strictly at Internet design with no true video or audio, research has identified several attention-eliciting structural features of Web pages. Readers do not appear to orient to the onset of a headline or even a boxed headline (Lang, Borse, Wise, & David 2002). Users did, however, orient to content that they selected. This suggests that when participants click on a link, they will automatically allocate cognitive resources to processing the resulting Web page. What about those pesky (or revenue generating, depending upon your perspective) banner ads? Static banner ads elicit no orienting; however, users do orient to animated banner ads (Lang 2000). Thus it appears that the inclusion of animation causes automatic allocation of cognitive resources to processing of the ad. In addition to animated banner ads, pop-up ads also elicit ORs (Diao & Sundar 2004).

Looking at Adobe Flash content, Schwartz (2005) combined work on animation with work on sound effects to see how these two features affected learning from multimedia content. As with previous work, animation exhibited a strong effect on cognition. The onset of animation led to an OR, but it also led to participants paying more attention over time. Thus, the animation both captured and maintained attention. Information presented during the animation also was better recognized and recalled. Sound effects that were related to the audio information also led to an OR and sustained attention over time. Unlike animation, however, sound effects led to better recall but not better recognition. This suggests that there may be a visual superiority. Perhaps the most interesting results came when comparing the combination of animation and sound. When paired together, recognition and recall were greatest for information presented with both animation and sound. Thus, it appears that when animation and sound are related to audio information in a multimedia presentation, cognitive processing is optimal. As work comparing information in the audio and visual channels has revealed, however, the key is for the information in both channels to complement the other channel.

AUDIO-VISUAL REDUNDANCY

The Internet and related applications bring with them exciting multimedia canvases. Increasingly Internet writing involves a mixture of the written word, spoken word, still image, and moving image. As technology continues to improve and online writers' skill sets widen, the potential for writing will extend far beyond the written word. Mainstream Web sites increasingly incorporate video in their presentations, and skill with convergent media is important for not just journalists but every writer.

When you are watching something in person, the audio is almost always synchronized with the video. That is, they happen at the same time. If you are at the zoo looking at exotic birds, as you see a macaw open its beak, you hear it squawk at the same time. In the natural, non-mediated world sights and sounds go together quite nicely. In the mediated world, however, it is very easy to say one thing and show another. When the audio and visual channels go together, we call this audio-visual redundancy. When they start to diverge, we call this audio-visual dissonance. As Internet writers increasingly include multimedia video with their presentations, it is important to understand the cognitive implications of audio-visual redundancy and dissonance.

If you are a big budget documentary producer, then you will have little trouble getting hours of background footage that you can match to the video. This will be especially difficult for the online writer trying to combine video with sound and the printed word. But even matching video to audio is not as simple as it sounds. Consider a documentary about the lives of African elephants. Obviously, elephants do not talk. And although they make a few sounds, this makes for pretty boring video. So even in the simplest case, the writer probably will write voice-over copy to go on top of the background video of elephants raising their young, looking for water, and splashing in the oasis once they find it. As soon as that voice-over copy starts to diverge from the background video, you have introduced dissonance. And if you do not diverge, then you have pretty much written a play-by-play account of elephants as if they were a football game, and no one is going to watch that. So one must diverge. Thus, as the viewers watch a young elephant calf nuzzle its mother, the announcer says, "This young one has had plenty of time to grow attached to his mother. The elephant's gestation period is 22 months, longest of any land animal." This is dissonant. The video is showing a young postpartum elephant calf, and the narrator is talking about a pregnant elephant. The director could show the calf being born, but that is not quite redundant either. And most people looking at a pregnant elephant would not know that she is pregnant.

Think of almost any scenario that you would like, and it quickly becomes clear that any interesting multimedia presentation is going to have dissonance. The question then becomes what happens when the audio and visual tracks begin to diverge. Given that most scholars acknowledge that human processing capacity is finite (Kahneman 1973; Lang 2000; Shiffrin & Schneider 1977), there is reason to believe that severe dissonance may temporarily overload our limited capacity perceptual systems. Consider the most extreme case where an editing mix-up has paired a totally unrelated audio narration with an unintended video source. So, for example, the audio track from a situation comedy has been placed over video from a crime drama. How well do you think that you could pay attention to that chaos? Would you look at the pictures, or would you strain to hear and understand what the characters were saying that triggered the audience laughter despite the bloody corpse in the video?

Few of these questions have been investigated in an online context; however, there is an extensive body of work on video and television processing. In one of the first studies of audio-visual redundancy, Drew & Grimes (1987) produced five newscasts. In the first newscast, the audio matched the video for all stories. In the second condition, half of the stories' audio matched the video, and half did not match. Although they did not match, the audio did not starkly contradict the video as in the situation comedy example above. The third condition had none of the audio matching the video. Finally, as a control, one group saw only the video, and another group heard only the audio. Following viewing one of the three newscasts, participants were tested for audio recall, visual recall, and comprehension. Not surprisingly, the low-redundancy condition had the poorest recall and comprehension. Taken as a whole, the data suggest that when the two channels are highly redundant, attention is focused primarily on the audio track while still attending to the video channel. However, as redundancy decreases, viewers appeared to give up and concentrate on the video channel. This is interesting because it suggests a primacy of the visual channel. If a writer picks a poorly matched photograph or embedded video, this suggests that the words will be lost for the sake of the poorly matched visual.

Grimes (1991) conducted a follow-up study once again looking at the effects of audio-visual dissonance on memory. Once again, when the two channels diverged even mildly, subsequent memory for the video information improved while memory for the audio information deteriorated. A second experiment in that same study once again confirmed the tendency for television viewers to give up on the audio when the channels conflict. This apparent competition between the audio and visual processing channels suggests that there is a single pool of cognitive resources for which both channels compete. If this were not the case, then attention and memory for audio, for example, should be relatively independent. If there is a single pool competing for resources, however, then it makes sense that increases in visual processing would come at the expense of audio processing.

Basil (1994a, 1994b) investigated this possibility with television viewers, requiring viewers to respond to tones while watching television. Rather than varying the redundancy, this study alternated which channel contained the most important information to comprehend the story. Furthermore, half of the time participants were told to pay the most attention to the audio channel, and the other half of the time they were told to attend closely to the visual channel. No matter the important channel or the instructed focus, the results were consistent and pointed toward a single bimodal pool of attentional resources. When the two channels are not purposely made dissonant, it appears that viewers actively attend to both channels in search of relevant information. This is similar to what we would expect as a viewer navigates a Web page with graphics and embedded video. The viewer is on a quest to understand the big picture, and he/she has no predisposed allegiance to either the audio or the visual channel. Readers will find meaning where it lies. If, however, poor design or bad writing make the Web page difficult to parse, then it appears that visuals receive preferential access to cognitive resources. This is likely due to the fact that visual processing is, in general, easier or lest costly in terms of cognitive resources. Across a wide variety of studies, visual processing appears to require fewer resources than auditory processing (Lang, Potter, & Bolls, 1999).

A recent study in the line of work on audio-visual redundancy suggests some of the challenges faced by online writers and Web designers. Bergen, Grimes, and Potter (2005) compared a traditional talking head newscast with the more cluttered look seen on cable news channels with information bars down the side of the screen and news crawls running under the video footage. This kind of clutter is far more reminiscent of the typical Web page environment. Despite the claims of multitaskers around the world, the data show little evidence that humans are very effective at competing cognitive tasks—and these experimental participants were college students. In a series of four experiments, the presence of competing graphics on the screen caused memory for the central stories to suffer. Even when the experimenters went to great lengths to encourage participants to focus on the newscasts—so much so that they were told that they would have to return to complete the experiment if they could not remember enough information from the newscasts—the additional visual complexity hurt the processing of the stories. Taken together, these data suggest that the online writer should use complexity knowingly and with caution. A visually complex Web page may be pleasing, but attention and memory for the information contained therein is likely to suffer.

"MEDIA EQUALS REAL LIFE"

Except for the youngest of children, everyone knows that computers, televisions, and video games are not real. A funny thing happens when we are not thinking about it, however. We treat mediated messages as if they were real. In an enlightening series of experiments, Reeves and Nass (1996) borrowed experiments from the social psychology literature and applied them to media. They dubbed this phenomenon "the media equation," and the equation is extremely simple: media equals real life.

Team Computer

Take, for instance, teamwork. People like to be on a team. We try harder in order not to let our teammates down. We say things like, "There's no 'I' in 'team.'" Humans are social creatures, and it just makes sense that we would form bonds with other teammates. It goes with our hunter-gatherer past, after all. But no one would form such a bond with a computer, would they? Reeves and Nass found out that indeed people will form such a bond.

Imagine being given a task to perform on a computer. First, however, you are assigned to the "blue team" and given a blue wristband. You are then seated in front of a computer with blue trim around the monitor and a label that says "blue team." Would you perform differently in that condition than if you have been given the same wristband with no mention of team and had been seated in front of a "green computer"? That is exactly one of the experiments performed by Stanford University professors Reeves and Nass.

So, would you have performed differently if you had been randomly assigned to the "team" condition? If you are like most people, you would swear that you would perform the same. That is why experimental scientists bring you into the lab to test hypotheses. Despite your gut feelings, you are a pretty poor judge of your cognitive behavior. What happened? By now you probably guessed that there was a difference.

The "blue team" said they felt more a part of a team when led to believe their performance was tied to the computer. Keep in mind that this was with a stand-alone PC computer, and these participants had often used a computer before. That is not especially surprising, but the participants also said they were more similar to the computer, and they said that the computer was friendlier. Take just a moment to think about that. These are very real, very human connections that people are readily making with a piece of hardware. There was no alluding to the person who programmed the software or a human on another terminal. It was clearly just the computer. And still participants formed an identification with the computer: not over weeks or months, but in a few minutes—with an inert piece of plastic, metal, and silicone. If a simple set of instructions at the beginning of an experiment can lead people to identify with a computer, then talented online writers can craft Web pages and multimedia messages that get readers to do more than read. Messages can get individuals to sign on with the team.

Play Nicely

The online writer must think of things that never confronted the traditional writer, things such as interfaces and avatars, in order to take full advantage of the online medium and the tools it offers. Even audio and video multimedia presentations fail to take full advantages of the powers of the medium. Instead, the Web page is the interface between the human user and the mediated world. Lots of experts invest countless hours tracking readers' eyes and studying usability. However, the media equation shows us that a successful interface is more than a usable interface. Interfaces also can be polite.

What happens when you are mildly angry with a co-worker? Do you march into his office and tell him what a jerk he is? Chances are you may sit in your own office fantasizing about just such an interaction. However, when you pass him in the hall and he asks, "How are you doing?" you are likely to smile, tell him that you are doing well, and ask him about his day. Why is this? Social psychologists will tell you that it is due to politeness. It would be an ugly world indeed if we all went around speaking our minds at every turn. So we are polite. You may tell one friend that another is a jerk, but you are a lot less likely to tell someone that to his/her face. What about a computer? What if you are working on an application, and the computer stops to ask you how it is doing? What would *you* say? You might imagine what Reeves and Nass thought would happen. They had participants rate a computer's performance on that actual computer or another computer nearby. The software interface was the same, and everything looked the same on the screen. However, when people had to rate a computer on the same computer, they gave more positive evaluations. Participants, apparently, felt that they could be honest with another computer, but they felt the need to be polite to the actual computer they were rating.

This politeness goes both ways. Interfaces and Web pages should keep in mind that the user-Internet exchange is not simply an information transaction. It is a social exchange, and the reader will be polite in response to being treated politely. Even if it seems far-fetched, the reader is treating the Web page like another person.

Computers Like Me

Are you rather laid back, or do you like to take charge? Some people are the first to voice their opinion, while others prefer to linger in the background and wait for their turn to speak. In the terms of the social psychologist, some people are dominant while others are submissive. What about the Web page you are reading, the avatar with whom you are communicating, or the computer in general. Can it be dominant or submissive? It turns out that it can. And it also turns out that people like their interfaces to be a lot like themselves. When the computer's personality matched the user's personality, users liked the computer better, said it was more social, and reported being more emotionally satisfied from the experience (Reeves & Nass 1996). It turns out the same thing is true when a shopping Web site is constructed to match a browser's personality (Coyle & Weir 2001).

These data suggest that writers in an interactive medium such as the Internet take into account personality factors of their audience members. Looking back at the "to whom" part of Lasswell's question, online writers appear to have an advantage that writers in traditional media did not enjoy: audience tailoring. By understanding for whom he/she is writing, the Internet writer can adapt messages and interfaces to maximize an audience's enjoyment with and identification of the message. Traditional mass communications followed a strictly sender-receiver model of communication. The writer talked, and the reader listened. The online medium increasingly allows for a conversation between writer and reader, and the writer should actively encourage the reader to be a dynamic participant in that engagement. In the experiments outlined here and in dozens of others, Reeves and Nass demonstrated that people have what almost can be described as a yearning to identify and connect with new media. The conscientious new media writer should help make this connection.

IMPLICATIONS FOR INTERNET WRITING

The intersection of mind and message is important to the online writer. In order to write effectively, understanding the cognitive and social psychological aspects of the audience are crucial. Once people decide to devote their attention to a Web page, you can assume that they will invest some cognitive resources on the task. But the writing, images, audio, and video on the page have a lot to do with whether that attention remains. Being aware of—and making use of—these structural features leads to better writing that will be better attended and well remembered. Currently the trend is to include an increasing amount of multimedia features within online presentations. The data here are clear. Related animations and other features, such as sound effects, enhance cognitive processing. When information in the audio and visual channels diverge, however, attentional capacity is quickly overloaded, and audiences appear to focus on the video at the expense of the audio. Finally, the media equation suggests that people willingly treat online content and the computers that deliver that online content as real people.

Appendix

Tips for Writing, Interviewing, and Blogging

100 WRITING TIPS

Writing tip #1. Do not stare down the blank screen. It will not blink. Just start writing; it does not even have to be at the beginning.

Writing tip #2. Do not take feedback personally. Filter what makes sense, and apply it so you can continually develop as a writer.

Writing tip #3. Do not add words to clarify or unconfuse. Subtract and use the right words only for clear and concise writing.

Writing tip #4. Do not send an emotional response to agent rejection—you might end up with one of their friends. It is a small (lit) world.

Writing tip #5. Pick a tense, and stay (and live) with it. Nothing choppier than present/past/future, and it stilts narrative and kills pacing.

Writing tip #6. Agents are gatekeepers to trade publications, like it or not. If you go it alone, at least have a lit-aware lawyer check the contract.

Writing tip #7. Write across genres. Not only does it make you more marketable and build a network, it helps you develop as a writer.

Writing tip #8. Family and friends are often the worst for feedback (praise); get someone who knows the language and/or has had some success.

Writing tip #9. Struggling with the novel? Making it a collection of (perhaps loosely) connected short stories is an option.

Writing tip #10. Writing is like knitting an afghan. A "plot-hole" cannot be patched. Add integrity first. Reweave with correct colors, yarn, pattern.

Writing tip #11. Flash drives, CDs—all are fine, but I also email myself ALL my projects at least weekly, and daily if it is current.

Writing tip #12. Character development is important. The proposal/idea is a page or two, at most. You have to do something with the other 200 or so pages.

Writing tip #13. I do not believe in writer's block—I cannot afford to. Sometimes the words find you, sometimes you must go find them.

Writing tip #13(a). Because to me, writer's block is equal parts a lack of direction, inspiration, and passion. Want it. Conceive it. Do it.

Writing tip #14. Imitation is not flattery—it is plagiarism/lameness in the writing world. Yet writing is a craft with tenets we all use.

Writing tip #15. In 24/7 real-time news cycle/blogosphere, lack of fact checking can be your doom if you sacrifice credibility for speed.

Writing tip #16. A great editor looks for coherence, narrative flow, arc of story before "drycleaning" for grammar and punctuation.

Writing tip #17. There is nothing wrong with an outline. You do not have to stick to it, but it can lay out a map to motivate and inspire you.

Writing tip #18. To bring texture to a story when writing dialogue, "listen phonetically" to how someone from a particular region speaks.

Writing tip #19. Do not rule out the landscape as a character. Jagged peaks, high forests, stark plains have roles in stories when relevant.

Writing tip #20. Interview a professional in the field for info for your character whether it is for knowledge, vernacular, habits, dress.

Writing tip #21. Diaries, even unpublished, are priceless for time-set pieces, and often find homes at local libraries.

Writing tip #22. "Hire" good editors for first reads: Mine are a librarian and a junior college English professor. Where I am weak, they are strong.

Writing tip #23. Great ideas are not great stories. Great characters are what people remember, and they move the plot along, not vice versa.

Writing tip #24. When writing a biography, start with the most detailed chronology of the subject's life—trust me on this one.

Writing tip #25. For bios, ask for transcripts, legal papers, pictures, records—whatever you can to verify, expand, or even narrow the story's focus.

Writing tip #26. Can you break the "rules" of writing? Sure, but only if you know the rules well enough.

Writing tip #27. Freelance writing is like being a contractor: Get work, use it to get OTHER work, then start the first one as others percolate.

Writing tip #28. Authors are not usually the best source on how to publish. How to write? Yes. How to find an agent? Certainly.

Writing tip #29. Before you bash agents, remember: They make money only if you do, so they do not turn down work they think will sell.

Writing tip #30. Web freelancing is a good start, especially for magazines that also publish hard copies and are part of a magazine conglomerate.

Writing tip #31. Blogging is fun. Informative is better than just the all-out rant, though rant plus research-supported info can also be a good read.

Writing tip #32. Think opening paragraph/page in your manuscript is important? It might be all an agent or editor looks at. Craft and hook.

Writing tip #33. Want to write better? Books on rhetoric, and the language, are of high value. Structure and syntax are valued commodities.

Writing tip #34. In *Portnoy's Complaint* I don't remember many uses of "said." Sure, it can be used, but other words can enliven dialogue.

Writing tip #35. Writing a story is not the same as speaking it. Stream of consciousness does not always translate to the written page.

Writing tip #36. Beat the deadline by as much as possible (still doing your best). Editors in a jam will give you more work as others fall through.

Writing tip #37. Details are important for character development— relevant details. Do not overdescribe, and use few, if any, adjectives.

Writing tip #38. Do not resubmit to an agent unless requested. But do take any feedback offered and apply it before submitting to another agent.

Writing tip #39. If an agent does not ask to represent you exclusively, do not volunteer. Exclusive does help get your agent's attention, but only if he/she represents your genre(s).

Writing tip #40. Cool it on spectacular events in prop. Earth only blows up once, and there are only so many diseases. Develop characters and narrative first.

Writing tip #41. Revision is good; learn to do it. Even if you "put things back," that intellectual elasticity will help you in the future.

Writing tip #42. What to do with no muse? Authors pay their own bills. Inspiration comes from keeping the lights on, literally.

Writing tip #43. For some book deals, you may not be the first choice— initially. Smile and thank them—other work may follow.

Writing tip #44. I am a one-medium pony—print. So when I had a documentary lightning bolt, I enlisted a visual storyteller to help me grow.

Writing tip #45. Finally found that one book on your topic? If you need more sources, there is likely a reference list with many more at the end.

Writing tip #46. Do not underestimate your editor; you can learn so much through 10 revisions.

Writing tip #46(a). Doing it longer does not mean you cannot do it better.

Writing tip #47. Do not start sentences, especially paragraphs, with "It is" or "There are." We call it "dead construction"—avoid it.

Writing tip #48. Ending is as important as the beginning. Turn a phrase; use a powerful quote. Last impressions stick like first impressions.

Writing tip #49. Avoid passive voice. Not the same as past tense. Passive voice is had/have plus form of to be plus an "-ed" ending verb.

Writing tip #50. Do not get overwhelmed or think of writing the "whole thing at once." Pick an idea, develop it, and see where it takes you.

Writing tip #51. Do not use big words unless they fit; do not go size 14 when an 8 leaves a smaller footprint but gets job done. Exceptions exist.

Writing tip #52. Like in news stories, book quotes should be timely, powerful, usually short, and graphically or uniquely articulate a point.

Writing tip #53. Nonfiction/fiction book writing is not similar to news writing. A book is a paced explication or unfolding, news a quick explanation.

Writing tip #53(a). Think of a news story as a small map. Think of a book as a globe. The former makes sense fast, the latter a long trip.

Writing tip #54. Key to first-person narrative when you are ghostwriting a biography? Capturing the subject's authentic voice.

Writing tip #54(a). If you get information from friends or family (and you will), you must have the subject regurgitate it in his/her own words in manuscript.

Writing tip #55. Keep running list of key numbers, records, facts, etc., to double-check after you have finished your first and last drafts.

Writing tip #56. Story slowing? How about adding the history of the area, how it was settled, major land barons, first politicians, industries?

Writing tip #57. Characters can take the shape of more than people, such as the weather does in many books on Wyoming. Vivid and ripe for detail.

Writing tip #58. Pinpointing the arc of any story is critical. As it unfurls, it explains the cause and consequence of events on its own.

Writing tip #59. Some biographies can become the inspiration for a collection of short stories: Mark Spragg's *Where Rivers Change Direction.* A haunting memoir of a Wyoming writer/antisocial.

Writing tip #60. "Turn a phrase" is completely different from a cliché. It is original, and associates or twists often dissimilar words.

Writing tip #61. Pay to publish/publish on demand (POD) is fine if your goal is to get "a book out." For a working writer, POD success stories are a micropercentage.

Writing tip #61(a). And I love guerilla/viral marketing—I use it, too: It is just that even a good POD book will not ever be on a store shelf.

Writing tip #62. Publishers and agents go by word count, not pages. A typical 225-page book (there are exceptions) is about 80,000– 90,000 words.

Writing tip #63. Have a biography handy, and put it on your Web site so you can send a link to it along with an attached (or hard) copy if needed.

Writing tip #64. If you collaborate to write someone else's book, you are the second author, even if he/she does not type. Smile, and cash the checks.

Writing tip #65. Not every chapter is high octane, walls burning—Reflection has great value in narrative when done right.

Writing tip #66. A harder part of a bio is getting the subject to look deep inside to come to some real truths, often for the first time.

Writing tip #67. For a first self-edit, read aloud. I learned it as "Reading to the wall" in school and I often do it to this day.

Writing tip #68. Do not query for freelance stories unless you have story suggestions included and even mapped out (sources, timelines).

Writing tip #69. Always include some sort of breakout box(es) with freelance stories. A graphic element makes the editor's job easier.

Writing tip #70. Ask your sources for copyright-free, high-resolution photos for you to include with your submission, but be sure about copyright.

Writing tip #71. Ask every source to suggest at least two more people to talk to. You may not need, but may use them in the future for a story.

Writing tip #72. Every person you talk to is in your network. Save contact info and a line or two about each on your computer.

Writing tip #73. Developing your own style and voice is important—and "voice" here has nothing to do with how you speak.

Writing tip #74. Watching or reading the news is a great time to make notes for characters, locations, and events to keep your story moving.

Writing tip #75. Never make an editor or agent wait. I respond in "real time." Be accessible, and you will land even more work.

Writing tip #76. Always attribute, whether it is directly or in footnotes. Do not rely on hyperlinks only, but cite as well. Links sometimes fade.

Writing tip #77. Highs and lows of book writing: The deal almost falls apart a half-dozen times from start to finish. Stay with it.

Writing tip #78. Once you finish an article or manuscript, do not wait for publication to start on the next project.

Writing tip #79. Go to writing conferences to learn the tricks of the trade from agents, publishers, and authors, and to build your network.

Writing tip #80. If doing a biography, get a collaboration agreement—it protects you from the moment you start investing your time and talent.

Writing tip #81. Escalator clauses, payment schedules, marketing support, deadlines, adaptations/options—all reasons to have an agent.

Writing tip #82. Take a reporter's notebook with you wherever you go. Inspiration can find you in the strangest places sometimes.

Writing tip #83. On long, solo car trips, take a digital recorder and dictate notes, images, interactions, and thoughts you may put in a story.

Writing tip #84. Rather than making the back story an entire chapter, you can subtly add it while introducing other characters and places.

Writing tip #85. How do you end a story? Usually, the arc of the story indicates that and it ends itself. Do not force an ending.

Writing tip #86. Use active, descriptive verbs, which has the additional benefit of helping you cut back on adjectives.

Writing tip #87. More possible characters to add texture to your narrative: An old house, an infamous body of water, a car.

Writing tip #88. When authors write more than they read, the writing eventually suffers. Enjoy a day and night with a really great book.

Writing tip #89. Get to know a good librarian. They find not only books but online documents and others.

Writing tip #90. A good editor should tell you what you are doing right as well as what needs improvement.

Writing tip #91. Do not do a lot of editing in galleys. That is where mistakes get inputted. Only fix essential, obvious (and easy) things.

Writing tip #92. For nonagented, nonfiction deals, university presses remain a good option, and they produce classy (though expensive) books.

Writing tip #93. Do not ever miss a delivery deadline. Unless you are a best-selling author, you will never get another deal with that publisher.

Writing tip #94. For fiction or nonfiction, do character sketches in a separate file. Give thorough detail on each to keep story consistent and believable.

Writing tip #95. Follow submission guidelines for publishers and agents to the letter. They really do want it exactly that way.

Writing tip #96. Learn multimedia skills, but also the difference in storytelling in each medium. Bells and whistles with no message are just noise.

Writing tip #97. If you make a mistake, own it, live it down, and do not make it again.

Writing tip #98. Keep a file of trends to avoid (overusing "that," verb-tense consistency, etc.). Refer to it when proofreading before submitting.

Writing tip #99. Save every interview, email, digital recording/tape, for bios. Great for fact-checking, and if needed, for legal reasons.

Writing tip #100. Take off the headphones, hang up, and observe the world around you. There are stories everywhere; hear them and write them.

TEN INTERVIEWING TIPS

Interview tip #1. Remember, no matter what you seek, and no matter what you get, there is never a reason for not giving them your respect.

Interview tip #2. Assemble chronology on person or issue. Keeps you focused, drives interview, leaves fewer stones unturned.

Interview tip #3. Ask for or find media packet on person. That way you can cite others on controversial or disputed topics rather than "confront."

Interview tip #4. Always start interview by getting three more names/numbers/emails of sources. Just in case. And for verifying or getting more info.

Interview tip #5. Do your homework. Respecting person or subject enough to research ahead of time gives you intellectual traction on topic.

Interview tip #6. Find comfortable, neutral setting. Might not be "their house" if they fear being judged or covering up secrets.

Interview tip #7. If something is unclear or undefined, ask for clarity, so that way it is their words explaining—not your own interpretation.

Interview tip #8. Be familiar with customs, cultures, even religions. Respect the environment you are entering to gather facts.

Interview tip #9. Avoid confrontational words, especially early in interview. Rather than cite "problem," refer to it as "challenge."

Interview tip #10. Ask open-ended questions only. Ask Yes-No questions and expect one-word answers. This is an easy one, but hard to keep in mind.

TEN TENETS OF BLOGGING (WELL)

Blogging tip #1. Do not plagiarize. Ever. Do not steal, just like your parents said. You will understand when it happens to you.

Blogging tip #2. Research credible sources. Synthesize all that information into an original thought, and cite references.

Blogging tip #3. Become well-versed in what you write about. This might involve interviews or even experiments, but know what you are writing about.

Blogging tip #4. If your blog is "musings" of your daily life, develop your characters—give some back story. Explain who they are—and why they are that way.

Blogging tip #5. Be vulnerable and humble. You do not always have to be the smartest one. That is smarmy and snarky. Be human. Readers like that.

Blogging tip #6. Set a schedule, and stick to it. If you promise two posts a week on certain days, deliver. Readers and customers will drift away if you do not.

Blogging tip #7. Rather than link, consider footnotes. It is more formal, and the reader is less likely to bail on your blog halfway through for a link.

Blogging tip #8. Few make a living doing humor well and often, like Dave Barry. Be versatile, but have themes you operate from, and branch out from there.

Blogging tip #9. Do not take feedback personally. Glean lessons from it, let readers hash out merits, but do not engage in back and forth. It leads to downward spiral.

Blogging tip #10. Rather than recycle clichés or cook up adjective soup, turn a phrase, express an original thought. Respecting writing equals respecting readers.

Bibliography

Aarseth, E. J. (1997). *Cybertext: Perspectives on ergodic literature.* Baltimore, MD: The Johns Hopkins University Press.

Albom, M. (April 1, 2005). Longing for another slice of dorm pizza. *Detroit Free Press.* Retrieved February 6, 2009, from http://apse.dallasnews.com/news/2005/040805albom5.html.

Arnheim, R. (1969). *Visual thinking.* Berkeley: University of California Press.

Babbie, E. (2007). *The practice of social research* (11th ed.). Belmont, CA: Thomson Higher Education.

Baehr, C. (2007). *Web development: A visual-spatial approach.* Columbus, OH: Prentice-Hall.

Baran, S. J., & Davis, D. K. (2008). *Mass communication theory: Foundations ferment and future* (5th ed.). Boston: Wadsworth.

Barry, A. (1998). *Visual intelligence.* Albany: State University of New York Press.

Barry, A. (2005). Perception theory. In K. Smith, S. Moriarty, G. Barbatsis, & K. Kenney (Eds.), *Handbook of visual communication: Theory, methods and media.* Mahwah, NJ: Lawrence Erlbaum Associates, Inc.

Basil, M. D. (1994a). Multiple resource theory I: Application to television viewing. *Communication Research, 21,* 177–207.

Basil, M. D. (1994b). Multiple resource theory II. Empirical-examination of modality-specific attention to television scenes. *Communication Research, 21,* 208–231.

Bedbury, S., & Fenichell, S. (2002). *A new brand world: Eight principles for achieving brand leadership in the 21st century.* New York: Viking-Penguin.

Bergen, L., Grimes, T., & Potter, D. (2005). How attention partitions itself during simultaneous message presentations. *Human Communication Research, 31,* 311–336.

Berker, T., Hartmann, M., Punie, Y., & Ward, K. J. (2006). *Domestication of media and technology.* New York: Open University Press.

Bok, S. (1999). *Lying: Moral choice in public and private life.* New York: Random House.

Bolter, J., & Grusin, R. (1999). *Remediation: Understanding new media.* Cambridge, MA: MIT Press.

Bradley, M. M., Codispoti, M., Cuthbert, B. N., & Lang, P. J. (2001). Emotion and motivation I: Defensive and appetitive reactions in picture processing. *Emotion, 1,* 276–298.

Bradley, S. D., Maxian, W., Wise, W. T., & Freeman, J. D. (2008). Emotion trumps attention: Using prepulse startle probe methodology to assess cognitive processing of television. *Communication Methods & Measures, 2,* 313–322.

Braiker, B. (2007). Poll: What Americans (don't) know. *Newsweek,* June 23, 2007.

Bruner, J. S., Goodnow, J., & Austin, G. A. (1956). *A study of thinking.* New York: John Wiley.

Carey, J. W. (1967). Harold Adams Innis and Marshall McLuhan. *Antioch Review, 21,* 214–238.

Christians, C. (1989). A theory of normative technology. In E. F. Byrne & J. C. Pitt (Eds.), *Technological transformation: Contextual and conceptual implications.* Dordrecht, The Netherlands: Kluwer Academic Publishers.

Chung, D. S., Kim, E., Trammell, K. D., & Porter, L. V. (2007). Uses and perceptions of blogs: A report on professional journalists and journalism educators. *Journalism & Mass Communication Educator, 62,* 305–322.

Clark, A. (1997). *Being there: Putting brain, body, and world together again.* Cambridge, MA: MIT Press.

Clark, D. (2008). Content management and the separation of presentation and content. *Technical Communication Quarterly, 17*(1), 35–60.

Clark, R. P. (April 11, 2005). Portrait of the columnist as a pampered athlete. *PoytnerOnline.com.* Retrieved February 6, 2009, from http://www.poynter .org/content/content_view.asp?id=80831.

Coyle, J. R., & Weir, T. (2001). Effects of interface personality on consumer attitudes. In C. R. Taylor (Ed.), *Proceedings of the American Academy of Advertising* (p. 272). http://www.aaasite.org/proceedings/2000.pdf.

Crawford, C. (2003). *The art of interactive design.* San Francisco: No Starch Press.

Crowley, D., & Heyer, P. (2003). *Communication in history: Technology, culture, society* (4th ed.). Boston: Allyn & Bacon.

Czitrom, D. (1982). *Media and the American mind; From Morse to McLuhan.* Chapel Hill: University of North Carolina Press.

Darwin, C. (1859). *On the origin of species by means of natural selection, or the preservation of favoured races in the struggle for life*. London: John Murray.

Dawkins, R. (1976). *The selfish gene*. Oxford: Oxford University Press.

Detenber, B. H., Simons, R. F., & Bennett, G. G. (1998). Roll 'em!: The effects of picture motion on emotional responses. *Journal of Broadcasting & Electronic Media, 21*, 112–126.

Diao, F., & Sundar, S. S. (2004). Orienting response and memory for Web advertisements: Exploring the effects of pop-up window and animation. *Communication Research, 31*, 537–567.

Donnelly, F. (April 8, 2005). Albom Column Sparks Criticism for Fabrication. *Detroit News*. Retrieved February 6, 2009, from http://apse.dallasnews.com/news/2005/040805albom2.html.

Drew, D. G., & Grimes, T. (1987). Audio-visual redundancy and TV news recall. *Communication Research, 14*, 452–461.

Ducate, L. C., & Lomicka, L. L. (2008). Adventures in the blogosphere: From blog readers to blog writers. *Computer Assisted Language Learning, 21*, 9–28.

Elman, J. L. (1990). Finding structure in time. *Cognitive Science, 14*, 179–211.

Eshet-Alkalai, Y. (2004). Digital literacy: A conceptual framework for survival skills in the digital era. *Journal of Educational Multimedia and Hypermedia, 13*(1).

Gallagher, B. (April 12, 2005). Mitch Albom's phony side revealed. *Niagara Falls Reporter*. Retrieved February 6, 2009, from http://www.niagarafallsreporter.com/gallagher209.html.

Garrett, J. J. (2003). *The elements of user experience*. New York: New Riders.

Geiger, S., & Newhagen, J. (1993). Revealing the Black Box: Information processing and media effects. *Journal of Communication, 43*(4), 42–50.

Gitlin, T. (2007). The murderer and the media. *Huffington Post*, April 22, 2007.

Golbeck, J. (2005). *Art theory for Web design*. Boston: Addison-Wesley.

Grimes, T. (1991). Mild auditory-visual dissonance in television news may exceed viewer attentional capacity. *Human Communication Research, 18*, 268–298.

Guadagno, R. E., Okdie, B. M., & Eno, C. A. (2008). Who blogs? Personality predictors of blogging. *Computers in Human Behavior, 24*, 1993–2004.

Gulliver, S. R., & Ghinea, G. (2004). Stars in their eyes: What eye-tracking reveals about multimedia perceptual quality. *IEEE Transactions on System, Man, and Cybernetics, 34*(4), 472–482.

Haas, C., & Hayes, J. R. (1986). What did I just say? Reading problems in writing with the machine. *Research in the Teaching of English, 20*, 22–35.

Hackos, J. (2002). *Content management for dynamic Web delivery*. Indianapolis: Wiley Publishing, Inc.

Hackos, J. (2007). *Information development: Managing your documentation projects, portfolio, and people*. Indianapolis: Wiley Publishing, Inc.

Hashway, R. M., & Duke, L. I. (1992). *Cognitive styles: A primer to the literature.* Lewiston, NY: Edwin Mellen Press.

Heider, F., & Simmel, M. (1944). An experimental study of apparent behavior. *American Journal of Psychology, 57,* 243–259.

Heim, M. (1998). *Virtual realism.* New York: Oxford University Press.

Heim, M. (1999). *Electric language* (2nd ed.). New Haven: Yale University Press.

Hirsley, M. (April 10, 2005). Peers, educators critical of Mitch Albom. *Chicago Tribune.*

Hirsley, M. (April 11, 2005). No one's defending renowned journalist. *ChicagoTribune.Com.* Retrieved February 6, 2009, from http://apse .dallasnews.com/news/2005/041105albom1.html.

Hobbs, R. (1998). The seven great debates in the media literacy movement. *Journal of Communication, 48.*

Huang, L., Chou, Y., & Lin, C. (2008). The influence of reading motives on the responses after reading blogs. *CyberPsychology & Behavior, 11,* 351–355.

Innis, H. (1950). *Empire and communication.* New York: Oxford University Press.

Innis, H. (1951). *The Bias of Communication.* Toronto: University of Toronto Press.

Internet Archive. (2009). *About IA.* Retrieved March 18, 2009, from http://www .archive.org/about/about.php.

Jacobs, S. (2006). *Beginning XML with DOM and Ajax: From novice to professional.* Berkeley, CA: Apress.

Jenkins, H. (2006). *Convergence culture.* New York: New York University Press.

Johnson, P. (April 13, 2005). Media mix: Will Albom's woes taint journalism? *USA Today.Com.* Retrieved August 27, 2008, from http://www.usatoday.com/life/ columnist/mediamix/2005-04-13-media-mix_x.htm.

Johnson, R. (1998). *User-centered technology.* Albany: State University of New York Press.

Johnson-Sheehan, R., & Baehr, C. (2001). Visual-spatial thinking in hypertexts. *Technical Communication, 48*(1), 22–31.

Josephson, S., & Holmes, M. (2002). Visual attention to repeated Internet images: Testing the scanpath theory on the World Wide Web. *Proceedings of the 2002 Symposium on Eye Tracking Research and Applications,* 42–49.

Joyner, James. (April 11, 2005). The Mitch Albom scandal: Much ado about nothing. *Outside the Beltway.* Retrieved from http://www.outsidethe beltway.com/archives/the_mitch_albom_scandal/.

Kahneman, D. (1973). *Attention and effort.* New York: Prentice-Hall.

Kant, Immanuel. (2003). *Critique of pure reason.* New York: Dover Publications.

Koffka, K. (1935). *Principles of Gestalt psychology.* New York: Harcourt Press.

Kostelnick, C. (1996). Supra-textual design: The visual rhetoric of whole documents. *Technical Communication Quarterly, 5*(1), 9–33.

Kostelnick, C., & Roberts, D. (1997). *Designing visual language: Strategies for professional communicators.* Boston: Allyn & Bacon.

Kruk, R. S., & Muter, P. (1984). Reading of continuous text on video screens, *Human Factors, 26*, 339–345.

Kulkofasky, S., Wang, Q., & Ceci, S. J. (2008). Do better stories make better memories? Narrative quality and memory accuracy in preschool children, *Applied Cognitive Psychology, 22*, 21–38.

Kurtz, H. (Host.) (April 17, 2005). *Reliable Sources.* (Television broadcast.) Washington, DC: CNN.

Labov, W. (1972). *Language in the inner city.* Philadelphia: University of Pennsylvania Press.

Lacy, D. (1996). *From grunts to gigabytes: Communication and society.* Urbana: University of Illinois Press.

Lai, L. S. L., & Turban, E. (2008). Groups formation and operations in the Web 2.0 environment and social networks. *Group Decision and Negotiation, 17*, 387–402.

Landow, G. (1992). *Hypertext: The convergence of contemporary critical thinking and technology.* Baltimore, MD: The Johns Hopkins University Press.

Landow, G., and Delaney, P. (1991). *Hypermedia and literary studies.* Cambridge, MA: Massachusetts Institute of Technology Press.

Lang, A. (1989). Effects of chronological presentation of information on processing and memory for broadcast news. *Journal of Broadcasting & Electronic Media, 33*, 441–452.

Lang, A. (1990). Involuntary attention and physiological arousal evoked by formal features and mild emotion in TV commercials. *Communication Research, 17*, 275–299.

Lang, A. (2000). The limited capacity model of mediated message processing. *Journal of Communication, 50*, 46–70.

Lang, A., Bolls, P., Potter, R. F., & Kawahara, K. (1999). The effects of production pacing and arousing content on the information processing of television messages. *Journal of Broadcasting & Electronic Media, 43*, 451–475.

Lang, A., Borse, J., Wise, K., & David, P. (2002). Captured by the World Wide Web: Orienting to structural and content features of computer-presented information. *Communication Research, 29*, 215–245.

Lang, A., Bradley, S. D., Chung, Y., & Lee, S. (2003). Where the mind meets the message: Reflections on ten years of measuring psychological responses to media. *Journal of Broadcasting & Electronic Media, 47*, 650–655.

Lang, A., Bradley, S. D., Park, B., Shin, M., & Chung, Y. (2006). Parsing the resource pie: Using STRTs to measure attention to mediated messages. *Media Psychology, 8*, 369–394.

Lang, A., Potter, R. F., & Bolls, P. D. (1999). Something for nothing: Is visual encoding automatic. *Media Psychology, 1*, 145–163.

Lang, A., Shin, M., & Lee, S. (2005). Sensation seeking, motivation, and substance use: A dual system approach. *Media Psychology, 7,* 1–30.

Lang, A., Sias, P. M., Chantrill, P., & Burek, J. A. (1995). Tell me a story: Narrative elaboration and memory for television. *Communication Reports, 8,* 102–110.

Lang, P. J., Bradley, M. M., & Cuthbert, B. N. (1999). *International affective picture system (IAPS): Instruction manual and affective ratings* (No. Tech. Rep. No. A-4). Gainesville: University of Florida, The Center for Research in Psychophysiology.

Lanham, R. (1993). *The electronic word.* Chicago: University of Chicago Press.

Lanham, R. (2007). *The economies of attention: Style and substance in the age of information.* Chicago: University of Chicago Press.

Lasswell, H. D. (1948). The structure and function of communication in society. In L. Bryson (Ed.), *The communication of ideas* (pp. 37–51). New York: Harper and Row.

Latour, B. (1987). *Laboratory life: The construction of scientific facts.* Princeton, NJ: Princeton University Press.

Lazarsfeld, P. F., Berelson, B., & Gaudet, H. (1944). *The people's choice: How the voter makes up his mind in a presidential campaign.* New York: Duell, Sloan & Pearce.

Levinson, P. (1999). *Digital McLuhan: A guide to the information millennium.* London: Routledge.

Lewis, R. (2008). *What is DRM and why should I care?* Retrieved March 18, 2009, from http://firefox.org/news/articles/1045/1/What-is-DRM-and-why-should-I-care/Page1.html.

Litman, J. (2006). *Digital copyright.* Amherst: Prometheus Books.

Littlejohn, S. W., & Foss, K. A. (2008). *Theories of human communication.* Belmont, CA: Wadsworth.

Logan, R. (1986). *The alphabet effect: The impact of the phonetic alphabet on the development of Western civilization.* New York: William Morrow & Co.

Logan, R. (2002). The five ages of communication. *Explorations in Media Ecology, 1* (1), 13–20.

Lowery, S. A., & DeFleur, M. L. (1995). *Milestones in mass communication research* (3rd ed.). White Plains, NY: Longman.

Lu, H., & Hsiao, K. (2007). Understanding intention to continuously share information on Weblogs. *Internet Research, 17,* 345–361.

Manovich, L. (2001). *The language of new media.* Cambridge, MA: MIT Press.

Marshall, P. D. (2004). *New media cultures.* London: Arnold.

Mason, M. (2006). *No one cares what you had for lunch: 100 ideas for your blog.* Berkeley, CA: Peachpit Press.

McLuhan, M. (1962). *The Gutenberg Galaxy: The making of the typographic man.* Toronto: University of Toronto Press.

McLuhan, M. (1964). *Understanding media: The extensions of man.* New York: McGraw-Hill.

McLuhan, M. (2003). Two selections by Marshall McLuhan. In N. Wardip-Fruin & N. Montfort (eds.), *The new media reader*. Cambridge, MA: MIT Press.

Mencher, M. (2000). *News reporting and writing* (8th ed.). Boston: McGraw-Hill.

Meyrowitz, J. (1985). *No sense of place*. New York: Oxford University Press.

Mill, John Stuart. (2007). *Utilitarianism*. Filiquarian Publishers.

Miller, G. A. (1956). The magical number seven, plus or minus two: Some limits on our capacity for processing information. *Psychological Review, 63*, 81–97.

Minocha, S., & Roberts, D. (2008). Social, usability, and pedagogical factors influencing students' learning experiences with wikis and blogs. *Pragmatics & Cognition, 16*, 272–306.

Mirel, B. (2003). *Interaction design for complex problem solving: Developing useful and usable software*. San Francisco: Morgan Kaufmann.

Miura, A., & Yamashita, K. (2007). Psychological and social influences on blog writing: An online survey of blog authors in Japan. *Journal of Computer-Mediated Communication, 12*, 1452–1471.

Morville, P. (2005). *Ambient findability*. Cambridge, MA: O'Reilly Media, Inc.

Muter, P., Kruk, R., Buttigieg, M. A., & Kang, T. J. (1988). Reader-controlled computerized presentation of text. *Human Factors, 30*, 473–486.

Muter, P., Latrzmouille, S. A., Treurniet, W. C., & Beam, P. (1982). Extended reading of continuous text on television screens, *Human Factors, 24*, 501–508.

Muter, P., & Maurutto, P. (1991). Reading and skimming from computer screens and books: The paperless office revisited? *Behaviour & Information Technology, 10*, 257–266.

Nelson, T. (1993). *Literary machines 93.1*. Sausalito, CA: Mindful Press.

Nielsen, J. (2008). *Eyetracking research into Web usability*. Retrieved December 18, 2008, from http://www.useit.com/eyetracking/.

Ong, W. (1981) [1967]. *The present of the word*. Minneapolis: University of Minnesota Press.

Ong, W. (1982). *Orality and literacy: The technologizing of the word*. New York: Routledge.

Open Source Initiative. (2006). *The Open Source Definition*. Retrieved March 17, 2009, from http://opensource.org.

O'Reilly, T. (2005). *What is Web 2.0: Design patterns and business models for the next generation of software*. Retrieved December 15, 2008, from http://www.oreillynet.com/pub/a/oreilly/tim/news/2005/09/30/what-is-web-20.html.

Pavlov, I. P. (1927). *Conditioned reflexes: An investigation of the physiological activity of the cerebral cortex*. Cambridge, U.K.: Oxford University Press.

Pearrow, M. (2000). *Web site usability handbook*. Rockland, MA: Charles River Media.

Perlmutter, D. D., & Schoen, M. (2007). "If I break a rule, what do I do, fire myself?" Ethics codes of independent blogs. *Journal of Media Ethics, 22*, 37–48.

The PHP Group. (2009). *PHP: Hypertext Preprocessor.* Retrieved March 25, 2009, from http://php.net.

Plume, T. (1988). Practical applications of optical disk image systems in document management. In P. A. Yates-Mercer (Ed.), *Future Trends in Information Science and Technology.* London: Taylor Graham.

Postman, N. (1979). *Teaching as a conserving activity.* New York: Delacorte.

Postman, N. (1985). *Amusing ourselves to death: Public discourse in the age of show business.* New York: Penguin Books.

Postman, N. (1992). *Technopoly: The surrender of culture to technology.* New York: Vintage Books.

Potter, R. F. (2000). The effects of voice changes on orienting and immediate cognitive overload in radio listeners. *Media Psychology, 2*, 147–177.

Potter, R. F., Lang, A., & Bolls, P. D. (2008). Identifying structural features of audio: Orienting responses during radio messages and their impact on recognition. *Journal of Media Psychology, 20*(4), 168–177.

Potter, W. J. (2001). *Media literacy* (2nd ed.). Thousand Oaks, CA: Sage.

Potter, W. J. (2004). *Theory of media literacy: A cognitive approach.* Thousand Oaks, CA: Sage.

Prince, R. (April 11, 2005). The Mitch Albom file: Free Press to look at past columns. *MaynardInstitute.Com.* Retrieved February 6, 2009, from http://www.maynardije.org/columns/dickprince/050411_prince/.

Reeves, B., & Nass, C. (1996). *The media equation: How people treat computers, television, and new media like real people and places.* Stanford, CA: CSLI.

Reinking, D. (1987). *Reading and computers: Issues for theory and practice.* New York: Teachers College Press.

Rockley, A. (2003). *Managing enterprise content: A unified content strategy.* Berkeley: New Riders.

Rogers, E. (1962). *Diffusion of innovations.* New York: Simon & Schuster/Free Press.

Saco, D. (2002). *Cybering democracy: Public space and the Internet.* Minneapolis: University of Minnesota Press.

Schneider, W., and Shiffrin, R. M. (1977). Controlled and automatic human information processing: I. Detection, search, and attention. *Psychological Review, 84*(1), 1–66.

Schwartz, N. C. (2005). *Integral or irrelevant? The impact of animation and sound effects on attention and memory for multimedia messages.* Unpublished doctoral dissertation, Indiana University, Bloomington.

Shapiro, M. A. (1991). Memory and decision processes in the construction of social reality. *Communication Research, 18*, 3–24.

Shapiro, M. A., & Chock, T. M. (2003). Psychological processes in perceiving reality. *Media Psychology, 5,* 163–198.

Shapiro, M. A., & Fox, J. R. (2002). The role of typical and atypical events in story memory. *Human Communication Research, 28,* 109–135.

Shenk, D. (1997). *Data smog: Surviving the information glut.* New York: Harper-Collins.

Shiffrin, R. M., & Schneider, W. (1977). Controlled and automatic human information processing: II. Perceptual learning, automatic attending, and a general theory. *Psychological Review, 84,* 127–190.

Sholle, D. (2002). Disorganizing the "new technology." In Greg Elmer (Ed.), *Critical perspectives on the Internet* (pp. 3–25). New York: Rowman & Littlefield.

Silverblatt, A. (2001). *Media literacy: Keys to interpreting media messages* (2nd ed.). Westport, CT: Praeger.

Silverblatt, A., Ferry, J., & Finan, B. (1999). *Media literacy: A handbook.* London: M. E. Sharp.

Silverman, C. (April 13, 2005). Mitch Albom suspended. *RegretTheError .Com.* Retrieved February 6, 2009, from http://www.regrettheerror.com/ newspapers/mitch-albom-suspended.

Silverstone, R. (2006). *Media and morality: On the rise of the Mediapolis.* London: Polity.

Skaalid, B. (1999). *Gestalt principles of perception.* Retrieved December 8, 2008, from http://www.usask.ca/education/coursework/skaalid/theory/gestalt/ gestalt.htm.

Smith, C. C. (2008). Technologies for transcending a focus on error: Blogs and Democratic aspirations in first-year composition. *Journal of Basic Writing, 27,* 35–60.

Smith, R. F. (2003). *Groping for ethics in journalism* (5th ed.). Ames, IA: Blackwell Publishing.

Steele, B. (April 9, 2005). From failure to professional malpractice. *The Dallas Morning News.* Retrieved February 6, 2009, from http://apse.dallasnews .com/news/2005/040905albom2.html.

Stefanone, M. A., & Jang, C. (2008). Writing for friends and family: The interpersonal nature of blogs. *Journal of Computer-Mediated Communication, 13,* 123–140.

Sternberg, R. J., & Berg, C. A. (1987). What are theories of adult intellectual development theories of? In C. Schaller & K. W. Schaie (Eds.), *Cognitive functioning and social structure over the life course* (pp. 3–23). Norwood, NJ: Ablex.

Strupp, J. (April 15, 2005). Should Albom be fired? At ASNE, editors say no. *EditorandPublisher.Com.* Retrieved February 6, 2009, from http:// apse.dallasnews.com/news/2005/041505albom1.html.

Sweetser, K. D., Porter, L. V., Chung, D. S., & Kim, E. (2008). Credibility and the use of blogs among professionals in the communication industry. *Journalism & Mass Communication Quarterly, 85*, 169–185.

Tewksbury, D., Moy, P. & Weis, D. S. (2004). Preparations for Y2K: Revisiting the behavioral component of the third-person effect. *Journal of Communication, 54*, 138–155.

Timiraos, N. (2006). Free, legal and ignored. *Wall Street Journal.* Retrieved March 18, 2009, from http://online.wsj.com/public/article/SB115214 899486099107-vuoIhGUthiYcFwsQK0DjegSRPwQ_20070706.html.

Tulving, E., & Thomson, D. M. (1973). Encoding specificity and retrieval processes in episodic memory. *Psychological Review, 80*, 352–373

Tyner, K. (1998). *Literacy in a digital world.* Mahwah, NJ: Lawrence Erlbaum Associates.

User Centric. (2009). *Eye tracking.* Retrieved March 31, 2009, from http://www .usercentric.com/services/eye_tracking.php.

Utt, S. H., & Pasternak, S. (1989). How they look: An updated study of American newspaper front pages. *Journalism & Mass Communication Quarterly, 66*, 621–627.

Vie, S. (2008). Digital divide 2.0: "Generation M" and online social networking sites in the composition classroom. *Computers and Composition, 25*, 9–23.

Voas, J. (October 8, 2005). Free Press for Mitch. *Detroit MetroTimes.* Retrieved March 23, 2007, from http://www.metrotimes.com/editorial/story.asp? id=5499.

What is RSS? RSS explained. Retrieved December 15, 2008, from http://www .whatisrss.com.

Wilkins, A. (1986). Intermittent illumination from visual display units and fluorescent lighting affects movements of the eyes across text. *Human Factors, 28*, 75–81.

Williams, A. L., & Merten, M. J. (2008). A review of online social networking profiles by adolescents: Implications for future research and intervention. *Adolescence, 43*(170), 253–274.

Williams, J. D. (2003). The implications of single sourcing for technical communicators. *Technical Communication, 50*(3), 321–327.

Winston, B. (1998). *Media Technology and Society: A History from the Telegraph to the Internet.* London: Routledge.

Witkin, H. A., & Goodenough, D. R. (1977). Field dependence and interpersonal behavior. *Psychological Bulletin, 84*, 661–689.

Witter, S. (2007). "That's online writing, not boring school writing": Writing with blogs and the Talkback Project. *Journal of Adolescent & Adult Literacy, 51*, 92–96.

Woodling, C. (April 12, 2005). Editor does KU proud. *Lawrence Journal World* (Kansas). Retrieved February 6, 2009, from http://apse.dallasnews.com/ news/2005/041205albom2.html.

World Wide Web Consortium. (2008). *The legal problems of social networks.* Retrieved March 18, 2009, from http://www.w3.org/2008/09/msnws/papers/NETWORKS_LEGAL_PROBLEMS.PDF.

World Wide Web Consortium. (2009). *Introduction to Web accessibility.* Retrieved March 25, 2009, from http://www.w3.org/WAI/intro/accessibility.php.

Wright, P., & Lickorish, A. (1983). Proof-reading texts on screen and paper. *Behaviour & Information Technology, 2,* 227–235.

Index

About the Authors

Craig Baehr has a Ph.D. in Professional Writing from the University of New Mexico and is Associate Professor of Technical Communication & Rhetoric at Texas Tech University. He is also author of *Web Development: A Visual-Spatial Approach* (Prentice-Hall, 2007), and various articles and chapters on Internet writing, online publishing, hypertext theory, corporate blogging, and visual communication. He is a recipient of the Distinguished Technical Communication Award from the Society of Technical Communication.

Bob Schaller has a Ph.D. in Mass Communications from Texas Tech University and is an Assistant Professor at Stephen F. Austin State University. He is the author of 40 books, including *Michael Phelps: The Untold Story of a Champion* and forthcoming Greenwood biographies on Bill Gates and Al Gore. Information about his work, and reviews of his books, are available at http://www.BobSchaller.com.

Samuel D. Bradley is the author of more than a dozen academic journal articles on the cognitive processing of media. He holds a doctoral degree in Mass Communications and Cognitive Science from Indiana University. He is an assistant professor at Texas Tech University.